Schooling for Democracy

Henry A. Giroux

Schooling for Democracy

Critical Pedagogy in the Modern Age

Routledge

First published in Great Britain in 1989 by
Routledge
11 New Fetter Lane
London EC4P 4EE

Printed in the United States of America.

British Library Cataloguing in Publication Data

Giroux, Henry A.
  Schooling for democracy: critical pedagogy
  in the modern age.
  1. United States. Educations. Sociopolitical
  aspects
  I. Title
  370.19'0973

  ISBN 0-415-03626-7

To the memory of Armand and Alice Giroux,
to my three sons, Jack, Brett, and Christopher,
and to Jeanne Brady-Giroux.

Contents

Acknowledgments

I would like to thank a number of people for sharing their ideas and time in reading parts of the manuscript for this book. Jim Giarelli was helpful on the issue of public philosophy; Roger Simon enabled me to better understand the concept of critical pedagogy; Bryan Deever found much of the work written by the social reconstructionists; Ralph Page forced me to think through many of the ideas in this book; Donaldo Macedo read the chapters on literacy and provided critical comments; Richard Quantz read a number of the essays and his comments were always useful; Stanley Aronowitz first encouraged me to write the book and then provided invaluable assistance in thinking through many of its central ideas; he also was a great source of support and a first-rate editor. Peter McLaren edited every chapter in this book; his friendship, scholarship, and criticism contributed strongly to its development. I would also like to thank Paul Smith and Jim Sosnoski for various comments and conversations on many of the issues raised here. Jeanne Brady shouldered a considerable amount of the social division of labor in our household during the last fifteen months. Without her help and support, I would never have been able to finish this project. She also was a source of invaluable intellectual and emotional inspiration. Finally, I would like to acknowledge the support of Jan Kettlewell, the Dean of the School of Education and Allied Professions at Miami University, and Professor Nelda Cameron-McCabe, the chairperson of my department, for their continued support and help.

Earlier versions of some of the material used in this book have appeared in *Educational Theory*, *Teachers College Record*, *Harvard*

Acknowledgments

Educational Review (with Peter McLaren), *Boston University Journal of Education*, *Interchange*, and *The Review of Education*. An earlier, abbreviated version of chapter 1 appeared in *In the Nation's Image: Civic Education in Japan, Soviet Union, United States, France, and Great Britain*, ed. Edgar Gumbert (Atlanta: Georgia State University, 1987). All rights to the original version of that article are expressly reserved by Georgia State University. All the chapters in this book have been revised, modified, and extended considerably; more specifically, the changes have resulted in revisions that bear little resemblance to the material published originally.

Preface

But the root of history is the working, creating human being who reshapes and overhauls the given facts. Once he has grasped himself and established what is his, without expropriation and alienation, in real democracy, there arises in the world something which shines into the childhood of all and in which no one has yet been: homeland.

—*Ernst Bloch,* The Principle of Hope

This book should have been finished in February of 1987. However, in 1986, Jeanne Brady and I became parents of three baby boys. My life was filled immediately with the kinds of daily tasks that add a new sense of urgency to one's views on childrearing, pedagogy, the future, and, needless to say, the social division of labor. Work on the book stopped for a number of months while I learned how to integrate what it meant to be a father, friend, lover, writer, and teacher. My interests shifted, and I found myself thinking about the future of this country more seriously and with more concern than I had ever done before. Amid the task of changing diapers, the exhaustion that comes from little sleep, and the inimitable sense of joy at being a father for the first time, I began to reflect on what type of world these three young men would inherit. Needless to say, it is not one that currently augurs well for humanity. But at the same time, it is not a world in which one can remain passive. Despair, poverty, militarism, and human suffering are increasingly becoming part of the text of daily life. And yet underlying such pain and suffering are memories of conflict and resistance by individuals whose spirits remained bolstered by the imperatives of hope and justice. It is in this tension between a social reality plagued by oppression and the narratives of historical and contemporary struggles that the terrain of resistance is both produced and acted upon. For it is within the dialectic of oppression and transformation that the language of critique and possibility as the precondition for resistance can be learned and practiced in the context of everyday life. It is this interplay of history, memory, and solidarity that leaves history open. More specifically, these categories can provide the basis for forms of historical consciousness through which men and women will be able to produce and subjectively experience the language, social relations, and pedagogy necessary for transforming community and public life according to the imperatives of a real democracy.

Of course, the reality and metaphor of birth represents more than the signification of a special event; it points to the ongoing struggle to renew, revitalize, and invent the logic and social practice of democracy. In some ways, the birth of my sons provided me with a renewed appreciation for the political and pedagogical value of those traditions of protest in the American experience which resonate with hope and possibility, but which are barely recognized or sympathetically engaged in "official" history. Ignored, in this case, are those visions, struggles, and popular expressions of a comprehensive democratic ideal forged in social movements and intellectual struggles that shaped the historical experience of brave men and women who also dreamed of a better future for their sons and daughters. Rethinking my own sense of history has raised new questions for me regarding how my subjectivity has been shaped by multiple layers of historical experience that constitute for better or worse what it means to grow up in the United States. The presence of children forces the issue of understanding and connecting one's own history with the history that one's children will both learn and experience. The ethical issue of how to live suddenly becomes intertwined with the reality of where one lives, or, to put it another way, the question of how one lives one's life is inextricably related to the historical sedimentations of biography and forms of historical consciousness that shape the political and social expectations which locate us as moral beings.

This renewed grasp of my own existential and historical location, together with my desire to teach my sons about the value and importance of America's subjugated history, raised new questions for me about the relationship between radical pedagogy, critical dissent, and the struggle for democracy. This need to think about history from the view of the resisters and victims—those men and women who in different ways said "no" to indignity and oppression and "yes" to what it meant to reaffirm fundamental, radical principles of American life—reminded me of an incident in the life of Antonio Gramsci, the Italian theorist. Writing from prison to his son, Delio, Gramsci shares with him the importance of history revealing how men and women can unite to fight for a better world. For me, Gramsci's letter took on the nature of a symbol for recovering and critically appropriating within the context of a radical theory of education those aspects of American history that provide a new language and set of insights through which to locate the past in the problems of the present and the present in the possibilities of the future.

In the most fundamental terms, this book represents an attempt to draw from, present, and advance those aspects of a radical politics and pedagogy that have been part of a long continuum of protest in the United States. In doing so, it attempts to reconstruct a tradition of risk and resistance that can be used to inform and extend the gains that have been made over the years by critical educators. The point, of course, is not to mimic the past as much as to recover the best of its radical and democratic traditions and link them to the voices and struggles of those educators currently attempting to reshape public schools within a new view of public life. Schools are one of the few sites within public life in which students, both young and old, can experience and learn the language of community and democratic public life. Similarly, it is impossible to overemphasize the need for educators to recognize the importance of such a consideration. For it is only through such a recognition that the theoretical and political differences that often separate Left educators and others will find a common ground in the struggle for a democracy with a radical intent, a struggle that recognizes in difference the elements of what it means not only to dialogue but also to embrace and work toward qualitatively improving the grounds on which life is lived. I hope that this book makes a contribution to such efforts. I also hope that the spirit of those who have struggled to reshape history in the interest of a better world will grow ever more present in the world in which Jack, Brett, and Chris will one day find themselves.

Schooling for Democracy

1
Introduction
Schooling, Citizenship, and the Struggle for Democracy

America is a land without memory. . . . Those of us who are middle-aged or older have all had the experience of talking to people in their twenties about some central part of our experience and finding an utter lack of recognition. In college classes today even a reference to Vietnam is likely to produce blank stares.[1]

Historical understanding teaches us to transform the seemingly fixed and internal in our lives into things that can be changed. It teaches . . . people that the structures surrounding them have been made and remade over and over. It teaches that we live in history.[2]

American patriotism has become a high priority in the present age. Like most current and oftentimes longstanding national pastimes, it represents part of a discourse[3] that historically has remained distinct from emancipatory versions of democracy, citizenship, and public life. The resurgent discourse of patriotism sweeping the United States is part of a wave of nationalistic chauvinism that has culminated in a series of recent events: the invasion of Grenada, the bombing of Libya, and the fervent fanfare surrounding the anniversary of the Statue of Liberty.

This is not to suggest that patriotism can be dismissed as an inherently reactionary ideology as much as to recognize that its radical possibilities have rarely been legitimated as part of the dominant discourse of American history. Moreover, the current wave of right-wing chauvinism is not without historical precedent. What is new in the 1980s is the absence of struggle over both redefining the meaning of patriotism and constructing a notion of citizenship that is consistent with the tenets of a critical democracy.[4] In fact, what is at work

3

in the 1980s is a newly created public philosophy that defines citizenship in a political vacuum, that is, as an unproblematic social practice sanctioned through an appeal to an equally uncritical reading of America's cultural heritage. What this discourse has produced has been a form of historical amnesia, one that is characterized by an intentional silence regarding the ongoing historical struggles that have been waged over the meaning and unrealized potentialities that underlie different conceptions of citizenship. Within the parameters of this new public philosophy, citizenship not only is removed from the terrain of historical contestation, it is also defined around a discourse of national unity and moral fundamentalism that drains from public life its most dynamic political and democratic possibilities. As part of this discourse, the notions of struggle, debate, community, and democracy have become subversive categories. In many respects, the ideological and political convictions of this philosophy are quite evident in the 1975 Trilateral Commission report, *The Crisis of Democracy*. In that report, one of the coauthors, Harvard political scientist Samuel Huntington, argues that the crisis in American democracy is due to the emergence starting in the 1960s of the increasing participation of a number of groups in the democratic process. According to Huntington, the willingness of the press, the universities, and grassroots movements to express their vitality as democratic institutions represent an unwarranted challenge to governmental authority. Or, as he puts it, "some of the problems of governance in the United States today stem from an excess of democracy."[5] The Orwellian implications of this form of right-wing "patriotism" and "citizenship" are clearly expressed in a position paper on a blueprint for conservative government presented to President Reagan in 1980 by the Heritage Foundation. The study urged the president to recognize: "the reality of subversion and [to put] emphasis on the un-American nature of much so-called dissidence," adding that "it is axiomatic that individual liberties are secondary to the requirement of national security and internal civil order."[6]

If America is quickly becoming "a land without memory," it is, in part, because the New Right has managed to develop a public philosophy that both resonates with and distorts the desires and experiences of many people in this country. That is, the New Right's appeal lies in its bold invocation of moral strength, its celebration of America's greatness, and its ability to speak a language of hope and promise, even while it systematically ignores major social problems and promotes dangerous levels of militarism. What the New Right has done is not merely retreat from the discourse of democracy while simultaneously pushing American society closer to the perils of fascism; less obviously, but equally important, it has filled the void at the level of collective desire and need through a celebration and mobilization of the public's repressed Dionysian dreams about community and collective affirmation, especially at a time when the latter no longer seemed possible. Of course, justice, democracy, and critical citizenship are beside the point for the New Conservatives. Under the rubric of acknowledging the problems that characterize everyday existence, they have further undermined the possibility of democratic public life by perpetuating what Bloch has called the "swindle of fulfillment."[7]

America's failure to give democratic legitimacy to the notions of citizenship and patriotism cannot be totally ascribed to the emergence of the New Right. It is also due, in part, to the failure of radical theory to exhibit a discourse of political imagination and possibility in reclaiming citizenship and patriotism as objects of struggle and redefinition. The contemporary agony surrounding radical politics is most evident in its failure to take seriously, and in some cases even acknowledge, the politics of citizenship over the past twenty years or, for that matter, to reconstruct a conception of radical democracy that could provide an alternative to the New Right's attempt at redefining the nature and quality of political life in the United States and elsewhere. In fact, attempts by Left critics to downplay and discredit the concept of citizenship as an emancipatory practice which links empowerment to forms of progressive social struggle has contributed to the ideological crisis at the very center of American democracy.[8] Not only must such a crisis be acknowledged, but it must also be willingly addressed by excavating and legitimating those forgotten traditions of moral and public discourse that were part of the pedagogical and political struggles of the past.

Citizenship, like democracy itself, is part of a historical tradition that represents a terrain of struggle over the forms of knowledge, social practices, and values that constitute the critical elements of that tradition. However, it is not a term that has any transcendental significance outside the lived experiences and social practices of individuals who make up diverse forms of public life. Once we acknowledge the concept of citizenship as a socially constructed historical practice, it becomes all the more imperative to recognize that categories like citizenship and democracy need to be problematized and reconstructed for each generation. Richard Hanson speaks to this well when he writes:

> By portraying meaning as a historical artifact it also reminds us that we, too, must establish the meaning of keywords like democracy for ourselves. The meaning of democracy is just as problematic for us as it was for our historical predecessors. Its meaning is not given to us, but must be taken by us, as we seek to understand the world and its human possibilities.[9]

What Hanson suggests is that the notion of citizenship needs to be reclaimed by progressives and radicals as an important terrain of struggle. Moreover, such a struggle needs to be seen as part of a wider effort to develop a public philosophy that provides legitimation for developing counterpublic spheres in which a critical notion of citizenship can be given expression through a radical model of citizenship education. In this case, the notion of citizenship must be removed from forms of patriotism designed to subordinate citizens to the narrow imperatives of the state. On the contrary, citizenship in this case becomes a process of dialogue and commitment rooted in a fundamental belief in the possibility of public life and the development of forms of solidarity that allow people to reflect and organize in order to criticize and constrain the power of the state and to "overthrow relations which inhibit and prevent the realization of humanity."[10]

At issue here is the need to develop a form of citizenship in which public language takes as a referent for action the elimination of those ideological and material conditions that promote various forms of subjugation, segregation, brutality, and marginalization, often expressed through social forms embodying racial, class, and sexist interests. Of course, an emancipatory form of citizenship not only would aim at eliminating oppressive social practices, but would also constitute itself as a new movement for moral reawakening and, in doing so, would work toward constructing nonalienating social relations whose goal would be to expand and strengthen the possibilities inherent in human life. Murray Bookchin is instructive on this issue:

> I would emphasize that more than ever, today, we need a new

movement for moral reawakening, not only for meeting human material needs-important as these are at all times. The great failing of contemporary "Leftist" movements, be they socialist or anarchist, is that a new society is conceived primarily as one that places "bread and beef" on the table, with the ironic result that the "Right" has gained the support of millions through moral appeals that give a sense of meaning to life in an increasingly meaningless society. I am thoroughly convinced that no new social movement will capture the imagination of people today without providing a sense of moral well-being, not only material well-being—indeed, of moral purpose, not only material improvement.[11]

To reclaim the notion of citizenship in the interest of an emancipatory public philosophy demands that the notion of citizenship be seen as a historical practice inextricably linked to relations of power and formations of meaning. In other words, if citizenship is to be dealt with in its broadest implications, it has to be analyzed as both an ideological process and a manifestation of specific power relations. As a manifestation of power relations, citizenship affirms and articulates between various public spaces and communities whose representations and differences come together around a democratic tradition that puts equality and the value of human life at the center of its discourse and social practices. The concept of citizenship must also be understood partly in pedagogical terms as a political process of meaning-making, as a process of moral regulation and cultural production, in which particular subjectivities are constructed around what it means to be a member of a nation state. In more specific terms, the concept of citizenship must be investigated as the production and investment of ideological discourses expressed and experienced through different forms of mass culture and in particular sites such as the schools, the workplace, and the family.

With the above theoretical qualifications in mind, I will first deal with the notion of citizenship as a historical construction and point briefly to its importance as part of a radical discourse for educators in the interwar period in the United States. I will then analyze some of the dominant ideological perspectives on citizenship that have developed in mainstream educational theory since the end of the Second World War and how these were challenged by radical social theorists. In developing this brief commentary, not only do I want to provide an ideological analysis of how schools have become increasingly conservative bastions of citizenship education in the 1980s, but I also want to describe how radical educators have failed to develop a programmatic discourse for reclaiming citizenship education as an important battleground around which to advance emancipatory democratic interests. Following this, I will provide a critical analysis of the ways in which citizenship is currently inscribed within the logic of dominant ideology, and how the latter is legitimated within mass cultural genres such as the Hollywood films and in some aspects of television programming. I will conclude with some theoretical considerations that can be used in developing an alternative theory of citizenship education.

Reclaiming the Historical Legacy of a Critical Theory of Citizenship

In the two decades before the outbreak of the Second World War, a small group of radical educators attempted to extend the work of Dewey and other progressives by redefining the meaning and purpose of schooling around an emancipatory view of citizenship. For educators like George Counts, Harold Rugg, Willystine Goodsell, Theodore Brameld, and others, the Deweyian notion that democratic public life required an ongoing attempt to reconstitute schools on the basis of democratic values posed an overwhelming challenge of pedagogical and political significance to American education. In part, this challenge emerged out of the recognition that schools were not value-free institutions that played a politically innocent role in transmitting an unproblematic democratic heritage to future generations. On the contrary, the reconstructionists viewed schools as deeply implicated in producing those aspects of dominant culture that served to reproduce an unjust and unequal society. At the same time, they recognized that schools were not merely bastions of domination that operated according to the logic of the state. Schools were also seen as contradictory sites, torn between the ideological imperatives of liberal democracy and the dominating values and practices of monopoly capitalism. Inherent in these contradictory ideologies were opportunities for political intervention and struggle. One of the central aims of the social reconstructionists focused on usurping pedagogical opportunities in schools for learning about the relation-

8

ship between democracy and empowerment. For the social reconstructionist, schools were not viewed as the only sphere for educational work, but, at the same time, public schools were seen as a crucial sphere around which to fight for the development of a particular kind of democratic citizen. In the first issue of *The Social Frontier*, a journal for social reconstructionist ideas, the importance of extending education beyond the realm of the school in the fight for democracy was made clear:

> *The Social Frontier* acknowledges allegiance to no narrow conception of education. While recognizing the school as society's central educational agency, it refuses to *limit* itself to a consideration of this institution. On the contrary, it includes within its field of interest all of those formative influences and agencies which serve to induct the individual—whether old or young—into the life and culture of the group. It regards education as an aspect of a culture in the process of evolution. It therefore has no desire to promote a restricted and technical professionalism. ... In the years and decades immediately ahead the American people ... must choose among diverse roads now opening before them. In particular they must choose whether the great tradition of democracy is to pass away with the individualistic economy to which it has been linked historically or is to undergo the transformation necessary for survival in an age of close economic interdependence.[12]

The terrain of struggle on which the social reconstructionists chose to fight focused around developing a public philosophy in which education was viewed as a form of cultural politics. That is, education was seen as part of an ongoing struggle to develop forms of knowledge and social practices that not only made students critical thinkers but also empowered them to address social problems in order to transform existing political and economic inequalities.[13] As a central feature of this vision of schooling, citizenship education was, in part, defined as an ongoing attempt to develop curricula that was critical of the injustices of American society. In other words, curricula development was linked to a theory of social welfare and reconstruction, one that both identified existing injustices and attempted to motivate students to change them through forms of social action. As early as 1927, Harold Rugg expressed the sentiments of this position in his description of how a curriculum should be organized:

Lacking a half-million dynamic teachers are we not forced to put into our schools a dynamic curriculum? A curriculum which deals in a rich and vivid manner with the modes of living of people all over the earth; which is full of throbbing anecdotes of human life? A curriculum which will set forth the crucial facts about the community in which people live; one which will interpret for them the chief features of the basic resources and industries upon which their lives depend in a fragile, interdependent civilization; one which will introduce them to the modes of living of other peoples.[14]

For Rugg, Brameld, and others, it was imperative that the curricula have an organic connection to the problems that students had to face in the outside world, and the problems that needed the most attention were those that violated the basic precepts of democracy. In short, the social reconstructionists wanted to develop forms of knowledge that were normatively based around a commitment to the "good society." They wanted knowledge and power to come together as a form of critical thinking that took as its object forms of cultural and political transformation. Moreover, they believed that at the core of citizenship education was a concept of teaching in which educators assumed the role of critical intellectuals who, in the words of Brameld, would:

solve our problems, not by conserving, not merely by modifying, nor by retreating; but by future-looking, by building a new order of civilization under genuinely public control, and dedicated to the fulfillment of the human values for which most men [sic] have been struggling, consciously or unconsciously for many centuries.[15]

Citizenship education in this view was defined as a referent not for defending—but rather for transforming—the existing social order; moreover, the job of teaching was defined around its social and political functions rather than in terms of an ahistoricized, apolitical notion of professionalism. Similarly, the role and purpose of public schooling was linked to a notion of public service committed to moral and political considerations designed to benefit often victimized and subordinated groups in American society.

Most important, the social reconstructionists understood that citizenship education was not merely about informing people or giving them critical skills, it was also about making choices based on ethical considerations and social concerns. John Childs stated the point well in 1935.

Strive as we may, we can never reduce education to the bare process of criticism. This, for the simple reason that criticism, in order to be significant, involves the use of standard, ethical judgments, and social values. Many educators believe that in a democratic society they should seek to actively nurture in the young the emotional and intellectual dispositions which will prompt them to put the welfare of the many above the privileges of the few. In doing this they recognize that they are using the school as a positive agency to bias the young in favor of the ethical values of social democracy. This is going beyond mere intellectual criticism. It is building the background of values and beliefs out of which the process of criticism is to operate.[16]

Moreover, citizenship education was also about empowering students to struggle against relations of power and privilege that transformed them and others into objects and instruments of oppression. Extending Dewey's belief that "intelligent social action held out the most promise for a better society,"[17] the social reconstructionists argued for a politics of social individuality in which citizenship education could take place not merely in the school but also in the wider social sphere through the political agency of counterpublics such as labor unions, churches, neighborhood organizations, journals, and so on. Beneath the logic of this position was an emphasis on the relationship between knowledge and power, doing and acting, and commitment and collective struggle. This notion of citizenship education and the public philosophy it grew out of reached its ascendancy during the depression and virtually slipped into oblivion by the 1950s. The reconstructionist legacy, while not without flaws, represents the most radical attempt by educators to develop a public philosophy and notion of citizenship education yet developed in the United States. Unfortunately, since the 1950s—with the ascendancy of the Cold War, the Sputnik crisis, and the increasing power of the cultural industry to shape public opinion—this legacy has been almost completely ignored by contemporary educators, even those working within the critical tradition.[18] It is worth reiterating that viewing democracy as both a sphere of struggle and a social movement gains theoretical credence through an analysis of the forms that struggle has taken within particular historical traditions. This makes it all the more instructive to examine briefly some of the forces at work in American society after 1945 that helped redefine both the role of public schooling in this country as well as the nature of citizenship itself in opposition to the tenets of a critical democracy. In this case, the work of C. Wright Mills is helpful.

Mills has argued that the post-1945 period in American history is significant because it marks in accelerated fashion the transformation of a community of publics, where people organized to debate and challenge major public issues, to a mass society marked by a growing political illiteracy and one-dimensional nationalist view of citizenship.[19] In many respects, Mills's analysis is useful not only in explaining what forces were at work in redefining the role of citizenship education in the schools but also in locating some of the ideological and material transformations that increasingly positioned people within a set of experiences and practices that undermined an emancipatory notion of what it means to be a critical and active citizen. In Mills' view, one of the most dangerous forces at work in American society was the growing culture industry, which included the electronic media of television, film, and radio, as well as the newspaper and magazine trade. For Mills, as well as for theorists such as Herbert Marcuse, Theodore Adorno, and Max Horkheimer, the growing centralization of power in the new media industry marked a narrowing of the range of ideas and interpretations available to the American people.[20] Moreover, these media were adopting programming formats and methods of presentation that often served to standardize and trivialize information. This was particularly true of the news media, with its superficial covering of important events, and Hollywood films with their endless formulas for producing particular genres. In any case, the end result was the emergence of a media that appeared to promote a new form of illiteracy, one that decried substantive information and debate for the glitter of the spectacle. The culture industry, so it was argued, had done more than undermine the possibility for serious public debate on a wide variety of issues; it had also become a powerful weapon in reproducing ideological interests that reinforced a growing Cold War ideology and an ethic of consumerism. Furthermore, it replaced the need for critical thinking with a rampant chauvinism and blurred the importance of moral responsibility with the pleasures mobilized by the advertising industry.

Another trend was the rise of the major metropolis and the growing influence of large urban life, both of which served to undermine the possibilities for community interaction and forms of sociality necessary for developing public life. Moreover, the growing invasion and colonization of the private sphere in the post-World War II period by new economic and political interests further undermined the possibility for blue-and white-collar workers to develop public spheres as extensions of neighborhoods, churches, and other kinship institutions which rooted them in a sense of place and struggle. This period was marked by a massive flight of the middle classes out of the cities to the suburbs and a growing separation between work and family as well as a retreat by many people from the public world of politics and community into the privatized world of suburban television culture. Fred Pfeil captures the spirit of this transformation:

> The most striking transformation ... for both middle and working classes in post-World War II America is precisely the invasion and colonization of its hitherto sacrosanct territory by new economic and political exigencies and concerns. Here I am referring first and foremost to that network of politico-economic strategies and decisions that underlay the mass movement out of the cities and into the suburbs in the 1940s and 1950s. Suburbanization, not affordable urban public housing, was the combined reply of business and state interests to the potentially dangerous popular demand for affordable space in the post-war years; and it proved a most effective solution. All those Levittowns and census tracts, loosely tied together by federally funded expressways and beltways, those interminable circuits of "living units" splayed out around the cities' decaying cores, not only made a fine living for whose hosts of speculators and developers—much of it, of course, on federally guaranteed low-interest mortgages and loans—by literally distancing both blue-and white-collar workers from their place of work, by snapping the nuclear family out and away from wider networks of neighborhood, kin and clan, they also boosted consumption while simultaneously shrinking both the private and public sphere. Workplace and neighborhood cultures effectively dried up and disappeared; so the attenuated family "unit" stayed home in its own private living room and watched TV.[21]

Finally, Mills believed, like Weber and Veblen, that the rise of bureaucratic structures of executive power undermined the possibility for both a democratic discourse and the exercise of democratic rights based on a critical public philosophy.

> The rise of bureaucratic structures of executive power, in the economic, the military, and the political orders, has lowered the

effective use of all these smaller voluntary associations operating between the state and the economy on the one hand, and the family on the other. It is not only that the institutions of power have become large scale and inaccessibly centralized; they have at the same time become less political and more administrative. It is within this great change of framework that the organized public has waned.[22]

Within this sociopolitical context, a variety of citizenship models developed in the United States during the 1945-80 period, and most of them incorporated a distinctly conservative or liberal logic. While it is not possible to outline these approaches here, it is worth noting that even the most liberal models of citizenship education failed to address the deep-seated inequalities that underlie the structure of American schools and American society, and generally substituted a focus on problem-solving and critical thinking for a pedagogy committed to overcoming the problems of sexism, racism, and chauvinism.[23] Moreover, in spite of the emergence of the radical student movement of the 1960s and the feminist movement of the 1970s, the language of individualism once again replaced the language of collective struggle in the late 1970s, and attempts to understand problems within their historical and socioeconomic contexts were replaced by pedagogies aimed at making students either good decision-makers or more fluid in the language of public debate.

In all these cases, the nature of citizenship is translated into the mastery of procedural tasks devoid of any political commitment regarding what is democratically just or morally defensible. Struggle generally is reduced to solving a problem or winning a debate. Lost here is the imperative of educating students to affirm moral principles that renounce social injustice and encourage students to become involved in the world in order to change it. In sum, what is missing from these approaches is any notion of a public philosophy that gives credence to an emancipatory form of citizenship that puts equality and human life at its center and equates democracy not with privileges but with democratic rights that ensure meaningful participation in the political, economic, and social spheres of society. At the same time, meaningful democracy and its attendant notion of emancipatory citizenship points to the construction of new sensibilities and social relations that would not allow for political interests to emerge in everyday life which support relations of oppression and domination.

Making the Citizen in the 1980s

Needless to say, the dominant ideology of citizenship is not automatically imposed or accepted by those who are positioned through its discourses. Between the needs that these discourses attempt to mobilize, and the expressions that they finally assume, there is a contradictory terrain of mediating forces that alter and modify their effects and, in some cases, actually reject their intended interests. For instance, the particular experiences of everyday life, various commonsense understandings, and a genuine capacity for critical analysis sometimes produce modifying, if not oppositional, readings of dominant ideologies. At issue here is the recognition that the lived effects of the dominant ideology are always problematic and must be seen as an object of inquiry rather than merely presupposed.

In the following analysis, I will argue that the power of the media to construct particular forms of subjectivities and citizens rests on their ability to restrict the power of alternative considerations and images regarding what it means to be a citizen. For example, this is particularly true for children who have been raised on the discourse of mass culture and have no grasp of history or other forms of alternative knowledge. Tony Wagner, for instance, points to recent surveys that discovered that the majority of young people in grades seven through twelve believed that some form of global catastrophe would take place in their lifetimes. At the same time, he found that in his own discussions with high school students across the country, very few of them believed that adults can effect any changes in democracy working as collective citizens. The point is that none of these students had studied an interpretation of history in which trade union struggles, civil rights struggles, or feminist struggles had any impact on changing the course of human history. Moreover, all these students seemed incapable of challenging a version of American life and history that suggests a conflict-free and ideal cultural narrative, one which in actuality smothers over the social contradictions born of racist, class-specific and gender-oriented forms of discrimination.[24] What is interesting in this observation is not merely the combination of despair and cynicism displayed by the students, but the fact that almost none of them Wagner talked to could provide a single example in history where citizens working together created important social changes and improved the quality of life. Wagner's study illuminates the ways in which the dominant ideology functions to organize and legitimate experiences so that people are positioned within a narrow range of discourses that limit their options for producing alternative visions and views of the world.

Citizenship education must be seen as a form of cultural production. That is, the making of citizens must be understood as an ideological process through which we experience ourselves as well as our relations to others and the world within a complex and often contradictory system of representations and images. Citizenship education involves more than simply analyzing the interests underlying particular forms of knowledge; it also involves the issue of how ideology functions through the organization of images, space, and time to construct a particular kind of subject and particular relations of subjection or rule. This will be illustrated through an analysis of the recent spate of educational reforms and through the representations of citizenship that are emerging in the film and television industries.

Schooling and the Flight from Citizenship Education

Since the beginning of the 1980s there has been an ideological restructuring both in the schools and in the wider society around the discourse of citizenship. This shift is characterized, on the one hand, by a language that has become more conservative and nationalistic. On the other hand, the formation and regulation of experience around a particular conception of citizenship is now being carried out in a more aggressive fashion in cultural spheres outside schools, particularly in a new genre of Hollywood films and in the ideological visions embodied in television programming.

Within the last five years the nature and character of American public education has undergone a major ideological shift. This shift is most evident in the gathering momentum of the current reform period to redefine the purpose of education so as to eliminate its citizenship function in favor of a narrowly defined labor market perspective. The essence and implication of this position is well stated by Barbara Finkelstein:

> Contemporary reformers seem to be recalling public education from its traditional utopian mission to nurture a critical and committed citizenry that would stimulate the process of political and cultural transformation and refine and extend the workings of political democracy. . . . Reformers seem to imagine public schools as economic rather than political instrumentalities. They forge no new visions of political and social possibilities. Instead, they call public schools to industrial and cultural service exclusively. . . . Reformers have disjoined their calls for educational reform from calls for a redistribution of power and authority, and the cultivation of cultural forms celebrating pluralism and diversity. As if they have had enough of political democracy, Americans, for the first time in a one-hundred-and-fifty-year history, seem ready to do ideological surgery on their public schools—cutting them away from the fate of social justice and political democracy completely and grafting them instead onto elite corporate, industrial, military, and cultural interests.[25]

Underlying the new conservative attack on the reforms of the last decade is a shift away from linking schools to the issues of equity and justice. Moreover, there is little concern with how public education will better serve the interests of diverse groups of students so they will be able to understand and gain some control over the sociopolitical forces that influence their destinies. In fact, the notion of citizenship is barely mentioned in the new educational reforms. In its place, there is a preoccupation with patriotism, which in this case is made synonymous with the tenets of economic productivity and national defense. This is painfully clear in one of the most important reform documents of the last decade, *A Nation at Risk*. In attempting to build a rationale for public support for education, the report argues:

> Another dimension of the public's support offers the prospect of constructive reform. The best term to characterize it may simply be the honorable word "patriotism." Citizens know intuitively what some of the best economists have shown in their research, that education is one of the chief engines of a society's material well-being. . . . Citizens also know in their bones that the safety of the United States depends principally on the wit, skill, and spirit of a self-confident people, today and tomorrow.[26]

Introduction

Within this discourse and its preoccupation with accountability schemes, testing, accreditation, and credentializing, educational reform has become synonymous with turning schools into "company stores" and defining school life primarily in terms that measure their utility against their contribution to economic growth and cultural uniformity. In effect, the ideological shift at work in the current school reform movement points to a definition of schooling that is so restricted that it almost completely strips public education of a democratic vision in which the politics of possibility and citizenship are given serious consideration. In other words, at the heart of this ideological shift is an attempt to reformulate the purpose of public education around a set of interests and social relations that define academic success almost exclusively in terms of the worst features of the dominant ideology. In this case, education for self and social formation gives way to a view of schooling reduced to the imperatives of corporate self-interest, industrial psychology, and cultural uniformity. Underlying the social relations that inform this notion of education is a view of the public as an aggregate of competing consumers whose commitment to justice, freedom, and human worth is defined primarily through the logic of material and economic considerations. Lost from this perspective is a notion of civic life that takes as its organizing principle the language of morality, civic courage, and social compassion.

It is important to note that in the new educational reform movement the discourse of citizenship has been reconstituted and reduced to a more blatantly conservative notion of patriotism. In effect, the grounds on which political socialization takes place have been defined within more narrow ideological parameters. In this case, a version of citizenship education emerges in which students rarely find themselves exposed to modes of knowledge that celebrate democratic forms of public life or that provide them with the skills they will need to engage in a critical examination of the society in which they live and work. Underlying the dominant trend in teaching and in learning, one that structures to a considerable degree the form and content of most public school curricula, are the principles of mastery, efficiency, and control. Under the rubric of "quality," the greatest challenge facing educational reform, according to President Reagan, is raising verbal and mathematical SAT scores at least fifty points within the next decade. Inherent in this argument is a call for pedagogies that reassert the primacy of traditional authority through an appeal to technocratic accountability models. Within this perspective, civic education no longer promotes the development of citizens who possess the social and critical attributes to improve the quality of public life. Instead, teachers are asked once again to promote character development in students, to teach them a clear sense of right and wrong, to promote skills of individual achievement, which translate into the virtues of "hard work, self-discipline, perseverance, industry, respect for family, for learning and for country."[27] This discourse invokes forms of institutional authority that says little about issues of equity or social justice; it is a view of authority rooted in an unproblematic appeal to the rules and to the imperatives of individual successes. For instance, there is no talk of conflict within this discourse, no mention of the "messy" social relations of sexism, racism, and class discrimination that underlie school and classroom relations. It is the discourse of uneasy harmony, one that smooths over the conflicts and contradictions of everyday life with an appeal to teaching tradition and character development. Underlying this call to harmony and tradition is a politics of silence and an ideological amnesia. A pedagogy of chauvinism dressed up in the lingo of the Great Books presents a view of culture and history as if they were a seamless web, a warehouse of great cultural artifacts. No democratic politics of difference is at work here. For within this vision difference quickly becomes labeled as a deficit, as "the other," deviancy in need of a psychological tending and control. In the meantime, the languages, cultures, historical legacies of minorities, women, blacks, and other subordinate groups are actively silenced under the rubric of teaching the dominant version of American culture and history as an act of patriotism. Within this language, the appeal to old-fashioned virtues is matched only by a similar appeal to old fashioned pedagogy. Teachers simply have to teach this warehouse of cultural wealth; students have to be regularly monitored, scrutinized, and measured in order to make sure they are succeeding; and school achievement is assessed and displayed in a dizzying array of numerical scores posted monthly in the local newspaper. Of course, nothing will be said about the 70-80 percent of drop-out rates for Puerto Rican students in the urban centers or the 48 percent drop-out rate for blacks, or the 65 percent drop-out rate for Native Americans in our schools. Nor will this type of pedagogy say anything about those teachers overburdened by deplorable working conditions, students silenced by administrators and teachers who believe they don't count, or those parents from subordinate groups who are ignored by school administrations because they lack the right cultural currency.

Underlying the emphasis on character development and patriotism in the new educational reform movement is the specter of a hegemonic ideology that celebrates the role of the expert, technocratic rationality, and a Cold War ethic. What is striking about the new public philosophy is that it contributes to the construction of a set of values that underlies a version of patriotism that is strongly consistent with what Daniel Yankelovich calls our prevailing social philosophy. He writes:

> The dominant philosophy held by the experts on whom we most depend — economists, defense analysts, bankers, industrialists, journalists, government officials — can best be described as a "missiles-and-money" sense of reality. This philosophy assumes that what really counts in this world are military power and economic realities, and all the rest is sentimental stuff. It has overly constricted the domain of what is real and transformed the large political and moral dilemmas of our time into narrow technical questions that fit the experts' own specialized expertise. This process of technicalizing political issues renders them inaccessible to public understanding and judgment because the public exists in the very domain of reality that is excluded.[28]

Within the current educational reform movement, the logic of self-interest coupled with a rationality that frames knowledge and learning in technical terms has become the hallmark of defining the meaning of "civic education" in America. In this context, students learn little about the language of community and public association, how to create and affirm their own stories along with those of others who inhabit different cultural, racial, and social positions, or how to balance their own individualistic interests with those of the public good. Justice is outside the critical range of the new public philosophy and its attendant pedagogical formulations. In fact, the new public philosophy has little to do with civic education in the emancipatory sense of the practice, one that stresses civic learning and public responsibility as part of the struggle to develop human capacities and social forms that extend rather than diminish new possibilities for democratic public life; instead, under the rubric of character development and moral regulation, it provides the basis for curricula and pedagogy that enshrine the virtues of possessive individualism, the struggle for advantage, and the legitimation of forms of knowledge that restrict the possibility for political understanding and action. When the language of moral responsibility is invoked, as, for instance, by William Bennett, former Secretary of Education, it is often trivialized or used as a weapon to admonish those ideological tendencies he disagrees with. Moral practice becomes important in addressing the drug problems in our nation's schools, or for berating liberal faculties in such "bastions of radicalism" as Harvard University. At the same time, moral practice is exorcised as a basis for addressing the instances of suffering and despair that often turn schools into warehouses, dead zones, and spaces, if you will, for minorities of race and class. This administration invokes the language of morality in order to trivialize it, to silence critics of society, to admonish critical intellectual practice, and to reduce teachers and educators to the moral gatekeepers of a Reaganlike evangelicalism. It should be noted that this in not the language of character development as much as it is the language of character underdevelopment; nor is this the practice of moral development as much as it is the practice of moral authoritarianism. In part this can be seen in the Reagan Administration's attempt to give moral and political support to Joe Clark, principal at Eastside High School in New Jersey. Clark drew the support of Bennett and others when he implemented a number of school policies that appeared to resonate with the Reagan Adminstration's view of educational leadership and discipline. One of the first things Clark did was to announce his educational philosophy with a sign on his office door which read "There's only one way—my way." True to form, Clark roamed the corridors of his school with a bullhorn, verbally assaulting students who either violated or criticized his policies. Clark suspended hundreds of students labeled as troublemakers, and when queried about refusing to notify the school board of the suspension of at least sixty students, Clark responded by arguing, "I'm tired of parasites, leeches and mutants who don't want to do anything to better themselves." Clark's relationship with his teachers is no less dictatorial. He has attempted to discipline them by denouncing over the loudspeaker system some of those who disagree with him, and he has threatened to get rid of any teacher who disagrees with his policies. Clark's relationship with the

Patterson Education Association is just as controversial. One report indicated the "PEA representatives have been assailed as 'spineless, gutless bastards,' and one, who, like Clark, is black, was attacked as 'half a black man.'"[29] Clark's view of learning appears to be consistent with his view of leadership and is in part exhibited by his pedagogical practice of teaching a new vocabulary word over the loudspeaker system each day. Clark defends this practice on the grounds that black and Hispanic youngsters have to earn their diplomas through rigorous academic training. More recently, he has drawn criticism from the Patterson School Board and also faces possible court action for chaining shut the schoolhouse fire doors against alleged drug pushers and troublemakers.

What are we to make of an administration that provides moral and intellectual support for petty educational demagogues like Joe Clark? Similarly, what is to be inferred from the actions of the Reagan Administration toward Patricia Lara, a noted Columbian journalist who has been critical of united States policy in Latin American? Lara has been detained and prevented from entering the United States on the grounds she might "engage in subversive activities." The parading of Joe Clark as a model of administrative leadership and the detention of Patricia Lara provide an important signal as to how this administration views intellectuals—teachers, students, and other who work with ideas and provide a social function essential to any free society. These seemingly insignificant events should not be taken lightly by teachers and others who believe that the best learning takes place amid the free flow of ideas, and that democracy itself is central to such an exchange.

In actuality, the new public philosophy "positions" students within a language of citizenship that represents a profoundly detrimental form of anticivic education. Within this educational philosophy, relations of power are implicated in the distribution and legitimation of particular forms of knowledge, and in the way time and space are organized so as to educate the body and construct the type of moral character that accepts the virtues of passivity, obedience, and punctuality as normal and desirable. Subjection to a particular type of authority and rule become normalized, so to speak, through the daily routines of school organization and classroom learning. Under these circumstances it is not difficult to understand why most Americans don't even bother to vote in national elections. Politics even in its most narrowly defined terms has no value as a public activity or sphere.

Patriotism is now a code word not only for the inculcation of politically acceptable knowledge, but also for administering needs and desires within forms of sociality that contribute to patterns of habit and character consistent with the interests of the state. In the logic of the new patriotism, rationality and character molding have become central considerations in developing forms of pedagogy by which to educate generations of future citizens. In many respects, the evangelicalism that constitutes the moral underside of the new public philosophy is captured in a speech that Ronald Reagan gave in 1984 to the National Association of Evangelicals.

> We saw the signs all around us. Years ago, pornography, while available, was mostly sold "under the counter." By the mid-70's it was available in virtually every drugstore in the land. Drug abuse used to be confined to limited numbers of adults. During the 60's and 70's it spread through the nation like a fever, affecting children as well as adults. Liberal attitudes viewed promiscuity as acceptable, even stylish. Indeed, the word itself was replaced by the term "sexually active." . . . But the Almighty who gave us this great land also gave us free will—the power, under God, to choose our own destiny. The American people decided to put a stop to the long decline, and today our country is seeing a rebirth of freedom and faith—a great national renewal.[30]

Celluloid Patriotism in Hollywood Films and Television Programming

The reactionary view of patriotism that has become part of the educational reform movement at both the state and federal levels of government has a counterpart in a growing number of Hollywood films and television programs. The latter are actively involved in the construction of a view of citizenship that is squarely located in the ideology of the new nationalism and chauvinism. Celluloid patriotism is the cultural stuff of "real American" men, obedient children, and women who know their place. Within these particular ideological constructions, audiences are positioned within a cultural vision of America that resonates with three interlocking discourses which I will label as follows: the new anti-Communism, the obedient children syndrome, and the rise of the new male.

Before I discuss these three ideological discourses, it is important to stress that any discussion about the mass media has to be premised around a rejection of orthodox, classical Marxist definitions of ideology. In this case, I want to argue that ideology cannot be reduced to the determining instance of the economic, nor can it be reductively defined as merely an instance of "false consciousness." Instead, ideology needs to be defined as the very production of meaning as it is structured and expressed in ideas, social relations, signifying practices, and within and through the construction of experience. It is worth repeating what Judith Newton and Deborah Rosenfelt say about this notion of ideology:

> What this means ... is that "ideology is not necessarily a direct
> expression of ruling-class [or gender] interests at all moments in
> history and that at certain conjunctures it may even move into
> contradictions with those interests." Ideology, then, is not a set of
> deliberate distortions imposed on us from above, but a complex and
> contradictory system of representations (discourse, images, myths)
> through which we experience ourselves in relation to each other and
> to the social structures in which we live. Ideology is a system of
> representations through which we experience ourselves as well, for
> the work of ideology is also to construct coherent subjects: "the
> individual thus lives his [or her] subject-ion to social structures as a
> consistent subject-ivity, an imaginary wholeness."[31]

Similarly, in arguing that viewers are "positioned" within a particular discourse, I am not suggesting that such viewers directly absorb the ideological message conveyed by a particular film or signifying practice. On the contrary, I am arguing that the production and reproduction of meaning and values represents an ideological construction of both sociality and subjectivity, a signifying practice "that produces effects of meaning and perception, self-images and subject positions for all those involved, makers and viewers; and thus a semiotic process in which the subject is continually engaged, represented, and inscribed in ideology."[32] And yet while viewers always mediate an ideological experience, they *do not* do so from a historically innocent position. For instance, the image of women as object of male desire is produced and reinforced within the mass media through a powerful, encompassing set of patriarchal ideologies. The historical weight of this patriarchal ideology not only limits how women are constructed in films, for instance, but also limits how audiences mediate and respond to these images. Put more simply, ideologies are not simply implanted in the viewers' subjectivity, but at the same time that the viewers response may be historically open, the choices that one can make are historically constructed and limited.[33]

A number of films, like *Rambo, Rocky IV, White Nights, Red Dawn, Invasion U.S.A.*, and *Moscow on the Hudson*, are constructed around the discourse of anti-Communism. In these films the world is generally divided into those who love freedom and those who don't. Here the images, editing, and pacing are more slick than their film counterparts in the 1950s, but the players are the same—the battle is between the free world, led by the United States, and the Communists, represented by the Soviets. Almost without exception, the exaggerations that structure these films eliminate the complexities of the events and histories they portray. Similarly, they exhibit a patronizing posture fueled by a moral evangelicalism that approaches the exigence of the Crusades. What it means to be a citizen and a patriot in these films is very clear. It is to be a man who is willing to fight the godless hordes in order to save all that is decent in the "free" world. There are no choices here, nor are there any reservations about the interrelation between means and ends. Rambo's violence, Rocky's overbearing and stoic drive to seek revenge, Chuck Norris's pathological ingratiations in maiming endless numbers of the enemy all take place against a brand of anti-Communism that paints the Soviet characters as less than human beings. For example, in *Rocky IV*, the pugilistic hero, Drago, is portrayed as a heartless robot filled with steroids and programmed to both win and kill. Similarly, the KGB agent in *White Nights*, who determines the fate of Raymond, the black American who went AWOL and joined the Russians, is a political Mephistopheles whose ruthlessness is matched only by his blind devotion to the ideological values of the totalitarian state. And so it goes. Dehumanization has its rewards in these films. Not only do these films function to position viewers within a logic that makes it easy to celebrate the ideologies of militarism, nationalism, and machismo, they also embody a cultural project that rereads the history of the past in an attempt to provide solutions to enduring crises in a manner that wipes clean any lingering doubts about the integrity

of American domestic and foreign policy. Of course, this offers a collectively cathartic exercise for those who need to be redeemed, but it
also represents the death of critical historical consciousness, and for
generations who are decades removed from an event like the Vietnam War it helps promote a powerful form of historical amnesia. Of
course, some of these films contain what appears at first glance to be
progressive ideological contradictions. Rambo, for instance, not only
hates the Russians but also disdains the new brand of computer-ori-
ented, government intelligence bureaucrats. But these contradictions are canceled out by a deeper ideological grammar. In the case
of Rambo, his hatred of the new computers and the morally weak
bureaucrats simply reinforces the image of his preindustrial moral
goodness, his representation of the virtues of a tradition long lost in
the United States, one currently represented by the like of national
leaders such as Reagan, Weinberger, and Bennett (Rambos with
white shirts and blue suits).

The second category of film that promotes a brand of celluloid
patriotism relies less upon the ideology of anti-Communism than
upon the celebration of certain traits that constitute the dominant
ideology's version of "real" masculine character and virtue. This is
the stuff of character building, or Americanism, in the manner of the
film *The Right Stuff*. In films such as *Top Gun* and *Iron Eagle*, a new
form of adolescent/man emerges. These are the military yuppies of
the 1980s, the young cadets out to set the record straight about the
role of young people in America and what it means to love the country and come home to father. *Iron Eagle*'s premise has an American
jet pilot shot down and placed on trial for violating the airspace of a
North African nation (Libya). When the State Department and the
army refuse to do anything to rescue the pilot, his teenage son teams
up with a black Colonel to steal a couple of F16s and take matters
into their own hands. Resistance takes a new twist in the film. Instead
of challenging the logic of militarism, the young people in this film
endorse it through what appears to be an act of superpatriotism. But
this is resistance that pays off. Dad is rescued in the end, and his son,
Doug, is admitted to the Air Force Academy, even though he has bad
grades. Of course, Doug's willingness to takes chances, and his alliance with a member of a subordinate group, strike a resonant note
with some audiences. But Doug's real high tech appeal is the introduction of rock music in the film. It seems that Doug can't hit a target

unless he has James Brown blaring out of the cassette deck in the F16. Right-wing patriotism isn't afraid to integrate popular culture into its logic.

Top Gun is also about the development of character and patriotism among young men who have decided to resist in the interest of Pax Americana. In this case, patriotism underscores the importance of competition, hyperachievement, and a form of excellence that disregards all vestiges of community and solidarity. The plot revolves around a pilot and his friend being sent to the nation's top fighter-weapons school in 1968. The term "top gun" refers to the ultimate pedagogical reward offered by the school to the pilot who scores the highest in his class. School, in this case, is about preparing for combat, about young men who frame their sexual desires around a love for high-powered jet technology, who talk of getting a "hard on" when they see the jets in action, and who learn how to collapse all vestige of ethics and choice into the logic of getting the job done. This film celebrates the military model of authority. Patriotism and citizenship in this film revolve around a love of war machines, an unflinching respect for the authority of the fathers, and a deep-seated resentment for any forms of sociality that undermine the virtues of competition and individual achievement. Women in films like *Top Gun* are second-rate characters, who appear faceless, sexless, and expendable. If anything, their presence simply serves to suggest that the men in the films are heterosexuals, in spite of their overall hatred and indifference to women.

In many respects, the denigrating portrayal of women within the discourse of the new patriotism is being mirrored in the resurrection of the new male in many new television shows. The new male portrayed in television programs like "Miami Vice," "Cheers," "Remington Steele," and "Moonlighting" represents the return and legitimation of an unreconstructed chauvinism. The new American male, as Peter J. Boyer points out, is:

> spontaneous, unhesitant, sure. In action drama, his antagonists are unqualifiedly bad, and he disposes of them accordingly, shooting first and getting in touch with his feelings later, if at all. In comedy, he is a womanizer.[34]

Although this perspective does not speak directly to the themes associated with patriotism, it does reconstruct social relations around forms of patriarchy and chauvinism that are essential to the right-wing notion of citizenship currently being mobilized in the electronic media. Citizenship in this case combines an appeal to traditional values with an ideology that legitimates a Reagan-type hypernationalism. Moreover, it reinforces a return to forms of institutional authority that refuse to tolerate dissent while promoting social relations in which chauvinism and sexism combine to redefine the meaning of masculinity and power.

Before addressing some general theoretical issues regarding the development of a critical theory of citizenship education, it is important to reiterate that the interests I have criticized as part of the dominant ideology of citizenship of schooling and the mass media should not suggest that such ideological interests are taken up in a relatively simple, straightforward manner. In many respects, the dominant ideology simply resonates with needs and experiences that not only are ambiguous but also contain elements of hope, lost potentials, and abortive dreams. In some cases, the ideologies that characterize the films I have discussed speak to the need for reaffirmation, to the need to have a voice, and to create larger-than-life figures who articulate the frustration and despair experienced by many people in this country. The point being, of course, that uncovering the mystifying aspects of the dominant ideology in these films is important but does not go far enough. A truly critical pedagogy would also uncover the latent possibilities, needs, and hopes that point to the possibility for further analysis and struggle.

Reclaiming Citizenship Education for Democracy

I want to conclude by reemphasizing and extending some theoretical considerations for developing a critical theory of citizenship education (the specifics of which will be taken up throughout the remainder of this book). Central to a politics and pedagogy of critical citizenship is the need to reconstruct a visionary language and public philosophy that put equality, liberty, and human life at the center of the notions of democracy and citizenship. There are four aspects to this language that warrant some consideration. First, it is important to acknowledge that the notion of democracy cannot be grounded in some ahistorical, transcendent notion of truth or authority. Democracy is a "site" of struggle and as a social practice is informed by competing ideological conceptions of power, politics, and community. This is an important recognition because it helps to redefine the role of the citizen as an active agent in questioning, defining, and shaping one's relationship to the political sphere and the wider society. As Laclau and Mouffe put it, the radical concept which democratic society introduces is that

> the reference to a transcendent guarantor disappears, and with it the representation of the substantial unity of society. . . . The possibility is thus opened up of an unending process of questioning: no law which can be fixed, whose dictates are not subject to contest, or whose foundations cannot be called into question. . . . Democracy inaugurates the experience of a society which cannot be apprehended or controlled, in which the people will be proclaimed sovereign, but in which its identity will never be definitely given but remain latent.[35]

Implicit in this position is a challenge to both liberal and right-wing notions of the concept of the political. That is, the notion of the political is not reduced to the liberal emphasis on following rules of legality and administrative procedure. Nor is it reduced to the right-wing view that politics is a private affair whose outcome has little to do with the public good and everything to do with the defense of the free-market economy and an individualist definition of rights and freedom. But it is important to stress that in redefining the notion of the political, the Left cannot merely reject out of hand the recent convergence of neoliberal and right-wing views of democracy. Instead, it must "deepen and expand it [the meaning of the political] in the direction of a radical and plural democracy."[36] For Laclau and Mouffe, this means acknowledging the importance of those fundamental antagonisms among women, diverse racial and sexual minorities, and other subordinate groups who have opened up radical new and different political spaces around which to press for the extension of democratic discourse and rights. The emergence of these new democratic struggles serves to demonstrate the need for a revitalized view of the meaning and importance of the concept of the political. Benjamin Barber has reinforced this view by rightly arguing that the American Left needs to ground the notion of the political in historical traditions that both reveal the subversive and dignifying power of democratic discourse and support the overarching importance of the autonomy of political discourse in understanding and influencing important aspects of our daily lives. He writes:

> The alternative [for the Left] is a revitalization of the autonomy of politics, and of the sovereignty of the political over other domains of our collective existence. The tradition that yielded the American constitution saw civic equality as the crucial equality. According to this tradition, politics can remake the world, and political access, political equality, and political justice are the means to economic and social equality. The Left's best weapons remain the American Constitution and the democratic political tradition it has fostered.[37]

Although Barber understates the problematic nature of relying on the American Constitution as a text for radical democracy (Robert Bork notwithstanding), he does recognize that democracy needs to be seen as an active social movement based on ideological and institutional relations of power that call for a vigorous participatory politics steeped in the traditions of a Jeffersonian democracy. In order to put a radical notion of democracy back on the agenda, the Left needs to redevelop a conception of active citizenship, which could be forcefully advanced against liberal and conservative spokespersons "who urge more moderation in democracy, measures to return the population to . . . a state of apathy and passivity so that 'democracy', in the preferred sense, can survive."[38] In radical terms, active citizenship would not reduce democratic rights merely to participation in the process of electoral voting, but would extend the notion of rights to participation to the economy, the state, and other public spheres. Thomas Ferguson captures this sentiment in his observation that

> the prerequisites for effective democracy are not really automatic voter registration or even Sunday voting, though these would help. Rather, deeper institutional forces-flourishing unions, readily accessible third parties, inexpensive media, and a thriving network of cooperatives and community organizations—are the real basis of effective democracy.[39]

Second, a radical language of citizenship and democracy entails a strengthening of the horizontal ties between citizen and citizen. This calls for a politics of difference in which the demands, cultures, and social relations of diverse groups are recognized as part of the discourse of radical pluralism. As a form of radical pluralism, the category of difference is not reduced to the possessive individualism of the autonomous subject at the heart of liberal ideology. On the contrary, a politics of difference in this form of pluralism would be grounded in various social groups and public spheres whose unique voices and social practices contain their own principles of validity while sharing in a public consciousness and discourse. Central to this form of radical pluralism is a public philosophy that recognizes the boundaries between different groups, the self and others, and at the same time creates a politics of trust and solidarity that supports a common life based on democratic principles that create the ideological and institutional preconditions for both diversity and the public good.[40]

This leads to my third consideration. A revitalized discourse of democracy should not be based exclusively on a language of critique, one that, for instance, limits its focus on the schools to the elimination of relations of subordination and inequality. This is an important political concern, but in both theoretical and political terms it is woefully incomplete. As part of a radical political project, the discourse of democracy also needs a language of possibility, one that combines a strategy of opposition with a strategy for constructing a new social order. Such a project represents both a struggle over historical tradition as well as the construction of a new set of social relations between the subject and the wider community. Put more specifically, the radical democrats need to situate the struggle for democracy in a utopian project, one that presupposes a vision of the future grounded in a programmatic language of civic responsibility and public good. Ernst Bloch paid significant attention to the importance of the utopian impulse in radical thought, and his notion of the production of images of that which is "not yet" is clearly captured in his analysis of daydreams.

> Dreams come in the day as well as at night. And both kinds of dreaming are motivated by the wishes they seek to fulfill. But daydreams differ from night dreams; for the day dreaming "I" persists throughout, consciously, privately, envisaging the circumstances and images of a desired, better life. The content of the daydream is not, like that of the night dream, a journey back into repressed experiences and their associations. It is concerned with, as far as possible, an unrestricted journey forward, so that instead of reconstituting that which is no longer conscious, the images of that which is not yet can be phantasied into life and into the world.[41]

As I see it, Bloch's insistence on incorporating the utopian notion of "unrealized possibilities" in radical theory provides a foundation for analyzing and constituting critical theories of schooling and citizenship. In this case, both schooling and the form of citizenship it legitimates can be deconstructed as a type of historical and ideological narrative that provides an introduction to, preparation for, and legitimation of particular forms of social life in which a vision of the future, a sense of what life could be like, is given a central place. Given the fundamental anti-utopianism that characterizes so much of radical discourse today, the incorporation of a utopian logic as part of a project of possibility represents an important advance in rethinking the role that teachers and others might play in defining schooling within a language of civic and public responsibility, one which views schools as democratic public spheres committed to forms of cultural politics aimed at empowering students and enhancing human possibilities.

Fourth, educators need to define schools as public spheres where the dynamics of popular engagement and democratic politics can be cultivated as part of the struggle for a radical democratic society. That is, educators need to legitimate schools as democratic public spheres, as places that provide an essential public service in the construction of active citizens, in order to defend them for their centrality in the maintenance of a democratic society and critical citizenry. In this case, schooling would be analyzed not only in terms of how it reproduces the logic and social practices of capitalism, but also for its potential to nourish civic literacy, citizen participation, and moral courage. As pedagogical principles that inform particular human capacities and social practices, civic literacy and citizen participation gain expression as forms of moral agency and political responsibility aimed at fashioning the practices and institutions of society around a democratic conception of collective life. The notion of citizen participation at work here goes far beyond the legal-abstract notion of citizenship celebrated in mainstream notions of democracy. As Barbara Finkelstein points out,

> citizens in a "just and friendly society" ... are social beings who in
> their public roles reveal their character and commitments. As
> citizens, they practice moral agency. If the conditions of modern life
> prevent the social exercise of moral agency—if the political economy
> precludes it, government ceases to require it, education fails to

model it—then freedom and justice are threatened. If people cannot, will not, or do not identify and socialize personal commitments in public acting, then they cease to be citizens. They are transformed into cunning rationalists, or mere functionaries, no longer the protectors of justice, freedom, or dignity. As a moral matter, their commitments to freedom, justice, and dignity become either empty pieties, or worse, demagogic invocations of socially disconnected rhetoric.[42]

As part of a radical democratic public philosophy, a theory of critical citizenship must begin to develop alternative roles for teachers as radical intellectuals to pursue both in and out of schools. This is an important issue because it highlights the necessity of linking the political struggle within schools to broader societal issues. At the same time, it underlies the importance of teachers using their skills and insights in alliance with others who are attempting to redefine the terrain of politics and citizenship as part of a wider collective struggle in alliance with various social movements. The role that intellectuals might play in such movements needs to be clarified, especially with respect to making the political more pedagogical and the pedagogical more political. Let me be more specific.

As critical teachers working in schools, we can make the *pedagogical more political* by clarifying how the complex dynamics of ideology and power both organize and mediate the various experiences and dimensions of school life. One possible approach might be to organize a radical pedagogy of citizenship around a theory of critical literacy. The linking of literacy to citizenship education provides a way of avoiding developing citizenship education as a separate course, and at the same time infuses its major concerns across the various subjects and disciplines. Fundamental to a pedagogy of critical literacy would be the opportunity for students to interrogate how knowledge is constituted as both a historical and social construction. In addition, students can be given the opportunity to address the question of how knowledge and power come together in often contradictory ways to sustain and legitimate particular discourses that define a notion of public good. This suggests everything from criticizing curricula content and classroom social relations to engaging in policy struggles over issues such as school leadership and state control. As part of the discourse of democracy and emancipatory citizenship, critical literacy can begin with analyses that focus on institutional dynamics and individual/group experiences as they unfold in all of their contradictions within particular social relations; furthermore, critical literacy can provide the theoretical basis for presenting students with the knowledge and skills necessary for them to understand and analyze their own historically constructed voices and experiences as part of a project of self and social empowerment. Central to this view of literacy is an understanding of how knowledge and experience are constructed around particular forms of intellectual, moral, and social regulation within the various relations of power that characterize schools, families, workplaces, the state, and other major public spheres.

As part of a broader theory of citizenship, literacy is about deconstructing knowledge in order to understand more critically one's own experiences and relations to the wider society. More specifically, it is part of a critical pedagogy designed to further understand how needs, emotional investment, and desire are regulated as part of the hegemonic project of the state in order to police and control the body as a site of surveillance and service. Although this point has been mentioned previously and will be taken up in later chapters, it is worth reemphasizing that a viable theory of citizenship has to do more than treat ideology as a way to interrogate the interests that structure particular forms of knowledge. Ideology is also rooted in those sedimented experiences learned practically through the mobilization and regulation of the body and emotions. Citizenship as a pedagogy implies the mobilization of knowledge and social relations, both of which serve to organize the body and emotions within particular regulations of space and time. This broader view of ideology represents an important form of learning that contributes to the formation of subjectivities and must become a fundamental object of inquiry for any critical theory of citizenship.

Reconstructed in these terms, critical literacy and citizenship education provide the rationale for developing schools as democratic public spheres. That is, as democratic public spheres, schools become places where students learn the knowledge and skills of citizenship within forms of solidarity that provide the basis for constructing emancipatory forms of community life. What this suggests is that a public philosophy is needed that links the purpose of schooling to the development of forms of knowledge and moral character in which citizenship is defined as an ethical compact, not a commercial contract, and empowerment is related to forms of self-and social formation that encourage people to participate critically in shaping public life.

A revitalized public philosophy also has to be grounded in a view of democracy based on relations that promote the realization of communities developed around forms of solidarity that advance the practices of critical citizenship and the quality of public life. Fundamental here is what it means to be human and to expand human possibilities for improving the quality of life and extending the meaning of freedom. At the risk of overstating the issue, citizenship education must be organized around a public philosophy that legitimates and provides the basis for developing democratic public spheres both within and outside the schools. It must be dedicated to the creation of a citizenry capable of expressing political and ethical leadership in the wider society. Public philosophy in this sense points to a view of citizenship education that reclaims the notions of struggle, solidarity, and hope around forms of social action that expand rather than restrict the notion of civic courage and public life.

As educators, we can help make the political more pedagogical by joining with social groups and movements outside schools that are struggling in order to address a number of important social problems and issues. Such alliances are important not only because they link the struggle for democratic public schooling to wider societal concerns and issues, but also because they demonstrate the possibility for intellectuals to work not merely as specific intellectuals in their respective work sites, but also as part of a number of separate but not unconnected struggles in which their theoretical and pedagogical skills can be put to use. Put another way, as critical educators, we can move beyond our social function as public/university/private school teachers so that we can apply and enrich our knowledge and skills through practical engagements in oppositional public spheres outside the schools.

Underlying this redefinition of teachers as both critical teachers and educators is a notion of citizenship that represents both the struggle over tradition as well as the construction of a new set of relations between school and the wider community. Inherent in such a task is the need to reconstitute a public philosophy that provides an ethical base for defining the meaning of democracy and the shaping of character around emancipatory interests. This means that citizenship education needs to be grounded in a public philosophy dedicated to uncovering sources of suffering and oppression, while legitimating social practices that uphold principles of sociality and community that are dedicated to improving the quality of human life.

In the chapters that follow, I attempt to generate a set of categories that link critique with possibility in the hope of providing a theoretical and programmatic discourse that gives some practical meaning to the idea of schooling as a form of cultural politics. I am acutely aware that my context is almost exclusively North American, but I believe that the radical discourse provided in this book can be used by educators in other countries and critically appropriated and selectively applied to the specific context in which they work and struggle. This is not to suggest that I am providing a recipe book as much as I am acknowledging that any discourse needs to be interrogated, mediated, and critically appropriated so that it can be used within specific contexts by those who see value in it. What this book represents is a particular way of seeing, a view of theory as a form of practice, one that rejects the fetish of defining the practical as the flight from theoretical concerns. On the contrary, theory as a form of practice points to the need for constructing a critical discourse to both constitute and reorder the nature of our experiences and the objects of our concerns so as to both enhance and further empower the ideological and institutional conditions for a radical democracy. The theoretical framework presented here makes no claim to certainty; it is a discourse that is unfinished, but one that may help illuminate the specifics of oppression and the possibilities for democratic struggle and renewal for those educators who believe that schools and society can be changed and that their individual and collective actions can make a difference.

2

Schooling and the Politics of Ethics: Beyond Conservative and Liberal Discourses

Within contemporary strands of radical educational theory a paradox surrounds the relationship between ethics, politics, and schooling. On the one hand, radical educational theory has exhibited a profound critique of, and moral indignation toward the social and political injustices that are reproduced in American public schools. On the other hand, it has failed to develop a moral and ethical discourse upon which to ground its own vision of society and schooling.[1] Moreover, it has failed to develop a theory of ethics that could legitimate and provide reflective mediation on emancipatory forms of classroom pedagogy. Caught in the paradox of exhibiting moral indignation without the benefit of a well-defined theory of ethics and morality, radical educational theory has been unable to move from criticism to substantive vision. In other words, radical educators have been unable to develop an ethical grounding and set of interests upon which to construct a public philosophy that takes seriously the relationship between schooling and a democratic public life.[2] In effect, moral indignation has often been expressed in a language paralyzed by skepticism and unable to move beyond the limited task of charting and registering the failure of American schooling.[3] Lost from this perspective is any attempt at recovering and building upon those forms of subjectivity and a collective struggle rooted in a creative, self-transforming, life-enhancing morality which the dominant culture so actively conceals and precludes whenever possible.[4] Bereft of a language of moral purpose, radical educational theory has been unable to posit a theoretical discourse and set of categories as a basis for constructing forms of knowledge, classroom social relations, and visions of the future that give substance to the meaning of critical pedagogy.

In many respects, the failure of radical educational theorists to develop a substantively grounded theory of ethics represents a flight not only from the discourse of hope but from the center of politics itself. That is, by failing to develop a language of morality and ethics, radical educational theory has generally conceded the high ground to a view of schooling and society that is fundamentally incapable of defining a notion of the public good. Lost is the ability to define a democratic vision or a view of authority upon which to establish a form of politics that combines the many virtues "found in ties of love, friendship, and association with a commitment to basic liberal values of freedom, respect, and self determination."[5]

The failure of radical educational theorists to formulate clear criteria on which to argue for particular forms of ethical behavior has also resulted in forms of historical inquiry that impede our understanding of how social movements develop around shared forms of moral discourse and vision. In other words, radical theorists have generally ignored the political necessity for illuminating historical traditions and experiences which serve to recover those lost moral visions and principles that give meaning to forms of self-and social transformation. What has been lost in this instance is a notion of historical inquiry that could show how the deep grammar of moral and ethical responsibility empowered social movements to struggle and fight for the imperatives of a democratic society and a liberating notion of public schooling. Limited in this way, historical inquiry has a strong tendency to collapse into an overly determined view of social control in which schools are viewed primarily as reflections of capitalist domination. What is missing from these perspectives is an adequate understanding of how moral and political agency come together to inspire both a discourse of hope and a political project that take seriously what it means to envision a better life and society.

By ignoring the centrality of morals and ethics in the struggle for human emancipation, radical educators have effectively removed themselves from the debate on schooling, politics, and values that has been gaining force in the United States within the last decade. In fact, it is becoming increasingly clear that one of the most important struggles for hegemony now being waged in American society is around the issue of the moral values underlying schooling. In the midst of a rampant moral relativism, the dissolution of democratic public life, and the dramatic increase in the suffering and exploitation of subordinate groups in American society, radical educational theory needs to develop a *moral discourse and theory of ethics*. Murray Bookchin captures the urgency of recovering a radical ethical stance in his comment:

> The reinstatement of an ethical stance becomes central to the recovery of a meaningful society and a sense of selfhood, a realism that is in closer touch with reality than the opportunism, lesser-evil strategies, and benefit-versus-risk calculations claimed by the practical wisdom of our time. Action from principle can no longer be separated from a mature, serious, and concerted attempt to resolve our social and private problems. The highest realism can be attained only by looking beyond the given state of affairs to a vision of what should be, not only what is. The crisis we face in human subjectivity as well as human affairs is so great, and its received wisdom is so anemic, that we literally will not be if we do not realize our potentialities to be more than we are.[6]

At the core of developing a critical theory of schooling around such an ethical stance is a twofold task. First, there is the need to constitute a protest against those existing ideological and social practices that further the mechanisms of power and domination at the level of everyday life; such a protest means moving beyond moral outrage and providing a critical account of how, within the immediate and wider dimensions of everyday life, individuals are constituted as human agents within *different* moral and ethical discourses and experiences. This raises important questions regarding not only how actions and discussions can be problematized in moral terms, but also how language, social practices, ideologies, and values work as part of the discourse of domination so as to legitimate authorities that both treat human beings as means and reproduce relations of domination, force, and violence. As a language of protest, radical ethics needs to provide a counterlogic to those relations of power and ideologies in capitalist society that mask a totalitarian ethics and strip critical ethical discourse from public life. Second, the task of developing a radical ethics as a vital part of a radical theory of education also involves developing a vision of the future, one rooted in the construction of sensibilities and social relations that give meaning to a notion of community life that understands democracy as a struggle for extending civil rights and seriously improving the quality of human life.

Central to this approach is the need for critical educators to develop a substantive moral rationality that moves beyond both the conservative reliance on an essentialist, a priori set of moral principles as well as the free-floating antifoundationalism so prominent in various forms of liberal postmodern and poststructuralist thought. In opposition to these positions, educators need to develop a provisional morality that corresponds to emancipatory social practices rooted in historical experience. Ethical discourse, in this case, needs to be given a historical referent that comprehends the historical consequences of what it meant to take an emancipatory position on the horror and suffering of the Gulag, the Nazi holocaust, the Pol Pot regime, and other historical events. Such events not only summon up images of terror, domination, and resistance, but also provide a priori examples of what principles have to be both defended and fought against in the interest of freedom and life.[7] Essential to my argument is the assumption that a critical discourse of ethics can be constructed around what I call a radical provisional morality. Such an approach is tied to those cultural and political traditions whose commitment is historically grounded in forms of moral agency and their accompanying social relations: the discourse of critical democracy, the discourse of an emancipatory politics of experience, and the discourse of possibility and hope. In opposition to some Marxian views of history as a linear and unambiguous trajectory of the unfolding of human events, educators must confront the uncertainty of historical outcomes and develop a provisional morality steeped in a frankly partisan reading of history. As Walter Benjamin implied in his essay "Thesis on The Philosophy of History,"[8] history has to be constructed from the point of view of the victims. For radical educational theory, this represents an appropriation of history steeped in a commitment to democracy, justice, and equality. It is important to stress that the ethical presuppositions that inform a progressive and critical theory of education and define its political project must be situated in a selective reading of critical historical traditions; moreover, the source of such presuppositions are to be located in the human capacity for political courage, rather than the doctrine of historical inevitability.

In what follows, I will argue that the current debate around ethics, schooling, public life, and politics has been primarily dominated by conservative and liberal discourses that share an anti-utopianism in which history remains abstracted from the language and discourse of hope. It is this stress on anti-utopianism that needs to be interrogated and critically transcended by an alternative notion of morality and ethics. Following a criticism of these positions, I will develop in the next chapter a theory of authority grounded in an ethics drawn from a selective reading of the debates on democracy and schooling that took place among social reconstructionists and progressives in the early part of the twentieth century; I will also selectively draw from feminist and liberation theology writings on ethics and community. In each case, I will examine how these traditions provide a basis for developing both a theory of radical ethics and for enlarging the meaning and practice of a critical theory of schooling and pedagogy.

Any attempt to develop a radical theory of ethics must begin with a dual recognition. First, dominant forms of educational theorizing within the last decade have been heavily influenced by forms of moral theory that share certain characteristics: an abstraction from everyday life; an indeterminacy and relativism that undermines the possibility for moral agency; and a refusal to link moral discourse with an emancipatory political project. In various ways these theoretical tendencies have affected the political discourses of both the Right and the Left and have made it increasingly difficult to develop an alternative radical theory of ethics and schooling rooted in the political and social imperatives of democratic citizenship. Second, a growing political illiteracy among the general populace, the increasing refusal of higher education to address the problems of citizenship and public life as a result of its increasing capitulation to the research demands of the marketplace, and the growing alienation and breakdown of public life reinforced by the dominant ideologies of individualism, consumerism, and scientific rationality have profoundly exacerbated a qualitative decline in the language and social practices of schooling, community, and family life.

Ironically, it has been those on the Right and not Left progressives and liberals who have been able to articulate most clearly and forcefully the problems associated with the breakdown of these areas. The Right has clearly recognized the need to develop a language of morality in its struggle to redefine its ethical and political vision of schooling, the family, and community life.[9] Its success has been astonishing, not to say disturbing. In the religious sphere it has mobilized millions of people through its use of television to spread the discourse of moral religious evangelicalism and fundamentalism. It has mounted a massive assault against feminism and against abortion rights, couching its attack in the language of morality. And, it has launched an increasingly successful attack on "secular humanism" in the schools in an attempt to promote either the teaching of religious fundamentalism or what it calls "character education."[10] In what follows, I focus specifically on the Right's attempt to revitalize the language of morality in the public schools. In my mind, this not only represents a dangerous attack on the most fundamental aspects of democratic public life and the obligations of critical citizenship, but also posits a terrain of struggle in which radical and progressive educators need to engage if schools are going to provide any possibility in the future for educating students to be critical and active democratic citizens.

Right Wing Ideology and the Ethics of Schooling

Since the advent of the Reagan administration, and especially since the appointment of William Bennett as Secretary of Education, various right-wing spokespersons, in and out of the government, have become quite aggressive in pushing a program for schools to address and teach a particular set of moral values and virtues. Despite the genuine diversity among these group at the level of theory, there is an underlying ideological unity to their political projects. I want to focus on three of these points of convergence: their restructuring of a mythical "golden age" in order to legitimate the teaching of specific values; their attack on the 1960s and the discourse of equity; and their criticism of existing liberal moral education programs in the public schools.

First, the ultraconservatives have constructed an unproblematic view of history in which it is argued that schools once acted as the moral gatekeepers of society, teaching good old-fashioned "republican virtues" embodied in texts like the McGuffey readers and in the old Latin classics curriculum.[11] For conservatives like Edward A. Wynne, the answer to today's educational problems is a return to the nineteenth-century mythical past in order to recover traditional American virtues and transmit them to students through what he openly calls indoctrination.[12] In an interesting sleight of hand, Wynne appropriates the left-wing critique of schools as institutions of social control and justifies public schooling precisely on these terms. That is, for Wynne, socialization should be the central focus of schooling and indoctrination the key pedagogical method through which to educate students. The goal is to ensure that students take their rightful places in the social and occupational order. As Wynne puts it, "The term 'social control' may have a pejorative sound to our modern ears, but it simply and correctly means that schools were concerned with affecting conduct, rather than transmitting informa-tion or affecting states of mind."[13] Wynne is, in fact, adamant about the pedagogical virtues of indoctrination: he views schools as places that should transmit values instead of critically appropriating, con-testing, and engaging them.

In a similar vein, educators such as Secretary of Education William Bennett and Superintendent for California public schools Bill Honig have urged public school educators to return to a conservative read-ing of history and the teaching of traditional values by reconstructing public school curricula around the central notion of character for-mation. Right-wing commentator Kevin Ryan finds that the most appealing aspect of the word "character," as used by Bennett and Honig, is that it brings the notion of socialization to the forefront of educational discourse. He writes:

In the Eighties, culture is once again viewed as a human achievement that should be transmitted to the young. To transmit the culture, however, we must introduce the young to its ethical principles and moral values. In other words, much of schooling should be vigorously devoted to teaching the young those things that the society has learned about how to live together in a civilized fashion.[14]

The values at the heart of such character formation have been pro-vided by Secretary Bennett in his listing of the Reagan administra-tion's most desirable moral characteristics. These include: "thought-fulness, kindness, honesty, respect for the law, knowing right from wrong, respect for parents and teachers, diligence, self-sacrifice, hard work, fairness, self-discipline, and love of country."[15] The ideological interests that structure these virtues are in part revealed in the authoritarian pedagogy designed to teach them. It is a pedagogy marked by a rigid view of knowledge, an uncritical view of American history, and a refusal to develop a theory of learning in which students are allowed to speak from their own traditions and voices. The underlying nature of the social practices and forms of power such virtues are designed to legitimate can also be seen in the right-wing celebration of the 1980s as a return to normalcy, to a period of conservative calm and patriotic virtue. One particular celebration of the 1980s is worth repeating in full:

> A society exhausted by change and internal strife now seems to be struggling to return to normal. President Carter, discouraged by the nation's ennui and paralyzed by the hostage crisis in Iran, was replaced in 1980 by a popular and upbeat President, Ronald Reagan. Church attendance began to rise. The divorce rate began to decline. "Preppy" came back into style; even the nihilistic punk movement has become just another fashion trend. The major television networks lost interest in Norman Lear and in the probing of social mores; they returned instead to situation comedies about recognizable families, e.g., "The Cosby Show" and "Family Ties." The national economy and the national spirit are flying high. The alienated, existential heroes of the Beat Generation and the articulate and angry young adults who led the various protest movements of the Sixties and the Seventies have been replaced by—and sometimes transformed into—Yuppies, who keep one eye on careers and the other on their stock portfolios.[16]

This description of the 1980s is oddly unencumbered by the slap-happy greed characteristic of the new Yuppie morality or the chauvinistic hypocrisy characteristic of United States foreign policy. It is appalling that within the right-wing view of contemporary society there is a careless silence about the homeless people everywhere present in our major cities, the growing division between the rich and the poor at all levels of society, the gun-running diplomacy at work in Central America, and the undermining of three decades' worth of civil rights legislation. In an era of militant chauvinism, with its celebration of Rambolike images of good and evil, along with an utter disregard for historically accumulated suffering, the conservative view of history and celebration of good old republican virtues appear to be nothing more than an apology for the status quo, an exercise of political clout in the era of "good feelings" and "good times."

A second unifying theme of the right-wing discourse on ethics centers on an attack on the social and educational reforms of the 1960s. According to this view, the educational upheavals and reforms that characterized the Sixties diluted academic standards and bequeathed a serious decline in academic achievement and competency. In the Right's view, the reforms of the 1960s contributed to the loss of United States superiority in the world economy and contributed to many of the major domestic and social problems of the 1980s. For instance, Franklin Parker argues that

> civil rights, freedom riders, free speech, student protests, Vietnam, Watergate, women's liberation. . . . These dislocations, plus rising crime and drug use, showed a discontent, anger, and drive for self-destruction that are still incomprehensible.[17]

Similarly, Wynne argues that the 1960s caused a breakdown in the moral consensus of the Great Tradition and that this is especially "significant in view of the increase . . . of youth disorder: suicide, homicide, and out-of-wedlock births."[18] Ryan extends this argument by claiming that the 1960s contributed to a "new anti-authority spirit" that further undermined the influence and power of teachers. As a result, teachers became morally confused and weak and wilfully retreated to the role of a hapless technician.[19] Ryan forgets that much of the deskilling that has characterized teacher work in the 1980s has little to do with the reforms of the 1960s and a great deal to do with the increased centralization of public school systems and the loss of teachers' control over the conditions of their work. In part this has happened through the imposition of "accountability models" of teaching and evaluation. Teachers have also lost power through the standardization of school curricula, including the adoption by many school systems of prepackaged, so-called teacher-proof curricula. If there is a crisis in teaching, it has little to do with a retreat from conservative moral values. Ira Shor speaks to some of the more immediate problems that public schools have faced.

> In reality, the current crisis resulted from budget cuts that left class sizes too large, school buildings shabby, instructional materials in

short supply, education programs unable to afford careful mentoring of student teachers, and aging academic departments deprived of new blood. Further, conservative educational policy in the 1970s imposed depressing programs of careerism and back-to-basics, making intellectual life in the classroom dull, vocational, and over-supervised.[20]

Shor's position is an important corrective to the right-wing attack on schools, but it too suffers from a refusal to analyze the long-term forces in the United States that have contributed to the crisis in public schooling. The rise of scientism and the social efficiency movement in the 1920s, the increasing impingement of state policy in shaping school curricula, the anticommunism of the l950s, the increasing influence of industrial psychology in defining the purpose of schooling, the racism, sexism, and class discrimination that have been reinforced through increasing forms of tracking and testing, and the failure of teachers to gain an adequate level of control over the conditions of their labor are all issues that have a long historical tradition in this country and that need to be included in any analysis of the problems that public schools are currently facing.

All of the arguments by the Right appear to share the notion that what is wrong with the schools is the result of what is new about them since the early 1960s. Of course, what is new has been partly a series of school reforms aimed at empowering disadvantaged minorities and linking issues of equity to issues of excellence as a central definition of school performance and success. The Right's attack on the early reforms is, in reality, merely a thinly disguised attack on the notion of equity itself. Its view of excellence is narrowly defined at the expense of empowering minorities; it supports forms of schooling that benefit the children of the white middle and upper classes. Its elitist view of schooling, parading under the dubious banner of meritocracy promotes antidemocratic tendencies based on a celebration of cultural uniformity, a rigid view of authority, a labor-market role for public schooling, and a distorted view of the success of the American school system prior to the 1950s.[21] The Right's view of history and equity has not gone unchallenged.

Mass education in its first half-century does not make today's failures look exceptional. Drop-out figures cited in urban school surveys conducted in the early 1900s are nearly identical to the figures cited in the 1979-1983 Chicago survey, although the incidence of failure was more likely to be at the elementary school level. Descriptions of traditional mass schooling present the familiar features of educational inequality: intense overcrowding, overworked and underpaid staff, grim and decaying facilities, insufficient and arcane textbooks, ethnic and racial hostility, and vast disparities in funding. The socialization that occurred was not a lesson in democratic values, but it was a convincing exposure to the hard realities of competition and social stigmatization. And repeatedly, the concept of meritocracy served to bridge the gap between elitist practice and democratic promise, by justifying the application of double standards, and by presuming that the disadvantaged were deficient rather than underserved.[22]

Another unifying theme in the Right's discourse on ethics and schooling centers on its attack on liberal models of moral education that have exercised some influence on school curricula during the last twenty years. The Right has attempted to develop its own theory of character education primarily through an attack on three dominant liberal approaches to moral teaching: the values-clarification approach; the Kohlbergian approach to moral reasoning; and the applied ethics approach.

The most sustained attack waged by the Right has been against the values-clarification approach developed by Sidney Simon and others.[23] In this approach, students are asked to clarify their own values through an analysis of often competing views of major social issues like poverty, war, crime, and drugs. The role of the teacher is to act as a mediator who has the dual task of both presenting problems and clarifying discussions. The theoretical and intellectual shoddiness of the values-clarification approach provides an easy target for right-wing criticism. Values-clarification fails for a number of reasons. Conservatives argue that by advocating choice as the basis for teaching and developing moral values, values-clarification theorists end up supporting a contentless pedagogy that tacitly endorses value neutrality. That is, students are given no criteria by which to discriminate between different and competing values. Conservatives also fault values-clarification for ignoring what the Right considers an unambiguous truth, namely that "a moral sensibility and social conscience are, in significant measure, learned by reading and discussing the classics."[24] Another criticism of the values-clarification approach is that it blurs an important distinction between moral and nonmoral values. The choice between different hairstyles, for example, is given as much moral weight as the choices offered people on the issue of abortion. There is nothing original in this criticism, and in many respects it simply serves as a polemical backdrop for the Right to advance their own agenda regarding ethics and schooling.

The second tradition in moral education attacked by the Right is Lawrence Kohlberg's approach to moral reasoning. Unlike the values-clarification approach, Kohlberg's perspective is developed around a complex and systematic theoretical discourse. Although the position is deeply flawed, the attack waged on Kohlberg by right-wing critics is often trivial and simplistic. My own criticism of Kohlberg's position is developed later in this chapter.

Kohlberg's cognitive-developmental approach argues that moral reasoning is rooted in the development of a person's cognitive abilities as he or she moves from lower to higher stages of complexity. Kohlberg holds that there are six stages of moral-cognitive development and that education should help students attain the highest stage compatible with their physical and cognitive structures. Underlying this approach to moral reasoning is the pedagogical task of promoting cognitive conflict through the examination of particular moral dilemmas.[25] It is through the repeated examination of such dilemmas that students will allegedly learn to reason at higher stages of moral thought. In applying his approach to social studies, Kohlberg provides an important commentary on the structure of his approach while criticizing a type of moral education that is similar to current right-wing approaches.

> The foundation of the old civic educator was the transmission of unquestioned truths of fact and of unquestioned consensual values to a passively receptive child. . . . In contrast to the transmission of consensual values, the new social studies have been based on Dewey's conception of the valuing process [which] postulates the need to focus upon situations which are not only problematic but controversial. . . . These objectives spring from the Deweyite recognition of social education as a process with forms of social interaction as its outcome. A Deweyite concern about action is not represented by a bag-of-virtues set of behavioral objectives. It is reflected in an active participation in the social process. This means that the classroom, itself, must be seen as an arena in which the social and political process takes place in microcosm.[26]

The right-wing attacks on Kohlberg focus on his emphasis on process at the expense of content—that is, on moral reasoning as opposed to the learning of specific virtues. Related to the latter is the claim that Kohlberg's approach promotes an unjustified disrespect for authority. Christina Hoff Sommers goes so far as to claim that Kohlberg indiscriminately attacks all forms of established authority and thus contributes to the ever-increasing breakdown of authority in the schools. She argues: "Kohlberg sees no need to question his assumption that established authority is intrinsically suspect. In any event, it is ironic that now, when teachers with authority are so rare, educational theorists like Kohlberg are proposing that authority itself is the evil to be combated."[27]

The attack on Kohlberg is further developed through the claim that contemporary college students exhibit forms of "half-baked relativism" and moral confusion. For example, Sommers draws on her own teaching experience in documenting the moral stupidity of the current generation. She says that when she asked one student if "she saw Nagasaki as the moral equivalent of a traffic accident, she replied, 'From a moral point of view, yes.'"[28] Another typical example comes from John Weiss who claims that in recent history seminars at Cornell, only "3 of 50 students understood a reference to the Sermon on the Mount, and only 8 of 75 knew of the book of Job."[29] Sommers's response to what she considers an example of moral nihilism and confusion fails to account for the ethics that underlie student thinking and behavior, but it does reveal the ideological interests that structure her own position. She argues:

> It is fair to say that many college students are thoroughly confused
> about morality. What they sorely need are some straightforward
> courses in moral philosophy and a sound and unabashed
> introduction to the Western moral tradition-something they may
> never have had before.[30]

Sommers sees no contradiction between unproblematically indoctrinating students with the warehouse of ethical and cultural values that she generously calls the "Western moral tradition" and the notion that as a precondition for all moral behavior, people should be able to think critically about the principles that inform their decisions and the actions of others. Moral agency in her view is reduced to the process of moral transmission, and learning is treated in reductionist fashion as "receiving" moral values. She ignores the important pedagogical issue of whether students get their moral education as a matter of received truth or as part of an intelligent engagement and reflective dialogue that considers the interrelated dynamics and effects of social class, gender, race, power, and history on their lives. Instead, she steadfastly focuses on the particular knowledge and virtues that are deemed important to "transmit." Missing from this perspective is any concern with the relationship between the content of the traditional values to be taught, the pedagogy to be used, and the relevance of the content and form for sustaining and advancing the imperatives of democratic life. In fact, the Right opposes the notion of moral education as a precondition for critically engaging with the wider society in order to promote and enhance human possibility. Conservatives generally see this emancipatory notion as a threat to their view of politics and human agency.

The Right's disdain for viewing moral agency as both a foundation and product of social and collective struggle becomes clearer when we look at the third area of moral education under attack by the Right, the applied ethics approach that is increasingly popular in the universities. University courses in which students debate the ethical consequences of principles and actions that inform such areas as medicine, law, social work, and schooling are currently under attack by the Right as either fostering an unjustified disrespect for established authority or diverting attention from the acquisition and practice of specific individual virtues. In this case, social criticism is dismissed and ethical judgment is reduced to the world of received virtues, sanctioned by a highly distorted reading of American history and, again, simplistically labeled as the Western Tradition.

There is a smothering silence in the Right's ethical worldview on the basic problems that face American society. Offering little or no critique of how existing social, political, and economic institutions contribute to the reproduction of unequal educational and social conditions, the Right ignores how power, ideology, and politics operate on and in schools so as to undermine the basic values of democracy and community.[31] Issues regarding forms of class, racial, and gender discrimination are conveniently ignored in favor of celebrating a mythical golden age of American history. Individual virtues are praised as the basis for moral behavior, but these virtues at best simply become a convenient and almost totally transparent apology for the status quo. Instead of analyzing the demands of critical citizenship, the Right retreats into an exalted past in order to reassert a view of traditional authority and morality as the best hope for social stability and for reconstructing schools as bastions of moral and social regulators of the existing order. In this position, individual capacities are conveniently adapted to existing social forms.[32] What are touted as important individual virtues become the basis for both a pedagogy and an ideology that excludes the language of social criticism and the discourse of possibility. Morality becomes the banner for a discourse that retreats into an unproblematic past in order to bolster unquestionable support for existing dominant social institutions and values.

In pointing to a recent conservative study arguing that youths who embrace traditional values make better high school students, Roger Simon highlights the reactionary ideology at work in this discourse of ethics and character.

> A clear example of the reduction of capacities by forms is the argument that "youth who 'embrace traditional' values make better high school students," putting the emphasis on school reforms that stress what is called "character development." What 'character development' means here is a particular narrowing of human capacities to fit particular forms. Such a position calls on studies that examine the relation between student values and high school success seeking to identify those human capacities that best fit the existing forms of schooling. The results of such studies are then read as identifying the desired norm—the desired sense of identity, values, and sensibility—that students must 'develop' to solve their school achievement problem. Those who fail to exhibit or, 'develop' such capacities are seen as deficient, lacking in appropriate character, simply of lesser worth. Taken to its logical conclusion such deficient human character is seen as a national danger! And yet again we have a community which renders natural its existing historical social forms—celebrating them as the epiphany of morality—and renders all versions of human possibility not in accord with the requirement of such forms as defective.[33]

In effect, Simon rightly argues that any discourse of ethics that limits individual capacities to existing social forms that are rendered unquestionable has little to do with the discourse of self-and social empowerment. Philip Corrigan has explored this issue as a central moral question for a radical Left politics of education.

[Social forms] are always sites of struggle in relation to the
differentiated human capacities which they of course in/form. But
there is always a moral question about these forms—and it seem to
me very necessary to discuss morality, a topic Marxists have been
scared of for too long. ... The moral question about social forms
implies no essentialism about human capacities; these are always in a
tendency of becoming. Instead, the moral question asks simply does
this or that form encourage, make possible, enable, differentiated
human capacities to be realised, to be practised; or does this or that
form disable, cripple, deny, dilute, distort those differentiated
capacities. By social forms I mean simply the ways that social actions
have to be done, the regulated pattern of the normal, expected and
obvious, the precisely taken-for-granted dominant features of a given
type of society. This also includes categories of thought and emotion
regarding social action, beliefs about means and ends and so on.
Forms are not perfect sets of action or categories, it is crucial to
grasp that they have different effects. Thus if we were to discuss the
standardized form of the family we cannot then remain silent about
the consequences of the form for different ages, but neither can we
isolate that form from its context of regulation. What happens there
is linked to what happens in schools, in workplaces, in forms of
cultural communication and so on.[34]

Extending Corrigan's point, a radical view of ethics needs to develop a provisional morality which provides the opportunity for individual capacities to be interrogated and examined so that they can
serve to both question and advance the possibilities inherent in all
social forms. Within this perspective, ethics becomes more than the
discourse of moral relativism or a static transmission of reified history; it becomes, instead, a continued engagement in which the
social practices of everyday life are interrogated in relation to the
principles individual autonomy and democratic public life, not as a
matter of received truth but as a constant engagement to sustain and
struggle within a project of possibility that enhances rather than
diminishes the traditions of democracy, community, and hope. But if
radical educators are to develop a defensible view of authority based
on a provisional morality that promotes individual autonomy within
the confines of democratic public life, they will have to do more than
interrogate and move beyond the Right's attempt to develop a discourse of ethics. They will also have to engage some of the basic
tenets of the dominant liberal discourse on ethics and education as
well as the more recent philosophical assault on all forms of moral

authority so fashionable in particular forms of postmodern thought. In addressing these issues, I will first analyze the liberal position.

Liberalism, Morality, and the Flight from a Politics of Daily Life

The broadly diffused liberal position on moral philosophy and educational ethics is the chief inheritor of the dual Enlightenment project of linking reason to freedom and linking social progress to the increasing development of scientific rationality. Emulating both Enlightenment and orthodox Marxian philosophies of history, liberal theorists of moral philosophy see a direct correlation between progress in the mastery of nature and the development and mastery of science in the service of social progress. At the risk of oversimplifying this position, I want to argue that liberal views on morality are most evident with respect to the professionalization of social theory and public philosophy within academic life, on the one hand, and the growing reliance upon a formalized discourse of rights and procedures on the other. Central to my position is the assumption that the liberal faith in reason, science, and instrumental rationality has played a decisive role in shifting liberal discourse away from the politics of everyday life while simultaneously grounding its analyses in the celebration of procedural rather than substantive issues.

The flight of liberal discourse from politics and from everyday life is especially evident in the growing legitimation of the ideology of professionalism within the university. This ideology is expressed particularly in the growth of mainstream analytical paradigms in philosophy, including the more narrowly defined philosophy of education.[35] Academic theorizing in philosophy tends to reduce theory to the imperatives of linguistic clarity and reduce logic to a demand for consistency and for empirical verification. Epistemological rigor and academic status in this ideological tendency labor under the shadow of the natural sciences and embrace a language of methodological inquiry and instrumental rationality that demoralizes and depoliticizes the relationship among ethics, society, and education. For example, liberal theorists within the analytical tradition make a fetish out of precise language clarification and the pinpointing of contradictory assertions within an argument. In doing so, they often end up divorcing the nature and applications of such techniques from any self-understanding of the political project that informs them as well as their own use of language, experience, and knowledge. Divorced from an emancipatory project of empowerment, methodological inquiry, used in this way, becomes hermetically sealed. It is incapable of developing a theoretical framework in which ethics and morality are understood as principles and practices that are constituted through the relationship between knowledge and power, on the one hand, and larger social, cultural, political, and economic considerations, on the other. Consequently, not only have liberal theorists diluted the potency of moral discourse within the university, they have also undermined the promise of the university to serve as a democratic public sphere where criticism and debate become institutionalized in the service of creating intellectuals capable of uniting vision and an ethical sensibility into a mobilizing political force. In his analysis of the link between the dominant analytic tradition and mainstream philosophy of education, Jim Giarelli posits a comment on the failure of this project:

> The last forty years have not been kind to this project. Since midcentury, the main tendency in philosophy of education, for example, has been toward increasing professionalism. Enthralled by the analytic paradigm, linguistic analysis became de rigeur and conceptual clarity was the clarion call. ... By any evidential account, it seems clear that philosophers of education, in their pursuit of professional rigor and status, have given up a place in the public educational conversation. Among the mainstream of American scholars, educational theory has been reduced largely to a subset of psychology and, similarly, educational policy to a subset of organizational theory, management science, and statistics. Educational ethics, further, has become a way of business—an apt metaphor—for professional ethicists who apply principles derived from a tradition of moral philosophy to the "problem" of education abstractly conceived—a tradition, I might add, which cannot even make sense of itself. At best, the belief that clarified concepts and more technically sophisticated research programs will foster substantive improvements in education and cultural life is an instance of uncritical hope.[36]

What is both interesting and ironic about liberal discourse on morality and ethics is that while it gives credence to the importance of educating teachers, students and others to become moral agents, it puts forward a strongly abstract and passive notion of rights and procedural justice. This emphasis can be clearly seen in the work of John Rawls and Kenneth A. Strike, who show no interest in developing a theory of ethics that encourages people to speak out of their own histories, traditions, and personal experiences.[37] Voice and historical and contextual specificity are not central categories in this brand of ethical theory. From such a perspective, the concept of justice is not defined by substantive results but rather through a fetishistic appeal to proper process. The complex relations of power along with the concrete problems of existing social and educational life in capitalist society often get lost in this work. The result is often little more than a simple-minded celebration of individualism and citizenship, taking for granted the ability of the capitalist state and its attendant market logic to address the suffering of subordinated and marginalized groups. The appeal that underlies this particular discourse of ethics is that it focuses on the fairness of the rules that govern existing society; absent from this view is any fundamental challenge to the moral and political viability of the society that legitimates such rules. Strike exemplifies this position:

> For liberals the state exists to regulate the competition among individuals for their private goods. ... The liberal conception of the state forbids the state from having a public notion of the good or from using its power to impose some concept of the good on its citizens. The legitimate role of the state must be understood in terms of regulating the competition among individuals for private goods. The theory of justice of a liberal state is intended to formulate the basic rules which govern this function of the state. Such a theory specifies what is to count as fairness in the rules according to which individuals cooperate and compete with one another in pursuing their own ends.[38]

In the work of both Strike and Rawls, an abstract orientation to rights and legal procedures buttresses a normative emphasis on rational consensus. Within this perspective the emphasis on procedural justice tells people how to order their lives and their relationship to the state. It is important to note, as Seyla Benhabib has pointed out, that the focus in this perspective is on the notion of freedom but not on questions regarding what constitutes the good life. Moreover, the category of freedom as posited in this view is based on notions of justice and rational consensus that are defined procedurally rather than substantively. Consequently, it says very little "about those qualities of individual life-histories and collective life-forms which make them fulfilling or unfulfilling."[39] It is worth repeating that there is little effort in this perspective to situate formal, liberal goals concretely in real histories, cultural traditions, and experiences that constitute communities of people. In other words, the ethical focus on procedural rights ignores the moral density of real or possible publics and public spheres. It ends up focusing on the reified "subject" who apparently lacks an engaged social history or on a community in which rights and laws are born out of the moral and political struggles of human beings operating within specific constructions of time, history, experience, and space. The "other" in this view of ethics is not a concrete entity but a transparent and empty vehicle for choosing one set of rules over others. Yet the concrete other is by its very definition not an abstraction reduced to actions in the public sphere but real human beings who define themselves through discourses of needs, desires, community, and dignity. The concrete other at the very least entails an ethical discourse in which the voices of subordinate groups, along with the sounds of human suffering and collective struggle, are not silenced. In true liberal fashion, formal rights replaces a politics of difference with the virtue of consensus, and in doing so manages to overlook the substantive morality of everyday life. Fred Siegel has rightly argued that this Rawlsian model of ethics and justice tells people how to live but ignores the dynamics involved in communities struggling to establish forms of democracy as a way of life. Underlying this position, Siegel says, is a decidedly anti-utopian discourse that isolates individuals through its inability to link ethics to the lived dynamics of democratic life.

> Modern society is divided between a romantic private life and a bureaucratic public sphere, but that split is alleviated in part by family and associational ties which bridge the gap. But for many in the sixties it was precisely those ties of family, church and neighborhood that were seen as the source of the nation's problems. Rawlsianism exhibits a similar hostility to those intermediate institutional forms. Like utilitarianism it is designed for a society of strangers: a mass of isolated individuals who enter into a contract with each other and the state which enforces the contract. For Rawls society is the relationship of each individual to the law; individuals have no non-contractual relations with each other.[40]

The emphasis on abstract rationality that informs liberal discourse on rights and justice is also evident in the work of Lawrence Kohlberg, Jürgen Habermas, and others.[41] In this case, a discourse of ethics is constructed around standards of rationality implicit in forms of communicative action. Through an appeal to theories of human development rooted in scientific psychology, Kohlberg's "natural law" theory of morality posits an optimistic view of education as a basis for improving the cognitive ability of students, which is seen as the precondition for increasing their capacity for moral reasoning. As is well known, Kohlberg argues that there is a universal, invariant sequence of stages in the development of moral judgment. These stages can be developed by problematizing particular moral issues and assessing how students respond to them, then engaging students in discussions that are not too far removed from their own levels of cognitive and moral reasoning.[42]

Even though Kohlberg recognizes that human beings develop in interaction with one another through the use of language and dialogue, his discursive ethics is no less reifying than the emphasis on procedural rights and justice advocated by Rawls and Strike. Kohlberg also separates the discourse of ethics and morality from the struggles, voices, and shared experiences that constitute a politics of difference in everyday life. Kohlberg's pedagogy provides little or no understanding of how voice and history come together within the ongoing asymmetrical relations of power that characterize the interplay of dominant and subordinate cultures. Practical argumentation, in this case, becomes the basis for a pedagogy and theory of ethics that ignores how individuals are formed through the material conditions that constitute the other side of culture. For Kohlberg and those who share his position, the virtue of scientific rationality and the operations of language become the basis for engaging abstract moral dilemmas and improving moral reasoning. History in this view is detached from moral reasoning and the dark side of scientific rationality is forgotten. Moreover, this approach gives high priority to consensus, cutting the possibility of developing a politics of difference which acknowledges the specificity of disadvantaged groups.

What is overlooked in this perspective, as Horkheimer has pointed out, is that the discourse of ethics is also about the nature of happiness and the good life. The latter cannot be separated from the issue of how a socialized humanity develops within ideological and material conditions that either enable or disable the enhancement of human possibilities. Horkheimer provides a referent for an alternative to the Kohlbergian position by arguing that it is important to stare into history in order to remember the suffering of the past and that out of this remembrance a theory of ethics should be developed in which solidarity, sympathy, and care become central dimensions of an informed social practice.[43]

In summing up this section, I want to stress that both the discourse of rights and cognitive moral reasoning fail to situate a theory of ethics in a notion of the good life that is attentive to the aspirations and hopes of those subordinate and marginal groups who occupy particular historical and social contexts. At the core of the liberal paradigm is the notion that the individual as a rights-bearing citizen can be addressed and understood outside the lived, connected, complex of human relations. A radical theory of ethics must reject this position as the starting point for developing a critical theory of education. Instead, educators should link a theory of ethics and morality to a politics in which community, difference, remembrance, and historical consciousness become foundational. In doing so, they can begin the task of developing an ethical discourse in which radical/utopian human satisfactions and needs, along with visions of the good life, can be constructed around historically informed and culturally specific aspects of struggle. Seyla Benhabib points to both the basis and importance for such a task when she discusses how the notion of the "concrete other" can be incorporated into a theory of ethics.

> The standpoint of the "concrete other," by contrast, requires us to view each and every rational being as an individual with a concrete history, identity, and affective-emotional constitution. In assuming this standpoint, we abstract from what constitutes our commonality and seek to understand the distinctiveness of the other. We seek to comprehend the needs of the other, their motivations, what they search for, and what they desire. Our relations to the other are governed by the norm of complementary reciprocity: each is entitled to expect and to assume from the other forms of behavior through which the other feels recognized and confirmed as a concrete, individual being with specific needs, talents, and capacities. Our differences in this case complement, rather than exclude one another. The norms of our interaction are usually private, non-institutional ones. They are the norms of solidarity, friendship, love, and care. Such relations require in various ways that I do, and

that you expect me to do in the face of your needs, more than would be required of me as a right-bearing person. In treating you in accordance with the norms of solidarity, friendship, love, and care, I confirm not only your humanity but your human individuality. The moral categories that accompany such interactions are those of responsibility, bonding, and sharing. The corresponding moral feelings are those of love, care, sympathy, and solidarity, and the vision of community is one of needs and solidarity.[44]

What is of particular interest in this position for a theory of morality and ethics is its concern with the materiality of human interaction, that is, with human needs shaped within existing social and political configurations. In this view, a moral framework for politics and daily life is rooted in both the material conditions and forms of solidarity that point to a better life as well as those formal principles and maxims that contribute to actualizing what Agnes Heller has called the universal values of life and freedom.[45] That is, a radical theory of ethics would not only embrace a politics of the concrete other based on norms of solidarity, sympathy, caring, friendship, and love, but would also struggle to define those maxims necessary for a provisional morality to discern the moral adequacy (i.e., goodness, badness, and moral indifference) of particular norms and rules. Such maxims would be part of a continuing attempt to provide what Michael Lerner has called an ongoing

vision of a moral American community. Such a vision should be idealistic and not pragmatic. It should paint a picture of what life should be, and insist that practical programs must be measured by the degree to which they tend towards creating this kind of society.[46]

Agnes Heller has actually attempted to initiate such a project. Although not unproblematic, her list of prohibitive and imperative maxims provides a starting point for debating what the nature of such maxims should be as part of a radical discourse of ethics:

a. Prohibitive maxims are:
1. Do not choose norms which cannot be made in public.
2. Do not choose norms the observance of which includes—for reasons of principle—the use of other human beings as mere means.
3. Do not choose norms which not everyone is free to choose.
4. Do not choose as moral norms (binding norms) norms the observance of which is not a goal-in-itself.

b. Imperative maxims are:
  1. Lend equal recognition to all persons as free and rational beings.
  2. Recognize all human needs, excepting the ones the satisfaction of which includes the use of other persons as means by definition.
  3. Respect persons solely on the basis of their virtues and (moral) merits.
  4. Keep your human dignity in all your doings.[47]

Developing a provisional morality that points to the adequacy of naming certain norms as emancipatory and others as repressive represents a major challenge for educators engaged in developing a view of authority and critical pedagogy grounded in a radical theory of ethics. No less challenging is the need to reconstruct and critically appropriate those historically constituted traditions of protest that might provide the basis for organizing everyday experiences around a language that promotes radical needs and emancipatory sensibilities. In effect, a major task for a critical theory of education is to analyze how historically constituted experiences of moral and political activity can contribute to developing an ethical discourse *with* an emancipatory political intent. That is, a discourse that can provide the basis for organizing and sustaining a community of public spheres inextricably connected to forms of self-and social empowerment that extend the project of human possibility and collective future happiness. Inherent in this ethical/political project is a Blochian notion of "not-yet," a view of the future that appropriates and modifies rather than denounces a provisional foundational morality. And yet, if a provisional morality is to become a central aspect of a radical theory of ethics, educators will have to address some current and important theoretical assaults against all forms of foundationalism currently being developed by postmodern philosophy.

Postmodern Philosophy and the Flight from Ethics

The cultural temper of the last decade has been marked by a radical break with the unifying principles and hegemonic logic that have characterized older mainstream traditions in philosophy. The totalizing and objectifying principles of modernist philosophy, which are characterized, in part, by its metanarratives of history, its faith in the teleology of science, its unwavering belief in the linear march of industrial progress, its defense of the human subject as an integrated and unified rationalist, and its reliance upon the "intentions" of a given text, are in a state of profound crisis. Various brands of postmodernism, poststructuralism, and neopragmatism have declared war on all the categories of transcendence, certainty, and foundationalism. First principles are now seen as mere relics of history. The unified subject, long the bulwark of both liberal and radical hopes for the future, is now scattered amid the valorizing of all decentering processes. Moreover, the attack on foundationalism has resulted in a one-sided methodological infatuation with deconstructing not simply particular truths, but the very notion of truth itself as an epistemological category. All attempts at defining a notion of the truth capable of sustaining a political project that engages rather than simply dismisses history and meaning have become suspect and part "of the baggage which poststructuralism seeks to abandon."[48] Subjectivity and ethics within this new philosophy are often voided in the indeterminacy of language, the celebration of difference, and the play of signifiers. What is most notable about this trend in postmodernist philosophy, in both its liberal and radical strains, is its refusal to link the language of critique to a viable political project. The flight from foundationalism is at the same time often a flight from politics.

This is not to suggest that all the theoretical projections that characterize postmodern philosophy need to be condemned in one totalizing sweep, as is done, for instance, in recent attacks by Fredric Jameson and Perry Anderson.[49] There are a number of oppositional elements in postmodern philosophy that constitute important critical interventions against the dominant cultural ideologies of late capitalism. Its emphasis on the importance of difference, conflict, and specificity cannot be dismissed in light of the refusal of certain versions of Marxism and dominant liberal theory to acknowledge the junctures, splits, and contexts that rub against their "overtotalizing" theories.[50] The incessant attack on the correspondence theory of truth, the hyperrationality of positivism, and the tidy notion of a unified, centered human subject *have* provided the basis for a more powerful language of critique in postmodern philosophy. But this is where the problem also begins. For postmodern philosophy in many instances is so wedded to demolishing the ideological edifice of meaning and certainty that it has failed to develop any firm moral, ethical, or political project upon which to justify its undoing of the text, subject, truth, and other such terrains which have been the traditional edifices of meaning and agency. This mad dance through the traditional constructions of meaning, history, and subjectivity appears at times as a whirlwind of complex theoretical discourse wreaking havoc but with no purpose in mind except to keep going.[51]

As a number of critics have amply pointed out, postmodern philosophy suffers from a number of major theoretical problems.[52] At the core of much postmodern philosophy is an overburdening stress on the decentering of the human subject and psyche. This one-sided emphasis on demolishing the autonomous bourgeois monadic subject translates into the death of the subject and with it the relinquishing of any notion of determinate human agency and collective struggle. Missing a human and subjective referent, this theoretical slide into a reified play of signifiers and deconstructionist strategies also takes its toll in the effacement of history itself. In Fredric Jameson's words,

> The past is thereby itself modified: what was once ... the organic
> genealogy of the bourgeois collective project has meanwhile itself
> become a vast collection of images, a multitudinous photographic
> simulacrum. Guy Debord's powerful slogan is now even more apt for
> the 'prehistory' of a society bereft of all spectacles. In faithful
> conformity to poststructuralist linguistic theory, the past as 'referent'
> finds itself gradually bracketed, and then effaced altogether, leaving
> us with nothing but texts.[53]

What is most disturbing is not only that a unidimensional language of critique holds the many ideological strands within postmodern philosophy together, but that the bruteness of its fundamentally anti-utopian character undercuts any possibility for the development of a potentially progressive and substantive political project. Without a language capable of recovering and reconstructing history, reconstituting subjectivity around an operational notion of human will and agency, and developing a political project based on a discourse of possibility, postmodern philosophy presents itself in opposition to any project designed to foster critique and hope in the service of an ethics and political philosophy linked to the construction of a radical democracy.

Postmodern philosophy, especially of the liberal American variety, has tended to sacrifice the development of a pedagogical discourse of ethics, agency, and politics for a language of critique aimed at demolishing all knowledge claims to certainty and first principles. The attack on foundationalism, the "myth of the given," and all other cultural codes that make an appeal to eternal or transcultural standards has also come under strong attack in the brand of American neopragmatism being developed in the work of Richard Rorty.[54] Rorty's version of liberal postmodern antifoundationalism is not restricted to a language of criticism that disparages any appeal to hope or to the defense of a set of social relations and vision of community. On the contrary, Rorty supports the modernist notion of continuing the tradition of Enlightenment faith in reason and dialogue as the basis for community life. For Rorty, the Enlightenment tradition at its best represents a form of cultural liberalism in which community is the embodiment of the Socratic virtue of the ongoing conversation. Rorty's postmodernism is also evident in his argument that the Western philosophical tradition has to be held at arm's length at all costs for it privileges the notions of necessity, universality, rationality, and objectivity and, in doing so, undermines the creation of dialogic communities; it also prevents the conversation of humankind from continuing. In this account, the anchoring of truth in any form of foundationalism is dismissed in favor of the notion of conversation defended neither as epistemology nor axiology but as practice in itself.

Central to understanding Rorty's view of *conversation, community,* and *politics* is his sweeping rejection of any attempt to ground one's judgments. For Rorty, neither the purpose nor the value of the conversation for humankind is to be appraised, for the latter requires some criteria of judgment and all judgments are tainted by the certainties that inform authoritative traditions.[55] Removed from the realms of power and politics, knowledge for Rorty is a matter of practicality and civility, whose virtue is simply its own existence. In similar fashion, society is also depoliticized as it primarily becomes a site or model for a conversational encounter. Most revealing is Rorty's view of the role of the intellectual in society. The ideological nature of Rorty's "conversation of mankind" begins to reveal its own ideological moorings as the role of the intellectual in this perspective is portrayed as the all-purpose hero ready "to offer a view on pretty much anything."[56] Available as a human archive for an unproblematic tradition,

> he [sic] passes rapidly from Hemingway to Proust to Hitler to Marx to Foucault to Mary Douglas to the present situation in Southeast Asia to Gandhi to Sophocles. He is a name-dropper, who uses names such as these to refer to sets of descriptions, symbol-systems, ways of seeing. His specialty is seeing similarities and differences between great big pictures, between attempts to see how things hang together.[57]

This is not the intellectual indebted to the notion of Sartrian engagement or Marxian struggle. In Rorty's perspective, the intellectual is reduced to simply being a somewhat privileged member of the community in the service of conversation, a member without a politics, a sense of vision, or a conscience. What is most striking about Rorty's view of conversation and community is the idealized pluralism that it supports. Treated as simply conventions, rather than as social practices that take place within asymmetrical relations of power, the notion of conversation is imbued with a false equality that glides over the issue of how specific interests and power relations actually structure the material and ideological conditions in which conversations are actually structured. Who is in the conversation? Who controls the terms of the dialogue? Who is left out? What interests are sustained beyond the abstract virtue of Socratic dialogue? Whose stories are distorted or marginalized? Why are some parts of the conversation considered more important than others? How does one decide between competing visions of community life as they are embodied in different strands of the conversation?

Rorty's cultural conservatism ignores these questions and in doing so provides a version of postmodern philosophy that is fundamentally anti-utopian in that it undermines and depoliticizes the Deweyian project of linking public will to the idea of radical democracy. Alfonso J. Damico explores the implications of Rorty's retreat from politics and his refusal to link the notion of conversation and community to the experimental democracy of self-consciously organized publics.

> Rorty [argues] . . . that "what matters is our loyalty to other human beings clinging together against the dark, not our hope of getting things right." This is, of course, a sentiment that is best

complemented by political complacency and quietism. There is a
sense, then, in which Rorty also depoliticizes the public will. From
Rorty's deconstructionist perspective, one can neither question the
purposes nor appraise the value of the conversation of mankind for
the strong reason that it has neither purposes nor merits—beyond
the fact that it is simply our virtue. .... In effect, this suggests that
there is something irrational about doubts that challenge in a strong
way the shared beliefs and values validated by the conventions of the
moment. If judging a practice requires some criteria of judgment that
do not simply reproduce the current practice, it is hard to see how
Rortyian citizens might assess and respond to disputes and
dissatisfactions where the meaning attached to various concepts of
the merits of established standards are themselves at issue among the
conversationalists. There is a 'givenness' about Rortyian conversation
that provides generalized support for the practice itself but that
leaves what goes on inside that practice obscure and beyond the
reach of critical or political deliberation.[58]

Although Rorty's antifoundationalism has some value in that it
encourages the cultivation of a critical attitude toward all traditions
and intellectual codes that legitimate themselves through one or
another form of transcendentalism, it ultimately ends up offering no
ethical or political grounds on which either to challenge the human
suffering and contradictions inherent in modern society or to exhibit
the moral and political courage necessary to struggle for a society
without exploitation. In the end, Rorty's conversation and moral relativism become the particular conversation of the liberal academic,
i.e., removed, insular, and apologetic. In fact, what begins as an attack
on all forms of foundationalism ends up being symptomatic of a particular type of intellectual and moral impotence characteristic of the
anti-utopianism so rampant in the American academy. Cornel West is
not far from the mark in suggesting that Rorty's antifoundationalism
may be slightly radical in the threat it poses to the legitimating logic
of the philosophical traditions in the academy, but it certainly presents no threat to the much more important role that the university
might play as an autonomous critical public sphere capable of challenging rather than adapting to the wider dominant society. In West's
terms

Rorty's neo-pragmatism provides not an earth-shaking perspective for
the modern West but rather is a symptom of the crisis in the highly
specialized professional stratum of educational workers in the

philosophy departments of universities and colleges. Rorty's antiepistemological radicalism and belletristic antiacademicism. . . . though pregnant with rich possibilities, remains polemical and hence barren. It refuses to give birth to the offspring it conceives. Rorty leads philosophy to the complex world of politics and culture, but confines his engagement to transformation in the academy and apologetics for the modern West.[59]

While there is a slightly subversive aspect to Rorty's work, it ultimately falls prey to a discourse of apologetics. That is, consistent with the current anti-utopianism that characterizes much of postmodern social theory, Rorty cancels out the character, methods, and dynamics of domination and power around a notion of conversation and community that hides more than it reveals. Difference and ethics in this position are construed as indifferent to human suffering and collective struggle. On the contrary, power, struggle, and transformation are canceled out in an ideology of pluralism that presupposes a society uncontaminated by the inequities of capitalist domination and exploitation. Rorty's neopragmatism leaves little room for an ethical discourse and political practice that interrogate political conditions beyond the conventions of conversational encounters. Hope now becomes dislodged from political struggle and ethical legitimacy and is reduced in Rorty's view to the play of interpretations underlying community life. As Rebecca Comay points out,

> "Hope" . . . becomes, in Rorty, the happy desire that we keep on going just the way we are. . . . "Community"—freed from global presumptions—becomes simply the place we are. "History"—freed from the constraining arche and telos—becomes the endless continuation of the same. . . . And philosophy, stripped of critical arrogance, becomes the cheerful affirmation of the "now."[60]

If the notions of moral discourse and political vision are to become more than just one more free-floating strand in the community of social conversations, critical educators will have to move beyond the theoretical and ideological limitations that underlie the various right-wing and liberal approaches to the related issues of schooling, morality, and authority. As it stands, even those radical educators who have recognized the need for developing a critical moral and ethical discourse have remained trapped within a decidedly liberal problematic. For example, Landon Beyer and George Wood take a decidedly Rortyian turn in arguing that a moral discourse is dependent on the interpretive community of which it is a part.[61] The problem with this position is that it fails to understand how human beings are constituted historically and materially within moral discourses and what these discourses mean regarding how they either sustain or challenge the forces of domination or freedom. Simply put, the grounds of an ethical discourse are not to be found in their social interpretative construction but in the question of how they affect the meaning and quality of life.

A much more theoretically sophisticated treatment of schooling and ethics can be found in the work of Jo Anne Pagano.[62] Pagano recognizes that at the heart of all competing educational discourses are moral interests and disagreements. But Pagano fails to link this insight to a pedagogical process that is substantive rather than procedural in nature. Assuming that a moral point of view is tantamount to a pedagogical imposition, she argues that educators need not specify a moral content. In this case, the learning of moral responsibility is shifted from the real world of commitments and solidarity to the process of introducing students to different views and letting them pick for themselves the moral discourse that suits their own lives and experiences. A critical pedagogy has to begin from the opposite position, and instead of concealing the interests that constitute one's own moral discourse or those that structure the suffering and exploitation within history, a critical educator can demonstrate his/her moral courage through a content that gives real meaning to ethical action while allowing students to read, debate, and align themselves with moral discourses brought to bear on the issues that become a legitimate object of discussion. Although a teacher cannot demand a student not be a racist, he/she can certainly subject such a position to a critique that reveals it as an act of political and moral irresponsibility related to wider social and historical social practices. This can be done in the spirit of debate and analysis, one that provides the pedagogical conditions for students to learn how to theorize, while affirming and interrogating the voices through which students speak, learn, and struggle. One important qualification must be made here. The positions that students often articulate are not forged in a single and coherent representation of the world. Such views are part of a deeper and fluid set of discourses that often place students in various complex and contradictory relations with the world. Students' perceptions are often riddled with conflicting and multiple semantic and "affective investments."[63] This suggests, of course, that students' voices need to be explored by radical educators at one level for their inherent semantic contradictions; one example would be in analyzing the ideological tension revealed by the student who claims he believes he is a "good" citizen but also registers racist or sexist remarks about women. At another level, student voices can be explored through the contradictions that emerge between the emotional investment that structures a given student's response to an issue and the obvious breakdown of any rationale defense for such a position. For example, a politics of pleasure may structure a student's response and defense of a film that he/she may overtly recognize as promoting a sexist or racist ideology. In both these examples, voice becomes a terrain of interrogation and struggle in which knowledge and power, on the one hand, and subjectivity and desire, on the other, provide the basis for analyzing how particular contradictory discourses and subjectivities are developed, regulated, and challenged, and how knowledge and desire can be constructed either to close off or to enable the possibilities for forms of democratic life.

It is important to note here that educators should consider defending their theoretical work both as a product of empowerment and as part of a continuing struggle for liberation. This is particularly necessary in order to counter the Rortyian-type claim among some educators that critical theorists have no right to impose their "language constructs" on others.[64] Surely, this is more than a misrepresentation of what critical educators are all about; in actuality, it is more akin to a theoretically flawed position that represents nothing less than a flight from serious politics and an apology for the status quo. It is theoretically flawed because it confuses the ideological interests inherent in developing a critical (or any other) political project with the pedagogical strategy to be used in conjunction with it. More specifically, educators have a moral and ethical responsibility to develop a view of radical authority that legitimates forms of critical pedagogy aimed at both interpreting reality and transforming it.[65] But what is at stake here is not just a struggle over authority and the production, distribution, and transformation of meaning, but also the equally important task of changing those forms of economic and political power that promote human suffering and exploitation. Developing an oppositional language needs to be judged in the context of a theoretical project that provides teachers, students, and others with the possibility for alternative readings of their own experiences and the nature of the larger social reality. Moreover, oppositional political projects, like any other political position, should be the object of constant debate and analysis. On the other hand, having a theoretically "correct" position gives no one the right to impose that position on another person in a way that serves to silence them. This raises the issue of how to construct a critical pedagogy that can both affirm and extend the possibility for self and social empowerment so as to create the conditions for a meaningful democracy in the United States. As Noam Chomsky puts it, "Meaningful democracy presupposes the ability of ordinary people to pool their limited resources, to form and develop ideas and programs, put them on the political agenda, and act to support them."[66] The issue here is how can educators make their own political commitments clear while developing forms of pedagogy consistent with the democratic imperative that students learn to make choices, organize, and act on their own beliefs. In part, Paulo Freire speaks to this issue in a dialectical fashion by recognizing that the political nature of education itself means that teachers have to take a position and make it clear to students, but at the same time such educators have to recognize that the fact of their own commitment does not give them the right to impose a particular position on their students. According to Freire,

> Because education is politicity, it is never neutral. When we try to be neutral, like Pilate, we support the dominant ideology. Not being neutral, education must be either liberating or domesticating. (Yet I also recognize that we probably never experience it as purely one or the other but rather a mixture of both.) Thus, we have to recognize ourselves as politicians. It does not mean that we have the right to impose on students our political choice. But we do have the duty not to hide our choice. Students have the right to know what our political dream is. They are then free to accept it, reject it, or modify it. Our task is not to impose our dreams on them, but to challenge them to have their own dreams, to define their choices, not just to uncritically assume them.[67]

Freire makes clear that the tension between the production of a radical theoretical position/political project and the pedagogical practice that should accompany it is an important issue that needs to be made problematic. To submit such a position to the reductionist notion that all oppositional language is a form of cultural imposition

69

curiously forgets how ideology constructs experience within asymmetrical relations of power and that the refusal to name the human suffering and exploitation caused by particular social and cultural formations is, in part, a stance that ultimately supports through its silence and ignorance the very dynamics of oppression. In many ways, the argument often expressed by mainstream educators that any form of oppositional discourse by default represents an imposition of one's views on somebody else is similar to the nineteenth-century ruling-class view that one could not raise one's voice, struggle politically, or promote social criticism because it violated the "gentlemanly" codes of civility. The resurrection of such a discourse among some academics strikes me as both shameful and perfectly appropriate for those who have become fully integrated into the ideological dynamics of higher education. Not only does such a discourse ignore the political nature of all schooling and pedagogy, it also represents an apology for forms of pedagogy that in their claims to neutrality merely voice the interests of the status quo and the logic of the dominant ideologies.

In the next chapter, I move to a more programmatic position on the discourse and pedagogy of morality and ethics. I develop a theory of emancipatory authority and ethics around the assumption that there are traditions of protest that provide a theoretical framework for developing a moral sensibility and set of pedagogical experiences consistent with the idea of radical democracy and an emancipatory view of community life. I attempt to reconstruct theoretical positions that can provide educators with a basis for constituting student experiences within forms of authority and moral discourse that exemplify the importance of critical democracy as a way of life, ethical practice as a discourse of solidarity and caring, and hope as an important precondition for a radical utopianism.

3
Authority, Ethics, and the Politics of Schooling

We live in a time when democracy is in retreat. Nowhere is this more obvious than in the current debate surrounding the relationship between schooling and authority. As is the case with most public issues in the 1980s, the new conservatives have seized the initiative and argued that the current crisis in public education is due to the loss of authority. The call for a reconstituted authority along conservative lines is coupled with the charge that the crisis in schooling is in part due to a crisis in the wider culture, which is presented as a "spiritual-moral" crisis. The problem is clearly articulated by Diane Ravitch, who argues that this pervasive "loss of authority" stems from confused ideas, irresolute standards, and cultural relativism.[1] As a form of legitimation, this view of authority appeals to an established cultural tradition, whose practices and values appear beyond criticism. Authority, in this case, represents an idealized version of the American Dream reminiscent of nineteenth-century dominant culture in which "the tradition" becomes synonymous with hard work, industrial discipline, and cheerful obedience. It is a short leap between this view of the past and the new conservative vision of schools as crucibles in which to forge industrial soldiers fueled by the imperatives of excellence, competition, and down-home character. In effect, for the new conservatives, learning approximates a practice mediated by strong teacher authority and a student willingness to learn the basics, adjust to the imperatives of the social and economic order, and exhibit what Edward A. Wynne calls the traditional moral aims of "promptness, truthfulness, courtesy, and obedience."[2]

What is most striking about the new conservative discourse on schooling is its refusal to link the issue of authority to the rhetoric of freedom and democracy. In other words, what is missing from this perspective as well as from more critical perspectives is any attempt to reinvent a view of authority that expresses a democratic concep-tion of collective life, one that is embodied in an ethic of solidarity, social transformation, and an imaginative vision of citizenship.[3] I believe that the established view of authority tells us very little about what is wrong with schools. But it does challenge critical educators to fashion an alternative and emancipatory view of authority and ethics as central elements in a critical theory of schooling. Agnes Heller states the problem well when she argues that "it is not the rejection of all authorities that is at issue here, but the quality of authority and the procedure in which authority is established, observed and tested."[4] Heller's remarks suggest a dual problem that critical educators will have to face. First, they will need a recon-structed language of critique in order to challenge the current con-servative offensive in education. Second, they will need to construct a language of possibility that provides the theoretical scaffolding for a politics of practical learning. In both cases, the starting point for such a challenge centers on the imperative to develop a dialectical view of authority and ethics which can both serve as a referent for critique and provide a programmatic vision for pedagogical and social change.

David Nyberg and Paul Farber point to the importance for making the concept of authority a central concern for educators by suggest-ing that "this question of how one shall stand in relation to authority is the foundation of educated citizenship: its importance cannot be overemphasized."[5] I want to extend this position by arguing that if all educators have either an implicit or explicit vision of who people should be and how they should act within the context of a human community, the basis of authority through which they structure class-room life is ultimately rooted in questions of ethics and power. Cen-tral to my concern is developing a view of authority and ethics that defines schools as part of an ongoing movement and struggle for democracy and teachers as intellectuals who both legitimate and introduce students to a particular way of life. In both instances, I want to fashion a view of authority that legitimates schools as democratic, public spheres and teachers as transformative intellectuals who work toward a realization of their views of community, social justice, empowerment, and social reform. In short, I want to broaden the definition of authority and ethics to include and legitimate educational practices that link democracy, teaching, and practical learning. The substantive nature of this task takes as its starting point the ethical intent of initiating students into a discourse and set of pedagogical practices that advance the role of democracy within the schools while addressing those instances of suffering and inequality that structure the daily lives of millions of people both in the United States and in other parts of the world.

In developing my argument, I focus on a number of considerations. First, I review briefly some major ideological positions on the relationship of authority and schooling. Second, I develop a theoretical rationale for giving the concepts of authority and ethics a central role in educational theory and practice. Third, I argue for a radical view of ethics and democracy that draws primarily from a selective reading of the debates on democracy, schooling, and ethics in which John Dewey and some prominent social reconstructionists engaged in the first half of the twentieth century. I focus on this particular tradition of protest and debate in order to recover and reconstruct a discourse that links democracy and schooling to a politics of risk, struggle, and possibility. I will then draw selectively from certain aspects of feminist theory and liberation theology in order to redefine how authority and ethics can be formulated in order to reconstruct the role that teachers might play as intellectuals engaged in criticizing and transforming both the schools and the wider society. Fourth, I present the broad theoretical outlines of a transformative pedagogy that is consistent with an emancipatory view of authority and ethics. Fifth, I argue that the notion of authority has to be developed within a language that is sensitive to wider set of economic, political, and social formations and practices in order for teachers to step out of their academic boundaries and enter into alliances with other progressive groups. At the heart of this position is the view that educators need to develop an emancipatory view of authority as part of an ongoing social movement whose purposes are both to analyze and to sustain the struggle for critical forms of education and democracy.

73

Authority As A Terrain of Legitimation and Struggle

The concept of authority can best be understood as a historical construction shaped by diverse, competing traditions which contain their own values and views of the world. In other words, the concept of authority, like any other social category of importance, has no universal meaning simply waiting to be discovered. As a focus of intense battles and conflicts among competing theoretical perspectives, its meaning has often shifted depending on the theoretical context in which it has been employed. Given these shifting meanings and associations, it becomes necessary to interrogate the way in which the concept has been treated by preceding ideological traditions, if we are to redefine its meaning for a critical pedagogy. Ideally, such an analysis should take into account the status of the truth claims that particular views of authority reflect as well as the institutional mechanisms that legitimate and sustain their particular version of reality. Only then does it becomes possible to analyze authority within such diverse ideological traditions for the purpose of revealing both the interests they embody and the cluster of power relations they support. Although it is impossible within this chapter to provide a detailed analysis of the various ways in which authority has been developed within competing educational traditions, I will highlight some of the more important theoretical considerations inherent in conservative, liberal, and radical analyses. For it is against this general set of criticisms that an argument for the relevance of developing an emancipatory view of authority in educational discourse can be situated.

In the new conservative discourse, authority is given a positive meaning and is often related to issues that resonate with popular experience. As an ideal that often embodies reactionary interests, this position legitimates a view of culture, pedagogy, and politics that focuses on traditional values and norms. Authority in this view presents a rich mix of resonant themes in which the notions of family, nation, duty, self-reliance, and standards often add up to a warmed-over dish of Parsonian consensus and cultural reproduction. In educational terms, school knowledge is reduced to an unproblematic selection from the dominant traditions of "Western" culture. Rather than viewing culture as a terrain of competing knowledge and practices, conservatives frame "culture" within the axis of historical certainty and present it as a storehouse of treasured goods constituted as canon and ready to be passed "down" to deserving students.[6] Not surprisingly, teaching in this instance is often reduced to the process of transmitting a given body of hallowed knowledge with student learning squarely situated in "mastering" the "basics" and appropriate standards of behavior.

Whereas the new conservatives view authority as a positive and inherently traditional set of values and practices, leftist educators have taken the opposite position almost without exception. In this view, authority is frequently associated with an unprincipled authoritarianism and freedom is something that is defined as an escape from authority in general. Authority within this perspective is generally seen as synonymous with the logic of domination. This position has been endlessly repeated by radical educational critics, who often portray schools as factories, prisons, or warehouses for the oppressed. For example, in the 1960s and 1970s radical educational critics such as Jerry Farber argued that the authority of classroom teachers was nothing more that a form of compensation for the powerlessness that most of them felt in other aspects of their lives. In Farber's terms,

> teachers ARE short on balls ... the classroom offers an artificial and protected environment in which they can exercise their will to power. Your neighbors may drive a better car ... your wife may dominate you; the State legislature may shit on you; but in the classroom by God, students do what you say—or else. The grade is a hell of a weapon. It may not rest on your hip, potent, and rigid like a cop's gun, but in the long run it's more powerful.[7]

There is a strong element of truth in the Marxian critique which argues that schools contribute to the reproduction of the status quo, with all of its characteristic inequalities; nevertheless, it is simply inaccurate to maintain that schools are merely agencies of domination and reproduction and that all forms of authority serve only to maintain such domination. This discourse understands neither the contradictions and struggles that characterize schools nor how authority might be used in the interests of a critical pedagogy. In addition, not only is this type of radical criticism of schooling and authority crudely reductionist, given its one-dimensional view of teaching, socialization, and power in schools; it also embodies a particular sexist view of authority. That is, the patriarchal nature of this critique of authority is evident in the language used by critics such as Farber, as well as in their smug refusal to recognize that the type of authority they are talking about almost without exception represented a form of power exercised by males. Consequently, radical critics who exercise this type of criticism often unwittingly reinforce the sexist notion that women are not smart or intelligent enough to legitimate forms of authority based on claims to scholarship, intelligence, and classroom practice. Within the last few years, feminist theorists have criticized this "radical" view of authority and the sexist practices it has helped to reproduce. Moreover, in more recent years, feminist educators have attempted to develop a view of authority that is consistent with feminist pedagogical principles. Susan Friedman provides a succinct analysis of both the problem of authority for feminist teachers and the attempt to redefine its meaning for a critical feminist pedagogy.

> Both our students and ourselves have been socialized to believe (frequently at a non-conscious level) that any kind of authority is incompatible with the feminine. That, fundamentally, is what patriarchy does in its definition of woman: deny women the authority of their experiences, perspectives, emotions and minds. The denial of intellect is particularly crucial for the scholar and educator who happens to be female. . . . As we attempt to move on to academic turf culturally defined as male, we need a theory that first recognizes the androcentric denial of all authority to women and, second, points out a way for us to speak with an authentic voice not based on tyranny. . . . I am arguing . . . for the inadequacy of masculine authority (based as it is on oppression) and the feminine (based as it is on oppression). We must move beyond both pedagogical models to develop a classroom based on the 'authority' radical feminism has granted to women in the process of subverting and transforming patriarchal culture. . . . Feminist pedagogy now needs to base the classroom more completely on the accomplishments of the movement. In our eagerness to be non-hierarchical and supportive instead of tyrannical and ruthlessly critical, we have sometimes participated in the patriarchal denial of the mind to women. In our radical and necessary assertion that the feminist teacher must validate the personal and the emotional, we have sometimes ignored the equally necessary validation of the intellect. In our sensitivity to the psychology of oppression in our students' lives, we have often denied ourselves the authority we seek to nurture in our students.[8]

Friedman's comments highlight the failure of radical educators to appropriate a view of authority that is able to provide the basis for both a critical and programmatic discourse within schools. One consequence of this position is that radical democrats are bereft of a view of authority that allows for the development of a theoretical strategy through which popular forces might wage a political struggle within schools in order to accumulate power and to shape school policy. Nor is there any indication how feminist, blacks, and other groups might develop a view of authority consistent with the nature of their oppression and their developing sense of history and power. The irony of this position is that the Left's politics of skepticism translates into an anti-utopian, overburdened discourse that undermines the possibility for any type of programmatic political action.[9]

Liberal theorists in education have provided the most dialectical view of the relationship between authority and education. This tradition is exemplified by Kenneth D. Benne, who not only has argued for a dialectical view of authority, but has also attempted to display its relevance for a critical pedagogy. Benne first defines authority as "a function of concrete human situations in which a person or group, fulfilling some purpose, project, or need, requires guidance or direction from a source outside himself or itself. ... Any such operating relationship—a triadic relationship between subject(s), bearer(s), and field(s)—is an authority relationship."[10] He elaborates on this general definition by insisting that the basis for specific forms of authority can be respectively found in separate appeals to the logic of rules, the knowledgeability of expertise, and the moral ethics of democratic community. Benne then makes a strong case for grounding educational authority in the ethical practices of a community that takes democracy seriously. He simultaneously points out the strengths and weaknesses of forms of authority based on either rules or expertise, but rightly argues that the highest forms of authority are rooted in the morality of democratic community. Benne's argument is important not only because it provides a working definition of authority but also because it points to ways in which the latter can be useful in developing a more humane and critical pedagogy. At the same time, it illustrates some weaknesses endemic to liberal theory that need to be overcome if the concept of authority is to be reconstructed in the interests of an emancipatory pedagogy.

While Benne makes an appeal to the ethics and imperatives of a democratic community, he exhibits an inadequate understanding of how power is asymmetrically distributed within and between different communities. By failing to explore this issue, he is unable to illuminate how the material and ideological grounding of domination works against the notion of authentic community through forms of authority that actively produce and sustain relations of oppression and suffering. In other words, Benne posits a formal dialectical theory of authority, which, in the final instance, remains removed from the lived social practices of students. As a consequence, we get no sense of how authority functions as a specific practice within schools shaped by the historical realities of social class, race, gender, and other powerful socioeconomic forces that sometimes prevent authentic forms of authority from emerging within public education. Simply put, Benne's analysis reproduces the shortcomings of liberal theory in general; that is, he unduly emphasizes the positive aspects of authority and in doing so ends up ignoring those "messy webs" of social relations that embody forms of struggle and contestation. By refusing to acknowledge the relations of domination and resistance, Benne effectively abstracts and disconnects the nature of authority from the concept of schooling as a site of contestation. We are left with a notion of authority trapped in the reified realm of abstract formalities.

In addition, Benne provides us with little understanding of how educational authority can be linked to the collective struggles of teachers both within and outside schools. His attempt to link authority to the notion of community neither informs us how teachers should organize in the interests of such a community, nor provides any referents for indicating what particular kinds of community and forms of subjectivity are worth fighting for.

In the end, what most conservative, liberal, and radical educational discourses manage to establish are either reactionary or incomplete approaches to developing a dialectical view of authority and schooling. Conservatives celebrate authority, linking it to popular expressions of everyday life, but in doing so they express and support reactionary and undemocratic interests. On the other hand, radicals educators tend to equate authority with forms of domination or the loss of freedom and consequently fail to develop a conceptual category for constructing a programmatic language of hope and struggle.

But to their credit, they do manage to provide a language of critique that investigates in concrete terms how school authority promotes specific forms of oppression. Liberals, in general, provide the most dialectical view of authority but fail to apply it in a concrete way so as to interrogate the dynamics of domination and freedom as they are expressed within the asymmetrical relations of power and privilege that characterize various aspects of school life.

At this point I want to argue, in the next section, for developing a radical theory of authority and ethics as part of a critical theory of education. In doing so, I insist that an emancipatory view of authority be grounded in a theory of ethics based on the principles of democracy, solidarity, and hope. I then offer a rationale for constructing a view of emancipatory authority and ethics. In addition, I attempt to recover vital elements within the radical tradition of democracy and education that dominated the social reconstructionists debates between the 1930s and the early 1950s.

Authority, Ethics and Schooling: A Rationale

It is important for educators to adopt a dialectical view of authority for a number of reasons. First, the issue of authority is an important critical referent and moral ideal for public schooling. That is, as a form of legitimation, authority is inextricably related to a particular vision of what schools should be as part of a wider community and society. In other words, authority makes both visible and problematic the presuppositions that give meaning to the officially sanctioned discourses and values that legitimate what Foucault has called particular "material, historical conditions of possibility [along with] their governing systems of order, appropriation, and exclusion."[11] For example, questions might be raised about the nature and source of authority which legitimates a particular type of curriculum, the way school time is organized, the political consequences of tracking students, the social division of labor among teachers, and the patriarchal basis of schooling. In this way, the concept of authority provides the basis for raising questions about the kinds of teaching and pedagogy that can be developed and legitimated within a view of schooling that takes democracy and critical citizenship seriously.

79

Second, the concept of authority raises issues about the ethical and political basis of schooling. That is, it calls into question the role that school administrators and teachers play as intellectuals in both elaborating and implementing their particular views or rationality; in other words, such a concept defines what *school* authority means as a particular set of ideas and practices within a historically defined context. In short, the category of authority reinserts back into the language of schooling the primacy of the political. It does so by highlighting the social and political function that educators serve in elaborating and enforcing a particular view of school authority.

Third, the concept of authority provides the theoretical leverage to analyze the relationship between domination and power by both questioning and elaborating the shared meanings that teachers use in order to justify their view of authority and the effects of their actions at the level of actualized pedagogical practices. In this case, authority provides both the referent and critique against which to analyze the difference between the legitimating claims for a particular form of authority and the way such a claim is actually expressed in daily classroom life.

A number of educational theorists have rightly argued that the relationship between authority and democracy needs to be made clearer if schools are to play a fundamental role in advancing the discourse of freedom and critical citizenship.[12] In the following section, I want to expand the logic of this argument by situating it in a tradition of protest that emerged in the earlier part of the century with the rise of the social reconstructionist movement, a movement which counted John Dewey, George Counts, and John Childs among its members. Writing against the background of the depression, the social reconstructionists actively attempted in the pages of *The Social Frontier* and other journals to demonstrate the importance of a discourse of democracy and ethics as central elements in the language of schooling.

Social Reconstructionism and the Politics of Ethics and Democracy

I argued in chapter 1 that America is becoming a land without memory and that one important function of the dominant ideology is to establish a society without a history of protest or a multiplicity of social and political discourses. As one way of challenging this ideology and the social practices that result from it, educators need to critically examine history as a form of "liberating remembrance." In this case, history needs to be resurrected not only as a site of struggle, but also as a theoretical resource for reconstructing an ethics of politics and possibility from the conflicts, discourses, and stories of those who chose to resist and reverse the mechanisms of oppression and domination. Grounded in communities of resisting discourses and social practices, radical historical traditions offer a definition of moral and political struggle as a form of responsible defiance and action. In this sense, the legacy and "stories" of social reconstructionism can serve as "subversive historical discourses" and become part of the dynamic of renewal and transformation central to a politics and pedagogy of ethics and democracy.

The debates on democracy in which the social reconstructionists were engaged in the first half of the twentieth century highlight the important insight that citizenship education has to be linked to forms of self-and social empowerment if the school is to become a progressive force in the ongoing struggle for democracy as a way of life. Such forms of empowerment would enhance the capacity for critical reason and individual autonomy, and create the possibility for transforming wider social and political structures. It is also important to stress that John Dewey and some of his social reconstructionist cohorts not only redefined the political and pedagogical significance of citizenship education, but also attempted to situate the relationship between democracy and schooling in an ethical foundation that has enormous significance today for the development of a critical theory of education. In their view, it was essential for educators to develop a normative foundation for linking authority, power, and learning to the practical task of developing forms of experience and community consistent with the political and social imperatives of democratic life. John Dewey, in particular, strongly argued that democracy as a way of life is a moral ideal that implies a form of community-in-struggle whose aim is to reconstruct human experience in the realization of such principles as freedom, liberty, and fraternity.

> Democracy as compared with other ways of life is the sole way of
> living which believes wholeheartedly in the process of experience as

end and as means; as that which is capable of generating the science
which is the sole dependable authority for the direction of further
experience and which releases emotions, needs, and desires so as to
call into being the things that have not existed in the past. For every
way of life that fails in its democracy limits the contacts, the
exchanges, the communications, the interactions by which
experience is steadied while it is also enlarged and enriched. The
task of this release and enrichment is one that has to be carried on
day by day. Since it is one that can have no end till experience itself
comes to an end, the task of democracy is forever that of a freer and
more humane experience in which all share and to which all
contribute.[13]

Dewey and other social reconstructionists strongly believed that
educational philosophy had to be seen as part of a wider social philosophy in which the issue of democracy as a way of life "expressed
the movement of the ethical world."[14] In this context, democracy
took on a political and ethical dimension that gave meaning and purpose to the form and content of education itself. Democracy would
now serve as the ideal against which to evaluate and change all those
institutions that make up public life, and schooling would become
the most important institution upon which to develop the authority,
knowledge, and social practices that expressed such an ideal. The
notion of democracy that emerged from this position went far
beyond the more limited liberal view of democracy as the terrain of
voting, elections, and government. In the work of many of the social
reconstructionists, democracy embraced all those institutions in
which authority and power were exercised in order to shape both
state policy and the ideological and material contours of everyday
life. Moreover, in this discourse democracy and ethics became interrelated as part of both a general theory of education and a theory of
social change. For social reconstructionists such as John Childs,
democracy provided the ethical foundation and political referent for
both social criticism and social transformation.

Democracy, as a social ideal, makes the individual the end and
institutions the means. Schemes of government, systems of
economics, forms of family-life and the institutions of religion are all
alike viewed as means for the enrichment of the lives of individuals.
The validity of each and every institutionalized practice is to be
tested by what it contributes to this supreme end. Society has no

good other than the good of its individual members, present and prospective. Democracy demands that these individuals, in their flesh and blood human form, be taken as the final objects of ethical consideration. It is a way of life, therefore, which by its inherent nature opposes regimentation, uniformity and totalitarianism. It prizes individuality and human uniqueness and seeks to provide the community arrangements which make for their richest possible development.[15]

By linking ethics, democracy, and politics to the meaning and purpose of schooling, the social reconstructionists attempted to create a public philosophy that would both challenge the prevailing social order and provide the basis for educators to deepen the intellectual, civic, and moral understanding of their role as agents of public formation. A number of important theoretical considerations emerge from this public philosophy regarding the meaning and purpose of schooling and the role that teachers might adopt as moral and political agents of social change.

First, the social reconstructionists believed, almost without question, that schooling was not a politically or morally neutral institution. Consequently, they focused their attention on providing an ethical discourse upon which to construct a viable democratic project for education. The central question in this project could be articulated as follows: "What is the purpose and social significance of education?" For Dewey, the central purpose of schooling was to develop in students a critical intelligence and disposition that would be consistent with their actions as socially responsible citizens. In this view, public schooling would derive its ethical criteria from a critically reconstructed ideal of democracy as a moral and political tradition.

The constellation of meanings and ideals which we call democracy constitutes the heart of the American ethical tradition. It is from these basic conceptions and ideals of democracy taken as a political, social and moral movement that the educator should derive his basic ethical criteria for the evaluation of social affairs.[16]

Second, although there was some debate among the social reconstructionists about the strengths and weaknesses of emphasizing the faith in intelligence within the wider progressive education movement, there was a general agreement that intellectual development had to be linked to a general theory of social welfare and could not be isolated as a goal for the sake of its own development.[17] The important issue here is that the development of a child's intelligence or capacity for critical thinking was not merely an epistemological or cognitive issue; it was also a moral undertaking and could not be removed from a wider social and political discourse. In his view, creative intelligence contained a utopian impulse and was an essential dimension in the formation of a democratic public. For Dewey, creative intelligence comes into being as part of the development of moral character, and it is this faith in intelligence that is a central precondition for a democracy. Dewey writes:

> Faith in the power of intelligence to imagine a future which is the projection of the desirable in the present, and to invent the instrumentalities of its realization, is our salvation. And it is a faith which must be nurtured and made articulate.[18]

Third, the social reconstructionists made a valuable pedagogical contribution in developing a view of democracy that linked a theory of ethics to the issue of moral character. For them, democracy as a moral ideal was not only about teaching students the capacity for critical thinking; it was also about the construction of experience and the formation of character as part of a general theory of social welfare. For Dewey, democratic community life as a pedagogical task had to be grounded in the face-to-face associations that stressed cooperation, solidarity, and social responsibility.[19] Democracy and moral behavior were learned in this sense as part of what some feminists have recently termed a politics of the body, that is, as something to be felt and internalized through the construction of experiences that produced particular forms of subjectivity. Equally important is the fact that the theory of ethics and democracy at work here not only linked intelligence and character around a politics of habit and the body, but also linked learning to a fundamental connection between the school and community life. It was around this issue that Dewey and others rejected the narrow emphasis on child-centered education that came to characterize the more conservative wing of progressive education. Jesse Newlon expresses well the view of Dewey and others regarding the relationship between schooling, community, and democracy.

> Democracy can be learned only through experience, through living. The home, the school, and the community must, then, provide youth with opportunities to work at genuine problems of democracy at the

level of their maturity. No wall can be erected between the school
and the community. Children and youth can learn to become
members of the community only by being members of the
community. It is obvious that merely to study about democracy is not
enough. It is equally obvious that the so-called child-centered school
goes into the ash can. Just as a democratic society is neither
child-centered nor adult-centered, so a school for democracy can be
neither child-centered nor adult-centered, nor "school" centered.[20]

Fourth, another fundamental contribution that the social reconstructionists provided in their attempt to interrelate ethics, schooling, and democracy was what I want to call a politics of difference.
Writing in the 1930s and 1940s for *The Social Frontier*, the social reconstructionists were acutely aware that one of the main features of the
ideology and practice of totalitarianism was an attempt to produce a
discourse that explicitly asserts the homogeneity of the social and
public sphere. Within this discourse, internal division is denied, and
where opposition or difference does exist it is labeled as a threat to
the welfare of the state. To use Claude Lefort's terms, "the other" in
totalitarian discourse is seen as the "Enemy of the People."[21] Dewey
and his cohorts strongly believed that a theory of dialogue and community had to be central to a theory of democracy, and dialogue and
communication in this sense was based on an appreciation of different voices and interests. In this case, a politics of difference grew out
of a fundamental recognition of the importance of the "other" and
the necessity of developing a common ground for linking the notion
of difference to a publicly shared language of struggle and social justice. The social reconstructionists's view of difference had little to do
with either the current poststructuralist version of the "free-floating"
signifier or the modernist concept of liberal pluralism.[22] Instead,
they argued for a recognition of genuine differences as part of an
attempt to develop the social forms of communication, mutual understanding, and solidarity that constitute a democratic public sphere.

The social reconstructionists also attempted to derive from their
theory of democracy and ethics a number of pedagogical principles
as a basis for defining both the role of the teacher and a critical pedagogy for democracy. Dewey was adamant in defining teachers as
intellectuals, that is, as reflective thinkers whose social function de-
manded that they be given the ideological and material conditions
necessary for them to make decisions, produce curricula, and act out

of their own point of view. For Dewey this meant, in part, giving teachers more power so that they could in turn create the classroom environments necessary for students to both experience and become knowledgeable about democracy as a way of life. For others such as John Childs, the teacher was to find his or her identity in the relationship between the need to educate students to be active, democratic citizens and the broader need to work outside schools as critically active citizens in order to transform the basic social and political injustices of society itself. In Child's view, the teacher as moral agent has both a pedagogical responsibility and a social responsibility to fulfill. Childs is quite clear on this point.

> The educator thus finds an identity between the broader educational need and the democratic social need. To meet these needs a drastic social reconstruction must be undertaken. The necessity for this social reconstruction becomes his controlling hypothesis. He continues to work for many specific reforms, but his deeper interest is the development of an economic and political movement which will attain the power to transform the historic economic system of the United States.[23]

Although the social reconstructionists were split on the issue of whether teachers should align themselves with the working class or align themselves with groups organized around broader social reforms in the struggle for democracy, there was a common sentiment in their overall dissatisfaction with capitalist society and in their underlying faith in what some have called the principles of militant democracy.

A number of principles for developing a pedagogy for democracy emerged in this discourse. Dewey made strong claims for the integration of theory and practice around the reconstruction of experience linked to forms of community life; George Counts and William H. Kilpatrick argued in different terms that democracy involves the studying of specific social problems and conditions and includes helping students develop a general theory of social welfare; John Childs argued vehemently for teachers to become aware of their own democratic points of view and to see these as strengths rather than as weaknesses; Boyd Bode made valuable contributions regarding the importance of democratic dialogue in the classroom and the necessity to expose students to a variety of points of view. In all these instances, pedagogy was seen as part of a cultural politics steeped in an ethical and democratic concern for linking school knowledge, student subjectivities, and classroom experience with the wider imperatives and needs of the social order. In this sense, the social reconstructionists developed a public philosophy of schooling, democracy, and ethics that is as important today as it was when it was first developed.

Emancipatory Authority and the Role of Teachers as Intellectuals

One of Antonio Gramsci's most important formulations regarding the political nature of culture was that intellectuals play a central role in the production and reproduction of social life. For Gramsci, the emerging role of intellectuals as a primary political force in maintaining the ideological rule of dominant groups signaled an important shift in the relationship between such central elements of cultural struggle as language, knowledge, and social relations on the one hand, and the dynamics of control and power, on the other.[24] In this case, intellectuals became producers of cultural capital, which as a deliberate analogue to material capital signifies the transformation of social relations from a fundamental reliance on the primacy of the policing function of the state to more subtle forms of control organized around forms of knowledge that name and construct everyday experience in accord with the logic of domination. Of course, Gramsci's emphasis on cultural hegemony has been developed by social theorists such as Pierre Bourdieu, Alvin Gouldner, and André Gorz.[25] But none of these theorists have furthered Gramsci's project of viewing intellectuals as elaborators of the dominant culture as well as a vital and fundamental social and political force in any counterhegemonic struggle.

As important as the emphasis has been in radical educational theory in elaborating the various ways in which cultural domination is played out within the different mechanisms and levels of schooling, I do not want to repeat that position here. Instead, I will redefine the role that teachers as intellectuals might play as producers of cultural forms and discourses that point to particular views of authority, ethics, and pedagogical practice whose underlying logic is consistent with a radical cultural politics. In other words, I redefine the role of teachers as intellectuals around a view of authority and ethics that points to the importance of specific forms of intellectual work and practice in any programmatic discourse for developing alternative forms of schooling. Such a stance is important because it posits an oppositional view of intellectual practice born of commitment and struggle. Furthermore, it provides a referent for analyzing and criticizing those intellectuals who have been reduced to either a technical intelligentsia performing a wide variety of functions in late capitalist society or those intellectuals who have become hegemonic intellectuals either unconsciously or consciously furthering the reproduction of the dominant society.

If the concept of authority is to provide a legitimating basis for rethinking the purpose and meaning of public education and critical pedagogy, it must be rooted in a view of community life in which the moral quality of everyday existence is linked to the essence of democracy.[26] Authority in this view becomes a mediating referent for the ideal of democracy and its expression as a set of educational practices designed to empower students to be critical and active citizens. That is, the purpose of schooling is now fashioned around two central questions: What kind of society do educators want to live in? What kind of teachers and pedagogy can be both informed and legitimated by a view of authority that takes democracy and citizenship seriously? Such a view of authority points to a theory of democracy that includes the principles of representative democracy, workers' democracy, and civil and human rights. It is, in Benjamin Barber's terms, a view of authority rooted in "strong democracy," and it is characterized by a citizenry capable of genuine public thinking, political judgment, and social action.[27] Such a view of authority endorses a concept of the citizen as more than a simple bearer of abstract rights, privileges, and immunities but as a member of any one of a diverse number of public spheres that provide a sense of communal vision and civic courage. Sheldon Wolin is worth quoting at length on this issue:

> A political being is not to be defined as ... an abstract, disconnected
> bearer of rights, privileges, and immunities, but as a person whose
> existence is located in a particular place and draws its sustenance
> from circumscribed relationships: family, friends, church,
> neighborhood, workplace, community, town, city. These relationships

are the sources from which political beings draw power—symbolic, material, and psychological—and that enable them to act together. For true political power involves not only acting so as to effect decisive changes; it also means the capacity to receive power, to be acted upon, to change, and be changed. From a democratic perspective, power is not simply force that is generated; it is experience, sensibility, wisdom, even melancholy, distilled from the diverse relations and circles we move within.[28]

As defined through the dynamics of concrete experience, institutional relations, and commitment to public life, authority becomes an important theoretical category for organizing and defending schools as democratic public spheres. That is, schools can now be understood and constructed within a model of authority that legitimates them as places where students learn and collectively struggle for the economic, political, and social preconditions that make individual freedom and social empowerment possible. Within this emancipatory model of authority, a discourse can be fashioned in which educators can struggle against the exercise of authority often used by conservatives to link the purpose of schooling to a truncated view of patriotism and patriarchy that functions as a veil for a suffocating chauvinism. In its emancipatory model, authority exists as a terrain of struggle and as such reveals the dialectical nature of its interests and possibilities; moreover, it provides the basis for viewing schools as democratic public spheres within an ongoing wider movement and struggle for democracy. For educators and others working in oppositional social movements, the dominant meaning of authority must be redefined to include the concepts of freedom, equality, and democracy.[29] Furthermore, the concept of emancipatory authority needs to be seen as the central category around which to construct a rationale for defining teachers' work as a form of critical, intellectual practice related to the issues, problems, concerns, and experiences of everyday life.

Here it is important to stress the dual nature of the emancipatory model of authority which I have been presenting. On the one hand, this model provides the basis for linking the purpose of schooling to the imperatives of a critical democracy, a position I have already discussed. On the other hand, it establishes theoretical support for analyzing teaching as a form of intellectual practice; moreover, it provides the ontological grounding for teachers who are willing to assume the role of transformative intellectuals.

The concept of emancipatory authority suggests that teachers are bearers of critical knowledge, rules, and values through which they consciously articulate and problematize their relationship to each other, to students, to subject matter, and to the wider community. Such a view of authority challenges the dominant view of teachers as primarily technicians or public servants, whose role is primarily to implement rather than conceptualize pedagogical practice. The category of emancipatory authority dignifies teachers' work by viewing it as a form of intellectual practice. Within this discourse, teachers' work is viewed as a form of intellectual labor that interrelates conception and practice, thinking and doing, and producing and implementing as integrated activities that give teaching its dialectical meaning. The concept of teacher as intellectual carries with it the imperative to judge, critique, and reject those approaches to authority that reinforce a technical and social division of labor that silences and disempowers both teachers and students. In other words, emancipatory authority establishes as a central principle the need for teachers and others to critically engage the ideological and practical conditions which allow them to mediate, legitimate, and function in their capacity as authority-minded intellectuals.

Emancipatory authority also provides the theoretical scaffolding for educators to define themselves not simply as intellectuals, but in a more committed fashion as transformative intellectuals. This means that such educators are not merely concerned with forms of empowerment that promote individual achievement and traditional forms of academic success. Instead, they are also concerned in their teaching with linking empowerment—the ability to think and act critically—to the concept of social transformation. That is, teaching for social transformation means educating students to take risks and to struggle within ongoing relations of power in order to be able to alter the grounds upon which life is lived. Acting as a transformative intellectual means helping students acquire critical knowledge about basic societal structures, such as the economy, the state, the workplace, and mass culture so that such institutions can be open to potential transformation. A transformation, in this case, aimed at the progressive humanization of the social order. Doug White, an Australian educator, is instructive on this issue:

In the broadest sense it is education—the bringing of knowledge into social life—which is central to a project which can turn possibilities into actualities. Radical teachers have not made a mistake in being too radical, but in not being radical enough. The task is for teachers, with others, to begin a project in which the forms of social institutions and work are considered and transformed, so that the notion of culture may come to include the development of social structures. The true nature of curriculum ... is the development of that knowledge, thought and practice which is required by young people to enable them to take part in the production and reproduction of social life and to come to know the character of these processes.[30]

As transformative intellectuals, teachers need to make clear the nature of the appeals to authority they are using to legitimate their pedagogical practices. In other words, educators need to clarify the political and moral referents for the authority they assume in teaching particular forms of knowledge, taking a stand against forms of oppression, and treating students as if they ought also to be concerned about the issues of social justice and political action. The social reconstructionists provide one referent for an emancipatory view of authority by developing a public philosophy in which the purpose of schooling and the legitimation and exercise of authority is rooted in the idea of democracy as a moral and political force. In the following section, I refer to the work of a number of writers within feminist and liberation theology traditions. I do not, however, attempt to provide an exhaustive analysis of either the theoretical differences that operate within and between these traditions, nor do I try to provide an extended analysis of the writers under discussion. My aim is simply to analyze their work with regard to a view of ethics that has important implications for further elaborating a discourse of emancipatory authority and the category of teacher as a transformative intellectual.

Feminist Ethics, Liberation Theology, and the Discourse of Memory, Narrative, and Solidarity

One of the major achievements of the feminist movement in the last decade has been to make indisputably clear the fact that no adequate understanding of contemporary social issues and problems can neglect the theoretical and political contributions of women. This has been partly the result of feminists having made serious theoretical and political interventions into almost every aspect of social and political life in their attempt to uncover, name, and challenge the ideology and practice of sexism.[31] In a similar fashion, a number of American writers have drawn from the diverse tradition of liberation theology and have begun to posit a critical and alternative discourse to the conservative and traditional ideologies and practices of the established churches.[32] Following the increasing political activism of church groups challenging United States foreign policy in Latin America and elsewhere, and its ruthless insensitivity to domestic problems, liberation theology in the United States is being forged within a set of historical and political circumstances that represent a unique American tradition of protest and struggle. What is important to recognize here is that both feminists and religious critics have increasingly contributed to developing a new language of critique, and uncovering forms of knowledge generally removed from the dominant public sphere; moreover, they have begun to redefine in critical and emancipatory terms the language of ethics, experience, and community. As a result, they have raised new questions, pointed to the possibility for constructing more viable and life-giving relationships, and, most important, revealed how the strength and power at the center of the lives of women and other oppressed groups can provide the foundation for a radical theory of ethics and moral principles. Of course, just as there is no overall theoretical unity in the feminist movement or in the ranks of the liberation theology movement, there is no unitary discourse that unproblematically constitutes a feminist or theological ethic. What does exist is a diverse body of writing on ethics, politics, and social theory that incorporates a number of important though sometimes contradictory strands. One of the most exciting theoretical accomplishments that has emerged in critical social theory is the development of a discourse that links certain strands of radical feminist theory with selected aspects of liberation theology. A body of work is emerging from the intersection of selected aspects of these two traditions which offers a number of important theoretical and moral referents for developing a view of authority based on an alternative set of moral principles and social practices. I will argue that the work being produced within the new tradition of feminist theology represents the most promising possibility for developing what Sharon Welch calls a feminist ethic of risk and resistance.[33] Central to this ethic are a number of elements that provide the possibility for teachers to both name the conditions that produce human suffering and pain as well as define a notion of responsible action. At the core of this ethic of risk and resistance is the attempt to develop a principled view of humanity, while bringing forth the ideological and structural basis for a life-enhancing, democratic community. I will now briefly name some of the basic themes that characterize this ethic of risk and resistance and then analyze its implications for teachers' work.

One of the most important insights developing within this work focuses on the experiences of women and the oppressed as the source of knowledge and moral principles. In this view, justice is bound less to abstract, conceptual rules and tied more closely to concrete forms of struggle and liberation that give priority to the well-being of people in their own historical locations. Justice in this perspective is not merely the application of procedural rules to varying contexts; it is an attempt to understand how moral sensibilities are formed amid human suffering and the struggle for liberation and freedom. What is just or true in this case is not how the latter are defined within the dominant historical discourse or within an abstract philosophical or theological position, but, instead, the meaning of these categories as they emerge out of those struggles shaped and informed by the lived experiences of women and other oppressed groups. Justice in this sense is not organized around an appeal to abstract principles but is rooted in a substantive project of transforming those concrete social and political structures that deny dignity, hope, and power to vast numbers of people. By making lived experience the source of ethical claims, feminists, in particular, have begun to raise serious questions about the ways in which experience is organized and legitimated so as to justify particular ethical discourses. The feminist theologian Beverly Harrison argues that the entry point of moral theology should begin with a collective naming process that is at once historical, affirmative, and transformative. She writes:

> Clarification of the group's concrete historical experience of
> oppression or subjugation, carried out communally, begins the work
> of ethics/theology. This collective "naming" process fosters the ability

to reflect on one's shared situation as structurally conditioned and also enables people to enter into the basic stance that precipitates ethical reflection itself: the power or capacity to be "the subjects of our lives." ... The methods of liberation theology and ethics must always be historical. ... It aids recovery of social memory and awareness of the struggles of our forebears. It aims to represent the past to us in a specific way. ... [it] enables us to see that the past has a human face, that human actions, patterned over time, are the source of social structures and institutional practices that have come to function as real, objective constraints on the lives of our forebears and on us. ... We need to remember that those who exercise privilege and control in the present also control "official" history. "Official" history suppresses the stories of resistance and dissent against the status quo and presents the past either as a triumph of the deserving or as inevitable. Critical history breaks open the past, in its full complexity, and re-presents that past as bearing a story of human struggle against domination. Even failed resistance bears powerful evidence of human dignity and courage that informs our contemporary vocations. Our remembered forebears and colleagues in struggle energize our lives as we live through the pressures and risks that real resistance to oppression always involves.[34]

Harrison's politics of experience represents a discourse of ethics that is both historical and transformative. It begins with a clear and prophetic option for examining the experiences of the "radical others" in history, and it also finds in the concept of historical memory the resources, stories, and struggles that reveal the possibility for a new vision of human community and identity for the oppressed.

The concern with the experience of the "radical and excluded others" in the work of feminist theologians serves to redefine the notion of justice. This work also calls into question the gender and moral basis for forms of rationality that define the social and sexual division of labor which constitute what is often viewed as the private and public spheres of everyday life. For instance, feminists as diverse as Nell Noddings and Jean Grimshaw have argued that the dominant conception of rationality and morality, with its instrumental logic of efficiency and self-interest, undermines a public morality in which it is considered obligatory to care for others and to alleviate needless forms of suffering and pain.[35] In this radical view, the rationality of the dominant public sphere adjudicates all norms and principles through the needs of the marketplace; morality is a function of the principles of supply and demand. Within this logic, the principles of morality and reason that determine public life are characterized by a belief in emancipation governed by increased control over nature and history, that is, in an evolutionary logic in which progress is defined in purely instrumental and quantitative terms as a linear progression from material scarcity to consumer abundance. For liberation theologians such as Johann Baptist Metz, the dominant rationality produces a distinction between the public and private spheres in which "private" values make no public demands, whereas public values deny the corporeality of desire, hope, and longing on the part of those who are oppressed and exploited within a machinery of domination rationalized through an appeal to the alleged evolutionary logic of science. For Metz,

> The modern world, with its technical civilization, is not simply a rational universe. Its myth is evolution. The silent interest of its rationality is the fiction of time as empty infinity, which is free of surprises and within which everyone and everything is enclosed without grace.[36]

Feminist theologians and others have raised new and important challenges to the ideology and morality that rationalizes the division between the private and public spheres in the Western democracies. At one level, they have argued that this rationality serves to mark gender distinctions that are oppressive and at the same time serve to undermine the possibility for an ethic of risk and resistance as the basis for public life. In the first instance, Jean Grimshaw argues the public is seen as paradigmatically the province of males and as such excludes those aspects of social life seen as attributes of women and the private sphere.

> Set against this conception of the public sphere is that of the private one of the intimacies of home and family. This is construed as the polar opposite of the world of impersonal instrumental rationality and self-interest. It is personal, particularistic, based on emotion and on care and nurturance for others. Each aspect of social life is defined by what it excludes. The public sphere thus excludes emotion, except insofar as this is transformed into rational self-interest. The private sphere of domestic life excludes reason, except insofar as this is represented by males who also figure in market relations.[37]

The morality and rationality that inform this view of experience not only discriminate against women, but also promote a view of public life that is at odds with the notion of radical democracy. Feminist theologians and others have attempted to challenge this view of rationality and morality. In doing so, they have attempted to develop a discourse that reunites the personal with the social and the political in order to question and then refuse the intellectual and objective barriers that prevent women and ethnic, racial, and minority men from appropriating the moral and political resources needed for self- and social empowerment. Central to this new discourse is an ethic of risk and resistance in which the mind/body duality is overcome through a politics of caring and sensuality. The politics of caring, following the work of Nell Noddings, Margaret Farley, and others,[38] suggests a number of important moral principles. First, it rejects all forms of rationality that treat human beings as merely means and reduce human suffering to quantitative analyses. Second, it points to the political and pedagogical obligation to develop a language of both critique and hope, that is, a language capable of both naming oppression and "keeping the power of relationships alive in our world."[39] Beverly Harrison develops this dialectical notion of critique and hope in her notion of the "work of radical love" and is worth repeating here in full:

> There is much more to be said about the envisionment of the work of radical love within a feminist moral theology that takes its signals from what is deepest and best in women's historical struggle. Certainly, more also needs to be said about the depth of sin and evil in the world. It is important to remember that a feminist moral theology is utopian, as all good theology is, in that it envisages a society, a world, a cosmos, in which, as Jules Giardi puts it, there are "no excluded ones." But feminist theology is also mightily realistic, in that it takes with complete seriousness the radical freedom we human beings have for doing good or evil. Since we acknowledge that we have, literally, the power to person-each-other into love—that is, into relationship—we can also acknowledge our power to obliterate dignity, respect, care, and concern for humanity from our world. All of that is within our power.[40]

The notion of the politics of sensuality represents an attempt to overcome the mind/body duality by recognizing that the politics of the mind/body split not only rejects the body and the emotions as a source of moral power, but also serves to fuel dominant ideologies bred by a hatred of nonwhites and women. More specifically, the subjugation of the emotions to the sphere of the intellect and reason represents a flight from morality and a refusal to honor a politics of difference in which communication with those who inhabit a different social and cultural terrain depends on embodied forms of mutuality and regard in the context of social justice. In this case, a politics of sensuality integrates the mind and the body as foundational to a morality in which people both understand *and* feel their connectedness to other human beings and living things. Our understanding of the world, in this discourse, is predicated on our ability to mediate it through our feelings, emotions, and perceptions. In Carol Robb's terms, the politics of sensuality represents a form of "embodied rationality" that has major implications for a feminist ethics of risk and resistance. She writes:

> The term "embodiment" with respect to feminist theory and specifically feminist ethics means, minimally: ... (1) Our sexuality and body-selves are to be celebrated rather than deprecated, and are to be respected as the ground of our personhood. (2) Mutuality, rather than control, ownership, or paternalism, is a major moral norm for social, including sexual, communication. (3) Sex role rigidity is destructive of possibilities for mature interpersonal relations; hence sex role fluidity is to be practiced. (4) We are to recognize and honor all expressions of sexual communication between people who care for each other in mutuality and equal regard, whether they are homosexual or heterosexual relations.[41]

Before analyzing how the ethic of risk and resistance might be used to redefine the work that teachers do as transformative intellectuals, I will briefly point to ways in which the categories of memory, narrative, and solidarity can be used to clarify and extend the possibilities for the politics of experience I have focused on in this section. Johann Baptist Metz argues that "identity is formed when memories are aroused."[42] For Metz, as well as for a number of feminists and theologians, memories are recalled in narratives that inform and transform our view and experience of history. Rebecca Chopp illuminates the importance of narrative as a structure of radical memory.

> Narrative, as the structure of theology, has two interrelated tasks. ... First, it is performative and practical as it forms and informs the human subject through dangerous memories. This is its

hermeneutical task, forming and transforming the lives of subjects through the recollection and interpretation of the memories of suffering. Second, it is critical insofar as these memories call into question the prevailing sociopolitical structures.[43]

Narratives are important because they provide the possibility for both reclaiming one's own "stories" and for forging bonds of solidarity with the living and with those who have suffered in the past. Solidarity, in this case, is forged through memories and hope; it is the recognition and identification of a different subject in history, that is, those poor and oppressed groups who have disrupted the historical narratives and ideology of linear progress of the dominant classes and groups. Through the categories of memory, narrative, and solidarity the foundation emerges for constructing an ethic oriented to a future without oppression and the massive denial of hope.

The notion of authority that begins to develop from this position rests on a commitment to a form of solidarity that addresses the many instances of suffering that are both a growing and threatening part of everyday life in America and abroad. Solidarity in this instance embodies a particular kind of commitment and practice. As a commitment, it suggests, as Sharon Welch has pointed out, a recognition and identification with "the perspective of those people and groups who are marginal and exploited."[44] As a form of practice, solidarity represents a break from the bonds of isolated individuality and the need to engage for and with oppressed groups in political struggles that challenge the existing order of society as being institutionally repressive and unjust. This notion of solidarity emerges from an affirmative view of liberation which underscores the necessity of working collectively alongside the oppressed. It is also rooted in an acknowledgement that "truth" is an outcome of particular power struggles that cannot be abstracted from either history or existing networks of social and political control. This position suggests that one's beliefs are always subject to a critical analysis and that the process of learning how to learn is always contingent on the recognition that one's perspective can be superseded. The politics of such a skepticism is firmly rooted in a view of authority that is not dependent merely on the logic of epistemological arguments, but which is deeply forged in "a creation of a politics of truth that defines the true as that which liberates and furthers specific processes of liberation."[45]

Teachers as Transformative Intellectuals

The category of transformative intellectual suggests that teachers begin with a recognition of those manifestations of suffering that constitute historical memory as well as the immediate conditions of oppression. The pedagogical rationality at work here is one that defines educators as bearers of "dangerous memory," intellectuals who keep alive the memory of human suffering along with the forms of knowledge and struggles in which such suffering was shaped and contested. Dangerous memory has two dimensions: "that of hope and that of suffering ... it recounts the history of the marginal, the vanquished, and the oppressed,"[46] and in doing so posits the need for a new kind of subjectivity and community in which the conditions that create such suffering can be eliminated. Michel Foucault describes the political project that is central to the meaning of dangerous memory as an affirmation of the insurrection of subjugated knowledges—those forms of historical and popular knowledge that have been suppressed or ignored, and through which it becomes possible to discover the ruptural effects of conflict and struggle. Underlying this view of dangerous memory and subjugated knowledge is a logic that provides the basis upon which transformative intellectuals can advance both the language of critique and the language of possibility and hope. Foucault:

> By subjugated knowledges I mean two things: on the one hand, I am referring to the historical contents that have been buried and disguised ... blocs of historical knowledge which were present but disguised within the body of functionalist and systematising theory and which criticism ... draws upon and reveals. ... On the other hand, I believe that by subjugated knowledges one should understand something else, something which in a sense is altogether different, namely, a whole set of knowledges that have been disqualified as inadequate to their task or insufficiently elaborated: naive knowledges, located low down on the hierarchy, beneath the required level of cognition of scientificity. I also believe that it is through the re-emergence of these low-ranking knowledges, these unqualified, even directly disqualified knowledges and which involve what I would call a popular knowledge ... a particular, local, regional knowledge ... which is opposed by everything around it—that is through the re-appearance of this knowledge, of these local

popular knowledges, these disqualified knowledges, that criticism performs its work.[47]

It is precisely the disqualified knowledges of working-class communities, women, blacks, ethnic minorities, along with the knowledges produced by critical theorists such as the social reconstructionists and others that should be the starting point for understanding how curriculum and schooling have been constructed around particular silences and omissions. Moreover, it is in this combination of critique, the reconstruction of the relationship between knowledge and power, and the commitment to a solidarity with the oppressed that the basis exists for a form of emancipatory authority that can structure the philosophical and political basis for a pedagogy that is both empowering and transformative. Of course, developing a legitimating basis for a form of emancipatory authority does not guarantee that a transformative pedagogy will follow. But it does provide the principles for making such a transformation possible. Furthermore, it establishes the criteria for organizing curricula and classroom social relations around goals designed to prepare students to relate, understand, and value the linkage between an existentially lived public space and their own practical learning. By public space, I mean, as Hannah Arendt did, a concrete set of learning conditions where people come together to speak, to dialogue, to share their stories, and to struggle together within social relations that strengthen rather than weaken the possibility for active citizenship.[48]

School and classroom practices in this sense can be organized around forms of learning in which the knowledge and skills acquired serve to prepare students to later develop and maintain those public spheres outside schools that are so vital for developing webs of solidarity in which democracy as a social movement operates as an active force. Maxine Greene speaks to the need for educators to create such public spaces in their own classrooms as a pedagogical precondition for educating students to struggle in an active democracy.

> We need spaces ... for expression, for freedom ... a public space ...
> where living persons can come together in speech and action, each
> one free to articulate a distinctive perspective, all of them granted
> equal worth. It must be a space of dialogue, a space where a web of

relationships can be woven, and where a common world can be brought into being and continually renewed. . . . There must be a teachable capacity to bring into being . . . a public composed of persons with many voices and many perspectives, out of whose multiple intelligences may still emerge a durable and worthwhile common world. If educators can renew their hopes and speak out once again, if they can empower more persons in the multiple domains of possibility, we shall not have to fear a lack of productivity, a lack of dignity or standing in the world. We will be in pursuit of the crucial values; we will be creating our own purposes as we move.[49]

Although Greene comes perilously close to advocating a form of liberal pluralism in which the celebration of difference becomes an end in itself, she does stress that the precondition for understanding democracy is to experience it as a set of social relations in which the other can be first recognized and heard so that the interests expressed amid different voices can then be interrogated around the issue of how they either disable or enable the possibility of democratic public life.

Emancipatory Authority and Practical Learning

Central to developing a critical pedagogy consistent with the principles of emancipatory authority is the need for educators to reconstruct the relations between knowledge, power, and desire in order to bring together what James Donald refers to as two often separate struggles within schools: the changing of circumstances and the changing of subjectivities.[50] In the first case, the central issue that needs to be explored by educators is identifying the kinds of material and ideological preconditions that need to exist before schools can be effective. This issue covers a wide range of concerns, such as active parent involvement in the schools, adequate health care and nutrition for students, high student morale, and adequate financial resources.[51] All these factors represent resources through which power is exercised and made manifest. Power in this sense refers to the means of getting things done and, as Foucault claims, "consists in guiding the possibility of conduct and putting in order the possible outcome to govern, in this sense, to structure the possible field of action of others."[52]

For teachers, the relationship between authority and power is manifested not only in the degree to which they legitimate and exercise control over student (a central concern of conservatives), but equally important through the capacity they possess to influence the conditions under which they work. As I repeatedly stress in this book and elsewhere, unless teachers have both the authority and power to organize and shape the conditions of their work so that they can teach collectively, produce alternative curricula, and engage in a form of emancipatory politics, any talk of developing and implementing progressive pedagogy ignores the reality of what goes on in the daily lives of teachers and is nonsensical.[53] The conditions under which teachers work are currently overtaxing and demeaning, and need to be restructured so as to both dignify the nature of their work and allow them to act in a creative and responsible fashion.

The major issues I will focus on here concern the ways in which teachers can create conditions for student self-and social empowerment through *what* they teach, how they teach, and the means whereby school knowledge can be made worthwhile and interesting. Central to both concerns is the linking of power to knowledge. This raises the issue of what kinds of knowledge educators can provide for students that will empower them not only to understand and engage the world around them, but also to exercise the kind of courage needed to change the wider social reality when necessary.

Educators need to begin with a certain amount of clarity regarding the kind of curriculum they want to develop at the different levels of schooling. I believe this should be a curriculum that gives a central place to the issue of "real" democracy. In developing such a focus, educators must rework those aspects of the traditional curriculum in which democratic possibilities exist, but in doing so they must also exercise an incessant critical analysis of those inherent characteristics that reproduce inequitable social relations. At issue here is the need for educators to recognize that power relations exist in correlation with forms of school knowledge that both distort the truth and produce it. Such a consideration suggests that any attempt to develop a curriculum for democratic empowerment must examine the conditions of knowledge and how such knowledge distorts reality; it also suggests that educators reconstitute the very nature of the knowledge/power relationship. In doing so, they need to understand that knowledge does more than distort. It also produces particular forms of life;

it has, as Foucault points out, a productive, positive function.[54] It is this function of knowledge that must be appropriated with a radical intent. It is important to recognize that although educators often refuse, subvert, and, where necessary, critically appropriate dominant forms of knowledge, this does not mean that they should continue working exclusively within the language of critique. On the contrary, the major thrust of a critical pedagogy should center on generating knowledge that presents concrete possibilities for empowering people. To put it more specifically, a critical pedagogy needs a language of possibility, one that provides the pedagogical basis for teaching democracy while making schooling more democratic.

In general terms, a critical pedagogy needs to focus on what Colin Fletcher calls themes for democracy and democracy in learning.[55] In the first instance, the curriculum should incorporate themes that recognize the urgent problems of adult life. Such knowledge should include not only the basic skills students will need to work and live in the wider society, but also knowledge about the social forms through which human beings live, become conscious, and sustain themselves, particularly with respect to the social and political demands of democratic citizenship. This relates to knowledge about power and how it works, as well as to analyses of those practices such as racism, sexism, and class exploitation that structure and mediate the encounters of everyday life.[56] Of course, the point here is not merely to denounce such stereotypes but rather to expose and deconstruct the processes through which these dominant ideological representations are produced, legitimated, and circulated in society. In many respects, the curriculum should be built upon knowledge that starts with the problems and needs of students. It must, however, be so designed that it can provide the basis for a critique of dominant forms of knowledge. Finally, such a curriculum should also provide students with a language through which they can analyze their own lived relations and experiences in a manner that is both affirmative and critical. R. W. Connell and his associates in Australia provide a clear analysis of the theoretical elements that characterize this type of curricula in their formulation of the kinds of knowledge that should be taught to empower working-class kids. They write:

It proposes that working-class kids get access to formal knowledge via learning which begins with their own experience and the circumstances which shape it, but does not stop there. This approach neither accepts the existing organization of academic knowledge nor simply inverts it. It draws on existing school knowledge and on what working-class people already know, and organizes this selection of information around problems such as economic survival and collective action, handling the disruption of households by unemployment, responding to the impact of new technology, managing problems of personal identity and association, understanding how schools work and why.[57]

Although I take up the following theme in detail in the next two chapters, it is important to mention that a curriculum based on an emancipatory notion of authority is one in which the particular forms of life, culture, and interaction that students bring to school are honored in such a way that students can begin to view such knowledge in both critical and useful terms. All too often students from the working class and other subordinate groups react to dominant school knowledge and ideas as if they were weapons being used against them. On the other hand, curricula developed as part of a critical pedagogy privileges subordinate knowledge forms and reconstructs classroom life as an arena for new forms of sociality. That is, instead of stressing the individualistic and competitive approaches to learning, students are encouraged to work together on projects, both in terms of their production and in terms of their evaluation. This suggests that students must learn within social forms that allow them to exercise a degree of self-consciousness about their own interactions as class, gendered, racial, and ethnic subjects. In addition to analyzing problems and issues that apply to the immediate contexts of students' lives, a critical pedagogy needs to critically appropriate forms of knowledge that exists outside the immediate experience of students' lives in order to broaden their sense of understanding and possibility. This means that students need to learn and appropriate other codes of experiences as well as other discourses in time and place that extend their horizons while constantly pushing them to test what it means to resist oppression, work collectively, and exercise authority from the position of an ever-developing sense of knowledge, expertise, and commitment. It also means providing the pedagogical conditions for raising new desires, needs, ambitions, and real hope, but always in a context that makes such hope realizable.

Giving students the opportunity to learn by understanding the mediations and social forms that shape their own experiences is important not merely because it provides them with a critical way to understand the familiar terrain of everyday practical life. It is also part of a pedagogical strategy that attempts to both recover and engage the experiences that students exhibit so as to understand how such experiences have been accomplished and legitimated within specific social and historical conditions. Michelle Gibbs Russell addresses this issue in the context of analyzing the political rationale behind her own teaching in a community college in Detroit. She writes:

> Political education for Black women in America begins with the memory of four hundred years of enslavement, diaspora, forced labor, beatings, bombings, lynchings, and rape. It takes on inspirational dimensions when we begin cataloguing the heroic individuals and organizations in our history who have battled against those atrocities, and triumphed over them. It becomes practical when we are confronted with the problems of how to organize food cooperatives for women on food-stamp budgets or how to prove one's fitness as a mother in court. It becomes radical when, as teachers we develop a methodology that places daily life at the center of history and enables Black women to struggle for survival with the knowledge that they are making history.[58]

For Russell, school is one of the places where historical and present connections can be made, where collective memory can be evoked in order to educate students to locate their own histories within new forms of understanding and new social relationships. That is, school becomes a place where a sense of memory, self, and the future is integral to a sense of cultural and political formation. How do we do this? Where do we begin? Again, Russell is vividly illustrative and helpful.

> We start where they are. We exchange stories of children's clothes ripped or lost, of having to go to school with sons and explain why he is always late and how he got that funny name. . . . Some of the stories are funny, some sad; some elicit outrage and praise from the group. It's a familiar and comfortable ritual in Black culture. It's called testifying. The role of the teacher? Making the process conscious, the content significant. Want to know, yourself, how the problems in the stories got resolved. Learn what daily survival

wisdom these women have. Care. Don't let it stop at commiseration. Try to help them generalize from the specifics. Raise issues of who and what they continually have to bump up against on the life-road they've planned for themselves. Make lists on the board. Keep the scale human. Who are the people who get in the way? . . . Get as much consensus before moving on. . . . Define a task for the next meeting.[59]

There is more wisdom in these excerpts from Russell's own teaching experience than is contained in most books on curriculum in the United States. What becomes central here is that educators understand how students' experiences are both constructed and engaged, because it is through such experiences that students produce accounts of who they are and constitute themselves as particular individuals. It is therefore imperative that teachers and other educators learn how to understand, legitimate, and interrogate such experiences. Not only does this mean understanding the cultural and social forms through which students learn how to define themselves, it also means learning how to engage critically such experiences in a way that refuses to disconfirm them or render them illegitimate. Knowledge has to first of all be made meaningful to students before it can be made critical. It never speaks for itself, but rather is constantly mediated through the ideological and cultural experiences that students bring to the classroom. To ignore such experiences is to deny the grounds on which students learn, speak, and imagine. Judith Williamson puts this issue well:

> Walter Benjamin has said that the best ideas are no use if they do not make something useful of the person who holds them; on an even simpler level, I would add that the best ideas don't even exist if there isn't anyone to hold them. If we cannot get the "radical curriculum" across, or arouse the necessary interest in the "basic skills," there is no point to them. But in any case, which do we ultimately care more about: our ideas, or the child/student we are trying to teach them to?[60]

Students cannot learn "usefully" unless teachers develop an understanding of the various ways in which subjectivities are constituted through different social domains. At stake here is the need for teachers to understand how experiences produced in the various domains and layers of everyday life give rise to the different "voices" students use to give meaning to their own worlds and, consequently, to their own existence in the larger society. Unless educators address the question of how aspects of the social are experienced, mediated, and produced by students, it will be difficult for educators to tap into the drives, emotions, and interests that give subjectivity its own unique "voice" as well as provide the momentum for learning itself.

One important question that emerges from a pedagogy that acknowledges the relationship between power and the construction of experience is what kinds of classroom relations can teachers and others establish based on the integration of critical knowledge, commitment, and a radical ethical discourse. I will take up the implications of this issue in greater detail in the following chapters; here, I want to illustrate the necessity and importance of developing a discourse of ethics as a foundation for the kinds of decisions about classroom knowledge and pedagogy that teachers often face on a daily level.

In one of my recent graduate courses I asked a number of public school teachers what criteria they used to defend or reject the introduction of certain materials either into their curricula or as part of a classroom discussion. In general, most of the teachers in the class answered that if people in the community or on the school board wanted the material included in the curriculum it should be there. Others argued that the knowledge selected should be judged on the basis of whether it contributed either to the development of an "academic" discipline or to the students' intellectual growth. In both cases, there was no attempt to defend what was to be taught in wider political and ethical terms. These answers are disturbing not only because they suggest a lack of theoretical depth and civic rigor on the part of these teachers but also because they indicate how vulnerable teachers might be to educational ideologies and practices that reduce them to merely carrying out the "orders" of wider interest groups. A discourse of ethics can respond to this problem on two counts. First, the purpose of schooling can be defined through a democratic public philosophy based on an ethical discourse that is critically attentive to the issues of public responsibility, personal freedom, and democratic tolerance, as well as to the necessity of rejecting norms and practices that embody and extend the interests of domination, human suffering, and exploitation. On the basis of such a public philosophy, teachers can defend the curriculum choices they make through a discourse that aims at developing an educated, empowered, and critical citizenry. Second, such a public philosophy provides the guidelines for carefully mediating between the imperative to teach and defend a particular selection and view of knowledge and the necessity of avoiding a pedagogy that silences the voices of students. The way in which such an ethics can be brought to bear by teachers can be illustrated by analyzing some issues involved in teaching a hypothetical lesson on a controversial subject such as the Holocaust.

At one level, a radical discourse of ethics would suggest that a teacher take a firm stand on the morality and human barbarism at the heart of the ideology, practices, and consequences of the Holocaust. In other words, the issue of whether or not the Holocaust was justified would not be an issue of pedagogical consideration and debate. In this instance, the teacher would not assume a position that suggested to students that supporting the Holocaust represented simply another point of view. At the same time, different voices in the class could be engaged around questions on how the Holocaust developed, the nature of the ideology that informed it, why people supported and/or directly participated in it, what such an event tells us about the present, and how a similar logic might be manifested in different social and cultural forms of contemporary daily life, and so on. In this way, the tension between taking a committed position on the selection and use of particular forms of knowledge can be defended by teachers while still providing a critical pedagogy that engages dialogue and the possibility for different voices to be heard. In this case, the choices that teachers make about both the curriculum knowledge and the classroom topics they select and legitimize along with the classroom pedagogy they develop are mediated through a public philosophy and ethical discourse that defends social forms that enhance and extend human competencies and capabilities that allow for the development of social identities within just and compassionate democratic communities.

Emancipatory Authority, Teachers, and Social Movements

For teachers to function as transformative intellectuals who legitimate their role through an emancipatory form of authority, they will have to do more than gain further control of their working conditions and teach critical pedagogy. They will have to open up every aspect of formal education to active, popular contestation from social movements and from other frontline groups and constituencies. These include community members, parents, support staff, youth advocacy groups, and others with vital interests in the schools. There are a number of reasons for arguing this position. First, it is impossible to argue for schools as democratic, public spheres if such institutions narrowly define and exclude various community groups from talking about educational concerns. Second, any notion of educational reform, along with its reconstructed view of authority and pedagogy, needs to focus on the institutional arrangements that structure and mediate the role of schooling in the wider society. Reforms that limit their focus to specific school problems or the politics of instruction ignore the ways in which public education is shaped, bent, and moved by wider economic, political, and social concerns. Third, educators need to make alliances with other progressive social movements in an effort to create public spheres where the discourse of democracy can be debated and where the issues that arise in such a context can be collectively acted on in a political fashion if necessary.

Teachers must be willing and prepared to make their schools more responsive to the wider community. In doing so, they will have to redefine the role and nature of authority as it is currently constituted around the ideology of professionalism, an ideology that is largely shaped by unions who often define themselves in opposition to wider school constituencies and community demands. As it stands, teachers tend to legitimate their roles as professionals through highly exclusionary and undemocratic appeals to knowledge and expertise. Professionalism as it is presently defined has little to do with democracy as a social movement. By creating active, organic links with the community, teachers can open their schools to the diverse resources offered by the community. By doing so, they can give the schools access to those community traditions, histories, and cultures that are often submerged or discredited within the dominant school culture. It is an unfortunate truism that when communities are ignored by the schools, students find themselves situated in institutions that deny them a voice. As Ann Bastion and her colleagues argue:

School isolation works to deny students a link between what they learn in the classroom and the environment they function in outside the school. The lack of relevance and integration is particularly acute for minority and disadvantaged students, whose social and cultural background is not reflected, or is negatively reflected, in a standard curricula based on a white, middle-class mainstream and on elitist structures of achievement. Isolation also denies communities the integrative and empowering capacities of the school as a community institution. Isolation denies schools the energy, resources, and, ultimately, the sympathies of community members.[61]

Community involvement in the schools can help foster the necessary conditions for a constructive, ongoing debate over the goals, methods, and service that schools actually provide for students in specific localities. Moreover, it is essential that teachers take an active role in organizing with parents and others in their communities in order to remove political power from the hands of those political and economic groups and institutions who exercise an inordinate and sometimes damaging influence on school policy and curriculum.[62]

If educators are going to have any significant effect on the unequal economic, political, and social arrangements that plague schools and the wider society, they have no choice but to actively engage in the struggle for democracy with groups *outside* their classrooms. Martin Carnoy reinforces this point by arguing that democracy has not been created by intellectuals acting within the confines of their classrooms.

Democracy has been developed by social movements, and those intellectuals and educators who were able to implement democratic reforms in education did so in part through appeals to such movements. If the working people, minorities, and women who have formed the social movements pressing for greater democracy in our society cannot be mobilized behind equality in education, with the increased public spending that this requires, there is absolutely no possibility that equality in education will be implemented.[63]

As transformative intellectuals, educational workers must define themselves as both teachers and educators. The former define their pedagogical and political role within the schools, whereas the latter speak to a wider sphere of intervention in which the same concern with authority, knowledge, power, and democracy redefines and broadens the political nature of their pedagogical tasks, which is to teach, learn, listen, and mobilize in the interests of a more just and equitable social order. By linking schooling to wider social movements, teachers can begin to redefine the nature and importance of pedagogical struggle and thereby provide the basis to fight for forms of emancipatory authority as a foundation for the establishment of freedom and justice. The next task is to organize and struggle for the promise a discourse of emancipatory authority offers to the schools, the community, and the wider society as a whole.

4
Schooling and the Politics of Student Voice

Within the last decade public schooling in the United States has been criticized quite strongly by both radical and conservative critics. Central to both positions has been a concern with what has been called the reproductive theory of schooling. According to the reproductive thesis, schools are not to be valued in the traditional sense as public spheres engaged in teaching students the knowledge and skills of democracy. On the contrary, schools are to be viewed in more instrumental terms and should be measured against the need to reproduce the values, social practices, and skills needed for the dominant corporate order. Of course, conservative and radical critics have taken opposing positions on the significance of schooling as a reproductive public sphere. For many conservatives, schools have strayed too far from the logic of capital, and because of this, are now held responsible for the economic recession of the 1970s, for the loss of foreign markets to international competitors, and for the shortage of trained workers for an increasingly complex technological economy. In response to this type of criticism, conservatives have argued that schools need to reform their curricula in order to serve the corporate interests of the dominant society more faithfully.[1] Underlying this theoretical shorthand is the demand that schools place a greater emphasis on character formation, basic skills, and corporate needs. In related fashion, a wave of new "cultural" conservatives have emerged who vigorously defend the public schools as well as higher education as reproducers of dominant cultural traditions. Arguing for curricula organized around the old Great Books or in more reductionist fashion, around a notion of literacy based on the mas-

113

tering of a list of knowledge and bits of information that "every American should know," this group of conservatives promote a particular form of cultural hegemony as the universal basis for both learning and literacy in the schools. Radical educators, on the other hand, have used the reproductive thesis to criticize the role that schools play in American society. In general terms, they have argued that schools are reproductive in that they provide different classes and social groups with forms of knowledge, skills, and culture that not only legitimate the dominant culture but also track students into a labor force differentiated by gender, racial and class considerations.[2]

Despite their differences, radical and conservatives alike have ignored John Dewey's vision of public schools as democratic spheres, as places where the skills of democracy can be practiced, debated, and analyzed. Similarly, both share a disturbing indifference to the ways in which students, from different class, gender, and ethnic locations, mediate and express their sense of place, time, and history, and their contradictory, uncertain, and incomplete interactions with each other and with the dynamics of schooling. In other words, both radical and conservative ideologies generally fail to engage the politics of voice and representation—the forms of narrative and dialogue—around which students make sense of their lives and schools. Although this is an understandable position for conservatives and for those whose logic of instrumentalism and social control is at odds with an emancipatory notion of human agency, it represents a serious theoretical and political failing on the part of radical educators.

This failing is evident in a number of areas. First, radical educational theory has abandoned the language of possibility for the language of critique. That is, by viewing schools as primarily reproductive sites, radical educators have been unable to develop a theory of schooling that offers the possibility for counterhegemonic struggle and ideological battle. Within this discourse, schools, teachers, and students have been written off as merely extensions of the logic of capital. Instead of viewing schools as sites of contestation and conflict, radical educators often provide us with an oversimplified version of domination that seems to suggest that the only political alternative to the current role that schools play in the wider society is to abandon schools as sites of struggle altogether. Since they view schools as ideologically and politically overburdened by the dominant society, they find unproblematic the moral and political necessity for developing a programmatic discourse for working within them. Thus, the role that teachers, students, parents, and community people might play in waging a political battle in the public schools is rarely explored as a possibility. One consequence is that the primacy of the political in this project turns in on itself and the defeatist logic of capitalist domination is accepted as the basis or starting point for a "radical" theory of schooling.

Second, in their failure to develop a form of educational theory that posits real alternatives within schools, radical educators remain politically powerless to combat the degree to which conservative forces adroitly exploit and appropriate popular concerns over public education. In other words, not only does the educational Left misrepresent the nature of school life and the degree to which schools *do not* merely ape the logic of corporate interests, it also unwittingly reinforces the conservative thrust to fashion schools in its own ideological terms. In short, radical educators have failed to develop a language that engages schools as sites of possibility, that is, as places where particular forms of knowledge, social relations, and values can be taught in order to educate students to take their place in society from a position of empowerment rather than from a position of ideological and economic subordination.

The major problem investigated in this chapter is how to develop a critical pedagogy that acknowledges the spaces, tensions, and possibilities for struggle within the day-to-day workings of schools. Underlying this problematic is the theoretical and political necessity to generate a set of categories that not only provide new modes of critical interrogation, but also point to alternative strategies and modes of practice around which such a pedagogy can be realized.

The basis for such a task lies at the outset in redefining the concept of power regarding the issue of everyday experience and particularly with respect to the construction of classroom pedagogy and student voice. For educators, power has to be understood as a concrete set of practices that produce social forms through which different sets of experience and modes of subjectivities are constructed. Power in this sense includes but goes beyond the call for institutional change or the distribution of political and economic resources; it also signifies a level of conflict and struggle that plays itself out around the exchange of discourse and the lived experiences that such discourse produces, mediates, and legitimates.

Another major assumption here is that discourse is both medium and a product of power. In this sense, discourse is intimately connected with those ideological and material forces out of which individuals and groups fashion a voice. As Bakhtin puts it:

> Language is not a neutral medium that passes freely and easily into the private property of the speaker's intentions; it is populated— overpopulated—with the intentions of others. Expropriating it, forcing it to submit to one's own intentions and accents, is a difficult and complicated process.[3]

Language is inseparable from lived experience and from how people create a distinctive voice. It is also strongly connected to an intense struggle among different groups over what will count as meaningful and whose cultural capital will prevail in legitimating particular ways of life. Within schools, discourse produces and legitimates configurations of time, space, and narrative, placing particular renderings of ideology, behavior, and the representation of everyday life in a privileged perspective. As a "technology of power," discourse is given concrete expression in forms of knowledge that constitute the formal curriculum as well as in the structuring of classroom social relations that constitute the hidden curriculum of schooling. Needless to say, these pedagogical practices and forms are "read" in different ways by both teachers and students. Nonetheless, as I suggested in the first chapter, within these socially constructed pedagogical practices are forces that actively work to produce a limited range of subjectivities that consciously and unconsciously display a particular "sense" of the world.

The importance of the relationship between power and discourse for a critical pedagogy is that it provides a theoretical grounding for interrogating the issue of how ideology is inscribed in those forms of educational discourse through which school experiences and practices are ordered and constituted. Moreover, it points to the necessity for accounting theoretically for the ways in which language, ideology, history, and experience come together to produce, define, and constrain particular forms of teacher-student practice. This approach refuses to remain trapped in modes of analysis that examine student voice and pedagogical experience from the perspective of the reproductive thesis. That is, power and discourse are now investigated not merely as the single echo of the logic of capital, but as a polyphony of voices mediated within different layers of reality shaped through an interaction of dominant and subordinate forms of power. By recognizing and interrogating the different layers of meaning and struggle that make up the terrain of schooling, educators can fashion not only a language of critique but also a language of possibility. This chapter engages that task. First, I critically analyze the two major discourses of mainstream educational theory. At the risk of undue simplification, these are characterized as conservative and liberal pedagogical discourses. Then, I attempt to develop a discourse appropriate for a critical pedagogy, one that draws on the works of Paulo Freire and Mikhail Bakhtin.

Conservative Discourse and Educational Practice

Schooling and Positive Knowledge

Conservative educational discourse often presents a view of culture and knowledge in which both are treated as part of a storehouse of artifacts constituted as canon. While this discourse has a number of characteristic expressions, a recent theoretical defense can be found in Mortimer J. Adler's *The Paideia Proposal*, E. D. Hirsch's *Cultural Literacy*, and Allan Bloom's *The Closing of the American Mind*.[4] Adler calls for schools to implement a core course of subjects in all twelve years of public schooling. His appeal is to forms of pedagogy that enable students to master skills and specific forms of understanding with respect to predetermined forms of knowledge. In similar fashion, conservatives such as E. D. Hirsch, Jr. and Allan Bloom have argued that students lack an awareness of mainstream history and the Great Books. Hirsch believes that public schools have overemphasized process at the expense of content, and in a gross and ill-considered attack on the ideas of John Dewey claims that Dewey's influence has extended to more than 16,000 school districts and as such have been responsible for a national literacy crisis. Hirsch argues that schools should provide students with a public language, but the core of such a language has nothing to do with teaching students how to question and analyze the varied and competing traditions that constitute both their own historical experiences along with those of

117

others who make up the diverse history of the United States. In fact, Hirsch unabashedly argues that schools are cultural institutions, and as such teachers should reject both the notion of value-neutrality as well as any form of cultural pluralism. Hirsch's position becomes decidedly political in that he further argues that teachers openly espouse and reproduce the dominant culture. Actually, Hirsch adopts the language, without the intent, of many radical educators and argues that mainstream culture should no longer be taught and legitimated as part of the hidden curriculum. In a curious twist of logic, he claims that mainstream culture should be openly embraced as the universal basis for learning in public schools. For Hirsch, such a curriculum can be organized around a list of dates, information, books, and events that every American should know. Hirsch's notion of literacy lacks any substantive argumentation, reads more like a phone book list, and has little to do with appropriating knowledge as part of a larger discourse of understanding, criticism, and self-and social formation.

Subordinate traditions, readings, histories, memories, stories, knowledge forms are simply dismissed by Hirsch as constituting forms of cultural deprivation. For Hirsch, minority and working-class students have failed in schools not because they have been silenced and marginalized through the transmission of a curriculum that ignores their histories and experiences; on the contrary, Hirsch, like Adler and Bloom, believes that such students have failed precisely because they have not mastered the inherited stock of knowledge that constitutes the dominant tradition. Bloom extends this argument by reiterating the now familiar conservative charge that radicals of the 1960s along with the rise of feminism and mass culture in the United States have undermined the authority and learning associated with the great texts of the past and share a strong responsibility for the failure of a system of education to provide students with a content consistent with a common knowledge gleaned from the old Great Books.

For Bloom, any notion of culture that does not become synonymous with his version of Western Civilization is at the heart of the crisis of decay and decline in American schools. In effect, it is the democratization of culture that represents, for Bloom, a source of ignorance and paralysis. Bloom has ho sympathy for culture as a form of self-formation and social empowerment for minorities, women, and youth. This is especially clear in his tirade against popular culture, which he views as potentially disruptive of existing circuits of power. Bloom argues that popular culture, especially rock and roll, has resulted in the atrophy of both nerve and intelligence in American youth. Rock and roll, and more generally popular culture, represents in Bloom's mind a barbaric appeal to sexual desire. Not to be undone by this insight, Bloom argues that popular culture is simply synonymous for turning "life . . . into a nonstop, commercially prepackaged masturbational fantasy."[5] Of course, what Bloom is truly disturbed by is the lack of respect for tradition that he sees in evidence among youth, the challenge to authority that emerged out of the student movements of the 1960s, and what he perceives as the leveling ideology of democratic reform characteristic of the discourse of radical intellectuals. What one actually gets in Bloom's book are unsupported statements rooted in an authoritarian tradition that appear to emulate the very convulsions he suggests characterizes the popular forms he attacks. He writes:

> The inevitable corollary of such sexual interest is rebellion against
> the parental authority that represses it. Selfishness thus becomes
> indignation and then transforms itself into morality. The sexual
> revolution must overthrow all the forces of domination, the enemies
> of nature and happiness. From love comes hate, masquerading as
> social reform. A worldview is balanced on the sexual fulcrum. What
> were once unconscious or halfconscious childish resentments
> become the new Scripture. And then comes the longing for the
> classless, prejudice-free, conflictless, universal society that necessarily
> results from liberated consciousness—"We Are the World," a
> pubescent version of *Alle Menschen werden Brüder*, the fulfillment of
> which has been inhibited by the political equivalents of Mom and
> Dad. These are the three great lyrical themes: sex, hate, and a
> smarmy, hypocritical version of brotherly love. Such polluted sources
> issue in a muddy stream where only monsters can swim.[6]

The "monsters" responsible for this version of contemporary madness are the Left, feminists, Marxists, anyone who uses a Walkman, and all those others who refuse to take seriously the canonical status that Bloom wants to attribute to the old Great Books that embody his revered notion of Western civilization. Bloom's discourse is based on the myth of decline, and its attack on popular culture is inextricably linked to the call for the restoration of a so-called lost classical heritage. Rather than a sustained attack on popular culture, this is the totalizing discourse of totalitarianism parading behind the veil of cultural restoration. Its enemy is democracy, utopianism, and the unrealized political possibilities contained in the cultures of "the other," that is, those who are poor, black, women, and who share the experience of powerlessness. Its goal is a type of education that presupposes forms of moral and social regulation in which the voice of tradition provides the ideological legitimation for a ministry of culture that echoes an ideological dogmatism and contempt for "the other" that is reminiscent of Hitler's Germany and Mussolini's Italy.

The educational theories of Bloom, Hirsch, and Adler all advocate a pedagogy that is consistent with their view of culture as an artifact, a pedagogy that Paulo Freire once called banking education. That is, a pedagogy that is profoundly reactionary and which can be summed up in the terms "transmission" and "imposition." These authors refuse to analyze how pedagogy, a deliberate attempt to influence how and what knowledge and identities are produced within and among particular sets of social relations, might address the reconstruction of social imagination in the service of human freedom. In this discourse, issues regarding what knowledge is of most worth, to what ends should students desire, and what it means to recognize that knowledge is a social construction so that students can learn to play an active part in its production both in and out of the classroom are ignored in the interest of "reproducing" history rather than learning how to make it. The vision that informs these positions is based on a view of excellence and learning that privileges the white, male, middle class and ignores everyone else. There is no sense of real struggle or social tension in the discourse of Bloom, Hirsch, and Adler. Instead, there is a current of political urgency rooted in the rhetoric of nostalgia and decline; pedagogy in these approaches becomes a memory machine anchored in a celebration and fabrication of history that sidesteps the disquieting, disrupting, interrupting legacies of racism, sexism, exploitation, and class subordination that now bear down so heavily on the present. This is the discourse of pedagogues afraid of the future, strangled by the past, and unaware of or refusing the complexity, terror, and possibilities in the present. This is the pedagogy of hegemonic intellectuals cloaked in the mantle of academic enlightenment and literacy.

In this view, knowledge appears beyond the reach of critical interrogation except at the level of immediate application. In other words,
there is no substantive political and ethical attempt to lay bare how
such knowledge gets chosen, whose interests it represents, or why
students might be interested in acquiring it. In fact, students in this
perspective are characterized as a unitary body removed from the
ideological and material forces that construct their subjectivities,
interests, and concerns in diverse and multiple ways.

I would argue that the concept of difference in this approach
becomes the negative apparition of "the other." This is particularly
clear in Adler's case since he dismisses the diverse social and cultural
difference among students with the simplistic and reductionistic
comment that "despite their manifold individual differences the children are all the same in their human nature."[7] In this view a predetermined and hierarchically arranged body of knowledge is taken as
the cultural currency to be dispensed to all children regardless of
their diversity and interests. Equally important is the fact that the
acquisition of such knowledge becomes the structuring principle
around which the school curriculum is organized and particular
classroom social relations are legitimated. It is worth noting that it is
an appeal to school knowledge exclusively that constitutes the measure and worth of what defines the learning experience. That is, the
value of both teacher and student experience is premised on the
transmission and inculcation of what can be termed "positive knowledge." Consequently, it is in the distribution, management, measure-
ment, and legitimation of such knowledge that this type of pedagogy
invests its energies. In his ethnographic study of three urban secondary schools, Philip Cusick comments on the problematic nature of
legitimating and organizing school practices around the notion of
"positive knowledge."

> By positive knowledge I mean that which is generally accepted as
> having an empirical or traditional base. . . . The assumption that the
> acquisition of positive knowledge can be made interesting and
> appealing in part underlies the laws that compel everyone to attend
> school, at least until their mid teens. . . . The conventional assumption
> would have it that the curriculum of a school exists as a body of
> knowledge, agreed upon by staff and approved by the general
> community and by district authorities who have some expertise, and

that it reflects the best thinking about what young people need to succeed in our society. But I did not find that.[8]

What Cusick did find was that school knowledge organized in these terms was not compelling enough to interest many of the students he observed. Moreover, educators locked into this perspective responded to student disinterest, violence, and resistance by shifting their concerns from actually teaching positive knowledge to maintaining order and control, or as they put it, "keeping the lid on."

> Not only did the administrators spend their time on those matters [administration and control], they also tended to evaluate other elements, such as the performance of teachers, according to their ability to maintain order. They tended to arrange other elements of the school according to how they contributed or failed to contribute to the maintenance of order. The outstanding example of that was the implementation in both urban schools of the five-by-five day, wherein the students were brought in early in the morning, given five periods of instruction with a few minutes in between and a fifteen-minute mid-morning break, and released before one o'clock. There were no free periods, study halls, cafeteria sessions, or assemblies. No occasions were allowed in which violence could occur. The importance of maintaining order in those public secondary schools could not be underestimated.[9]

Student voice and experience is reduced to the immediacy of its performance and exists as something to be measured, administered, registered, and controlled. Its distinctiveness, its disjunctions, its lived quality are all dissolved under an ideology of control and management. In the name of efficiency, the resources and wealth of student life histories are generally ignored. A major problem with this perspective is that the celebration of positive knowledge does not guarantee that students will have any interest in the pedagogical practices it produces, especially since such knowledge appears to have little connection to the experiences of the students themselves. Teachers who structure classroom experiences out of this discourse generally face enormous problems in the public schools, especially those in the urban centers. Boredom and/or disruption appear to be primary products. To some extent, of course, teachers who rely on classroom practices that exhibit a disrespect for both students and critical learning are themselves often victims of specific labor conditions that virtually make it impossible for them to teach as critical educators. At the same time, these conditions are determined by dominant interests and discourses that provide the ideological legitimation for promoting hegemonic classroom practices. In short, not only do such practices involve symbolic violence against students by devaluing the cultural capital that they possess, they also tend to position teachers within pedagogical models that legitimate their role as white-collar clerks. Unfortunately, the notion of teachers as clerks is part of a long tradition of management models of pedagogy and administration that has dominated American public education.

Conservative educational discourse is not all of one piece; there is another position within this perspective that does not ignore the relationship between knowledge and student experience. It is to this position that I now turn.

Schooling and the Ideology of Positive Thinking

In another important variation of conservative educational theory, the analysis and meaning of experience shift from a preoccupation with transmitting positive knowledge to developing forms of pedagogy that recognize and appropriate the cultural traditions and experiences that different students bring to the school setting. The theoretical cornerstone of this position is developed around a modified view of the concept of culture. That is, the static notion of culture as a storehouse of traditional knowledge and skills is replaced here by a more anthropological approach.

In its revised form, culture is viewed as a form of production, specifically, as the ways in which human beings make sense of their lives, feelings, beliefs, thoughts, and the wider society. Within this approach, the notion of difference is stripped of its "otherness" and accommodated to the logic of a "polite civic humanism."[10] Difference no longer symbolizes the threat of disruption. On the contrary, it now signals an invitation for diverse cultural groups to join hands under the democratic banner of an integrative pluralism. The specific ideology that defines the relation between difference and pluralism is central to this version of conservative educational thought in that it serves to legitimate the idea that in spite of differences manifested around race, ethnicity, language, values, and life-styles, there is an underlying equality among different cultural groups that allegedly disavows that any one of them is privileged. At work here is an attempt to subsume the notion of difference within a discourse and set of practices that promote harmony, equality, and respect within and between diverse cultural groups. Beneath this model of egalitarianism is a pedagogy whose aim is to ultimately weave these different cultural groups into an ideological tapestry that in fact supports a dominant Western tradition and way of life characterized by its alleged *respect* for the expression of different cultural traditions while ignoring the asymmetrical relations of power within which these different traditions operate.

This is not meant to suggest that conflict is ignored in this approach; I am not suggesting that the social and political antagonisms that characterize the relationship between different cultural groups and the larger society are altogether denied. On the contrary, such problems generally are recognized but as issues to be discussed and overcome in the interest of creating a "happy and cooperative class," which will, it is hoped, play a fundamental role in bringing about a "happy and cooperative world."[11] Within this context, cultural representations of difference as *conflict and tension* become pedagogically workable only within a language of unity and cooperation that legitimates and supports a false and particularly "cheery" view of Western Civilization. Consequently, the concept of difference turns into its opposite, for difference now becomes meaningful as something to be resolved within *relevant* forms of exchange and class discussions. Lost here is a respect for the autonomy of different cultural logics and any understanding of how such logics operate within asymmetrical relations of power and domination. In other words, the equality associated with different forms of culture as lived and embodied experiences serves to displace political considerations of the ways in which dominant and subordinate groups interact and struggle both in and outside schools.

The pedagogical practices deriving from this notion of difference and cultural diversity are suffused with the language of positive thinking. This becomes clear in curriculum projects developed around these practices. These projects generally structure curriculum problems so as to include references to the conflicts and tensions that exist among diverse groups, but rather than encouraging students to critically understand the ways in which various groups struggle within relations of power and domination as these are played out in the larger social arena, they subordinate these issues to pedagogical goals that promote a mutual respect and understanding among various cultural groups in the interest of fostering national unity. The apologetic nature of this discourse is evident in the kinds of educational objectives that structure its classroom practices. The complexity and sweat of social change are quietly ignored.

In more sophisticated versions, conservative educational theory recognizes the existence of racial, gender, ethnic, and other types of conflict among different groups but is more ideologically honest about why they should *not* be emphasized in the school curriculum. Appealing to the interests of a "common culture," this position calls for a pedagogical emphasis on the common interests and ideals that characterize the nation. As one of its spokespersons, Nathan Glazer, puts it, the choice of what is taught "must be guided . . . by our conception of a desirable society, of the relationship between what we select to teach and the ability of people to achieve such a society and live together in it."[12] What is troubling in this position is that it lacks any sense of culture as a terrain of struggle; moreover, it does not pay any attention to the relationship between knowledge and power. In fact, underlying Glazer's statement is a facile egalitarianism that assumes but does not demonstrate that all groups can actively participate in the development of such a society. While appealing to a fictive harmony, his unitary "our" suggests an unwillingness to either indict or interrogate existing structures of domination. This harmony is nothing more than an image in the discourse of those who do not have to suffer the injustices experienced by subordinated groups. In short, this version of conservative educational theory falls prey to a perspective that idealizes the future while stripping the present of its deeply rooted contradictions and tensions. This is not merely the discourse of harmony; it is also a set of interests that refuses to posit the relations between culture and power as a moral question demanding emancipatory political action.

Liberal Discourse and Educational Practice

Liberal discourse in educational theory and practice has a long association with various tenets of what has been loosely called progressive education in the United States. From John Dewey to the Free School Movement to the 1960s and 1970s to the present emphasis on multiculturalism, there has been a concern with taking the needs and cultural experiences of students as a starting point from which to develop relevant forms of pedagogy.[13] Since it is impossible to analyze in this chapter all the theoretical twists and turns this movement has taken, I focus exclusively on some of its dominant ideological tendencies along with the way in which its discourses structure the experiences of both students and teachers.

Liberal Theory as the Ideology of Deprivation

In its most commonsense form, liberal educational theory favors a notion of experience that is equated either with "fulfilling the needs of kids" or with developing cordial relations with students so as to be able to maintain order and control in the school. In many respects these two discourses represent different sides of the same educational ideology. In the ideology of "need fulfillment," the category of "need" represents an *absence* of a particular set of experiences. In most cases, what educators determine as missing are either the culturally specific experiences that school authorities believe students must acquire so as to enrich the quality of their lives or, in more instrumental terms, the fundamental skills they "need" in order to get jobs once they leave the public schools. Underlying this view of experience is the logic of cultural deprivation theory, which defines education in terms of cultural enrichment, remediation, and basics.

In this instrumentalist version of liberal pedagogy there is little recognition that what is legitimated as privileged school experience often represents the endorsement of a particular way of life, signified as superior by the "revenge" that befalls those who do not share its attributes. Specifically, the experience of the student as "other" is cast as deviant, underprivileged, or "uncultured." Consequently, not only do students bear the sole responsibility for school failure, but also there is little or no theoretical room for interrogating the ways in which administrators and teachers actually create and sustain the problems they attribute to students. This view of students, particularly of those from subordinate groups, is mirrored by a refusal to examine the assumptions and pedagogical practices that legitimate forms of experience embodying the logic of domination. One glaring example of this was brought home to me by a secondary school teacher in one of my graduate courses who constantly referred to her working-class students as "low life." In her case, there was no sense of how language was actively constructing her relations with these students, though I am sure the message was not lost on them. One practice that sometimes emerges from this aspect of liberal educational ideology places teachers in the position of simultaneously blaming students for their perceived problems and humiliating them in an effort to get them to participate in classroom activities. The following incident captures this approach:

> The teacher after taking attendance for fifteen minutes, wrote a few phrases on the board: "Adam and Eve," "spontaneous generation," and "evolution," and told the students that: "For the next forty minutes you are to write an essay on how you think the world started, and here are three possibilities which you know, we discussed last week. I did this with my college prep class and they like it ... It will do you good. Teach you to think for a change, which is something you don't do often."[14]

Liberal Theory as the Pedagogy of Cordial Relations

When students refuse to surrender to this type of humiliation, teachers and school administrators generally face problems of order and control. One response is to promote a pedagogy of cordial relations. The classic instance of dealing with students in this approach is to try to keep them "happy" either by indulging their personal interests through appropriately developed modes of "low status" knowledge or by developing good rapport with them. Defined as the "other," students now become objects of inquiry in the interest of being understood so as to be more easily controlled. The knowledge, for example, used by teachers with these students is often drawn from cultural forms identified with class, race, and gender specific interests. But relevance, in this instance, has little to do with emancipatory concerns; instead, it translates into pedagogical practices that attempt to appropriate forms of student and popular culture in the interests of maintaining social control. Furthermore, it provides a legitimating ideology for forms of class, race, and gender tracking. The practice of tracking at issue here is developed in its most subtle form through an endless series of school electives that appear to legitimate the cultures of subordinated groups while actually incorporating them in a trivial pedagogical fashion. Thus, working-class females are "advised" by guidance teachers to take "Girl

Talk," a course dealing with television soap operas, whereas middle-class students have no doubts about the importance of taking classes in literary criticism. In the name of relevance and order, working-class males are encouraged to select "industrial arts" whereas their middle-class counterparts take courses in chemistry. Students are not merely tracked into different courses; they are actually placed in classes that differentially offer on the basis of racial, class, ethnic, and gender considerations the possibilities for self-and social empowerment. Jeanne Oaks in her extensive study of high-and low-level English classes illuminates how students in these different classes are socialized into different and unequal forms of pedagogy. She writes:

> In both English and math classes, we found that students had access to considerably different types of knowledge and had opportunities to develop quite different intellectual skills. For example, students in high-track English classes were exposed to content that can be called "high status knowledge." This included topics and skills that are required for college. High-track students studied both classic and modern fiction. They learned the characteristics of literary genres and analyzed the elements of good narrative writing. These students were to write thematic essays and reports of library research, and they learned vocabulary that would boost their scores on college entrance exams. It was the high-track students in our sample who had the most opportunities to think critically or to solve interesting problems. Low-track English classes, on the other hand, rarely, if ever, encountered similar types of knowledge. Nor were they expected to learn the same skills. Instruction in basic reading skills held a prominent place in low-track classes, and these skills were taught most through workbooks, kits, and "young adult" fiction. Students wrote simple paragraphs, completed worksheets on English usage, and practiced filling out applications for jobs and other kinds of forms. Their learning tasks were largely restricted to memorization or low-level comprehension.[15]

The practices and social forms along with the divergent interests and pedagogies that are produced through tracking have been analyzed extensively elsewhere and need not be repeated here.

Liberal Theory and the Pedagogy of Child Centeredness

In its more theoretically argued forms, liberal educational discourse provides a more "supportive" view of student experience and culture. Within this perspective, student experience is defined by the individualizing psychology of "child centeredness." Understood as part of a "natural" unfolding process, student experience is not tied to the imperatives of rigid disciplinary authority but to the exercise of self-control and self-regulation.[16] The focus of analysis in this discourse is the child as a unitary subject, and pedagogical practices are structured around encouraging "healthy" expression and harmonious social relations. Central to this problematic is an ideology that equates freedom with "the bestowal of love" and what Carl Rogers calls "unconditional positive regard" and "emphatic understanding."[17] The liberal pedagogical canon demands that teachers emphasize self-directed learning, link knowledge to the personal experiences of students, and attempt to help students interact with one another in a positive and harmonious fashion.

How student experiences are developed within this perspective is, of course, directly related to the larger question of how they are constructed and understood within the multiple discourses that embody and reproduce the social and cultural relations that characterize the larger society. This issue is ignored not only in liberal views of educational theory, but in conservative discourses as well. The silence regarding forms of race, class, and gender discrimination and how these are reproduced in relations between the schools and the larger social order is what links conservative and liberal theories of education, constituting what I call the dominant educational discourse. Although I have already criticized some of the assumptions that inform the dominant educational discourses, I want to elaborate on these before I turn to the issue of how a critical pedagogy can be fashioned out of a theory of cultural politics.

Dominant Educational Discourses

Dominant educational discourse falls prey to a deeply ingrained ideological tendency in American education as well as in the mainstream social sciences to separate culture from relations of power. By analyzing culture uncritically either as an object of veneration or as a set of practices that embody the traditions and values of diverse groups, this view depoliticizes culture as a social construct and practice. More specifically, there is no attempt in this view to understand culture as shared and lived principles of life characteristic of different groups and classes as these emerge within inequitable relations of power and fields of struggle. Actually, culture remains unexplored as a particular relation between dominant and subordinate groups expressed in the form of lived antagonistic relations that embody and produce particular forms of meaning and action. In effect, these discourses exclude the concept of "dominant" and "subordinate" culture altogether and by doing so fail to recognize the importance of wider political and social forces on all aspects of school organization and everyday classroom life.

By refusing to acknowledge the relations between culture and power, the dominant educational discourses fail to understand how schools themselves are implicated in reproducing oppressive ideologies and social practices. Rather, they assume that schools can analyze problems faced by different cultural groups and out of such analyses students will develop a sense of understanding and mutual respect that will in some way influence the wider society. But schools do more than influence society; they are also shaped by it. That is, schools are inextricably linked to a larger set of political and cultural processes and not only reflect the antagonisms embodied in such processes but also embody and reproduce them. This issue becomes clearer in statistical studies that reveal that "one out of every four students who enrolls in ninth grade (in the U.S.) drops out before high school graduation. Drop out rates for Black students are just under twice as great for White students; those for Hispanic students are just over twice as great. . . . In 1971, 51 percent of all White and 50 percent of all Black high school graduates went to college. In 1981, the rate of young Black high school graduates enrolled in college had fallen to 40 percent, in October of 1982, it fell to 36 percent."[18]

The importance of these statistics is that they point to ideological and material practices that are actively produced within the day-to-day activities of schooling, though their origins are in the wider society. They also point to the silence on a number of questions pertaining to how schools actually work to produce class, race, and gender differentiations and the fundamental antagonisms that structure them. One issue the statistics point to is how wider forms of political, economic, social, and ideological domination and subordination might be invested in the language, texts, and social practices of the schools as well as in the experiences of the teachers and students themselves. An equally important concern centers on the issue of how power in schools is expressed as a set of relations that treats some groups as privileged while disconfirming others. Some important questions that could be pursued here include: What is the ideology at work when children are tested in a language they do not understand? What interests are being sustained by tracking black children who have no serious intellectual learning disabilities into classes for the educable mentally handicapped? What are the ideologies underlying school practices reflected in urban schools in which the drop-out rates are 85 percent for Native Americans and between 70-80 percent for Puerto Rican students?[19] The important point illuminated by these figures is that dominant educational discourses lack not only an adequate theory of domination, but also a critical understanding of how experience is *named, constructed, and legitimated* in schools.

Another major criticism of dominant educational discourses focuses on the political nature of school language. Defined primarily in technical terms (mastery) or in terms that argue primarily for its communicative value in developing dialogue and transmitting information, language in this perspective is abstracted from its political and ideological usage. For instance, language is privileged as a medium for exchanging and presenting knowledge and, as such, is removed from its constitutive role in the struggle of various groups over different meanings, practices, and readings of the world. Within dominant educational theory there is no sense of how language practices can be used to actively silence some students, or of how favoring particular forms of discourse can work to disconfirm the traditions, practices, and values of subordinate language groups; similarly, there is a failure to have teachers acquire forms of language literacy that would translate, pedagogically, into a critical understanding of the structure of language and a capacity to help students develop a form of literacy in which they can both validate and critically engage their own experiences and cultural milieus. This is an issue I discuss in the next chapter.

It is not surprising that within dominant educational discourses questions of cultural difference are sometimes reduced to a single emphasis on the learning and understanding of school knowledge, in particular, as presented through the form and content of curriculum texts. Lost here are the ways in which power is invested in institutional and ideological forces that bear down on and shape social practices of schooling in a manner not evident, for instance, through a singular analysis of curriculum texts in their isolated moment of classroom usage. There is no clear understanding, for example, of how social relations operate in schools through the organization of time, space, and resources, or of the way in which different groups experience these relations through their economic, political, and social locations outside schools. Not only does dominant educational theory fail to understand schooling as a cultural process that is inextricably linked to the inescapable presence of wider social forces; it also appears incapable of recognizing how forms of teacher and student resistance might emerge in schools as part of a refusal to either teach or accept the dictates of dominant school culture.[20]

In more specific terms, dominant educational discourses fail to analyze how the school as an agent of social and cultural control is mediated and contested by those whose interests it does not serve. In part, this is due to a functionalist view of schooling which sees schools serving the needs of the dominant society without questioning either the nature of that society or the effects it has on the daily practices of schooling itself. The theoretical price paid for this type of functionalism is high. One consequence is that schools are seen as if removed from the tensions and antagonisms that characterize the wider society. As a result, it becomes impossible to understand schools as sites of struggle over power and meaning. Furthermore, there is no theoretical room in this approach to understand why subordinate groups may actively resist and deny the dominant culture as it is embodied in various aspects of daily classroom life.

Critical Pedagogy as a Form of Cultural Politics

In this section I want to develop a perspective that links critical pedagogy with a form of cultural politics. In doing so, I draw principally from the works of Paulo Freire and Mikhail Bakhtin and attempt to construct a theoretical model in which the notions of struggle, student voice, and critical dialogue are central to the goal of developing a critical pedagogy.[21] Bakhtin's work is important because he views language usage as an eminently social and political act linked to the ways individuals define meaning and author their relations to the world through an ongoing dialogue with others. As a theoretician of difference, dialogue, and polyphonic voice, Bakhtin rightly empha-

132

sizes the need to understand the ongoing struggle between various groups over language and meaning as a moral and epistemological imperative. Accordingly, Bakhtin deepens our understanding of the nature of authorship by providing analyses of how people give value to and operate out of different layers of discourse. He also points to the pedagogical significance of critical dialogue as a form of authorship since it provides the medium and gives meaning to the multiple voices that construct the "texts" constitutive of everyday life.

Paulo Freire both extends and deepens Bakhtin's project. Like Bakhtin, Freire offers the possibility for organizing pedagogical experiences within social forms and practices that "speak" to developing more critical and dialogical modes of collective learning and struggle. But Freire's theory of experience is rooted in a view of language and culture that links dialogue and meaning to a social project emphasizing the primacy of the political. In this case, "empowerment" is defined as central to the collective struggle for a life without oppression and exploitation.

Both authors employ a view of language, dialogue, and difference that rejects a totalizing vision of history. Both argue that a critical pedagogy has to begin with a dialectical celebration of the languages of critique and possibility—an approach which finds its noblest expression in a discourse that integrates critical analysis with social transformation. Similarly, both authors provide a pedagogical model that begins with problems rooted in the concrete experiences of everyday life. In effect, they provide valuable theoretical models from which educators can selectively draw in order to develop an analysis of schools as sites of conflict actively involved in the production of lived experiences. Inherent in these approaches is a problematic characterized by the way in which various pedagogical practices represent a particular politics of experience. Or, more specifically, it characterizes a cultural field where knowledge, language, and power intersect in order to produce historically specific practices of moral and social regulation.

This work of Freire and Bakhtin points to the need to inquire how human experiences are produced, contested, and legitimated within the dynamics of everyday classroom life. The theoretical importance of this type of interrogation is linked directly to the need for educators to fashion a discourse in which a more comprehensive politics of culture, voice, and experience can be developed. At issue here is the recognition that schools are historical and structural embodiments of ideological forms of culture. They signify reality in ways that are often experienced differently and actively contested by various individuals and groups. Schools in this sense are ideological and political terrains out of which the dominant culture in part produces its hegemonic "certainties"; but they are also places where dominant and subordinate voices define and constrain each other, in battle and exchange, in response to the sociohistorical conditions "carried" in the institutional, textual, and lived practices that define school culture and teacher/student experience. In other words, schools are not ideologically innocent; nor are they simply reproductive of dominant social relations and interests. At the same time, schools produce forms of political and moral regulation intimately connected with the technologies of power that "produce asymmetries in the abilities of individuals and groups to define and realize their needs."[22] More specifically, schools establish the conditions under which some individuals and groups define the terms by which others live, resist, affirm, and participate in the construction of their own identities and subjectivities. Roger Simon illuminates some of the important theoretical considerations that have to be addressed within a critical pedagogy:

> Our concern as educators is to develop a way of thinking about the construction and definition of subjectivity within the concrete social forms of our everyday existence in a way that grasps schooling as a cultural and political site that [embodies] a project of regulation and transformation. As educators we are required to take a position on the acceptability of such forms. We also recognize that while schooling is productive it is not so in isolation, but in complex relations with other forms organized in other sites. . . . [Moreover,] in working to reconstruct aspects of schooling [educators should attempt] to understand how it becomes implicated in the production of subjectivities [and] recognize [how] existing social forms legitimate and produce real inequities which serve the interest of some over others and that a transformative pedagogy is oppositional in intent and is threatening to some in its practice.[23]

Simon rightly argues that schools as sites of cultural production embody representations and practices that construct as well as block the possibilities for human agency among students. This becomes clearer if we recognize that one of the most important elements at work in the construction of experience and subjectivity in schools is language: language intersects with power in the way particular linguistic forms structure and legitimate the ideologies of specific groups. Language is intimately related to power, and it constitutes the way in which teachers and students define, mediate, and understand their relation to each other and the larger society.

As Bakhtin has pointed out, language is intimately related to the dynamics of authorship and voice.[24] It is within and through language that individuals in particular historical contexts shape values into particular forms and practices. As part of the production of meaning, language represents a central force in the struggle for voice. Schools are one of the primary public spheres where, through the influence of authority, resistance, and dialogue, language is able to shape the way various individuals and groups encode and thereby engage the world. In other words, schools are places where language projects, imposes, and constructs particular norms and forms of meaning. In this sense, language does more that merely straightforwardly present "information"; in actuality it is used as a basis both to "instruct" and to produce subjectivities. For Bakhtin, the issue of language is explored within the context of a politics of struggle and representation, a politics forged in relations of power pertaining to who decides and legislates the territory on which discourse is to be defined and negotiated. The driving momentum of voice and authorship is inseparable from the relations between individuals and groups around which dialogue begins and ends. In Bakhtin's terms, "the word is a two-sided act. It is determined ... by those whose word it is and for whom it is meant. ... A word is territory shared by both addresser and addressee, by the speaker and his interlocutor."[25] At issue here is the critical insight that student subjectivities are developed across a range of discourses and can only be understood within a process of social interaction that "pumps energy from a life situation into the verbal discourse, it [life] endows everything linguistically stable with living historical momentum and uniqueness."[26]

With the above theoretical assumptions in mind, I will now argue in more specific terms for the development of a critical pedagogy as a form of cultural politics. In effect, I want to present the case for constructing a pedagogy of cultural politics around a critically affirmative language that allows educators to understand how subjectivities are produced within those social forms in which people move but which are often only partly understood. Such a pedagogy makes problematic how teachers and students sustain, resist, or accommodate those languages, ideologies, social processes, and myths that position them within existing relations of power and dependency. Moreover, this pedagogy points to the need to develop a theory of politics and culture that analyzes discourse and voice as a continually shifting balance of resources and practices in the struggle over specific ways of naming, organizing, and experiencing social reality. Discourse can be recognized as a form of cultural production, linking agency and structure through public and private representations that are concretely organized and structured within schools. Furthermore, I understand discourse as an embodied and fractured set of experiences that are lived and suffered by individuals and groups within specific contexts and settings. Within this perspective, the concept of experience is linked to the broader issue of how subjectivities are inscribed within cultural processes that develop with regard to the dynamics of production, transformation, and struggle. Understood in these terms, a pedagogy of cultural politics presents a twofold set of tasks for educators. First, they need to analyze how cultural production is organized within asymmetrical relations of power in schools. Second, they must construct political strategies for participating in social struggles designed to fight for schools as democratic public spheres.

In order to realize these tasks, it is necessary to assess the political limits and pedagogical potentialities of the different but related instances of cultural production that constitute the various processes of schooling. It is important to note that I call these social processes "instances of cultural production," rather than using the dominant Left concept of reproduction. While the notion of reproduction rightly points to the various economic and political ideologies and interests that are reconstituted within the relations of schooling, it lacks a comprehensive, theoretical understanding of how such interests are mediated, worked on, and subjectively produced.

A critical pedagogy that assumes the form of a cultural politics must examine how cultural processes are produced and transformed within three particular, though related, fields of discourse: *the discourse of production*, *the discourse of text analysis*, and *the discourse of lived cultures*. Each of these discourses has a history of theoretical development in various models of leftist analysis, and each has been subjected to intense discussion and criticism. These need not be repeated here.[27] I want to look at the potentialities exhibited by these discourses in their interconnections, particularly as they point to a new set of categories for developing forms of educational practices that empower teachers and students around emancipatory interests.

Educational Practice and the Discourse of Production

The discourse of production in educational theory has focused on the ways in which the structural forces outside the immediacy of school life construct the objective conditions within which schools function. This strategic framework can provide us with illuminating analyses of the state, the workplace, foundations, publishing companies, and other embodiments of political interests that directly or indirectly influence school policy. Moreover, schools are understood within a larger network of connections that allows us to analyze them as historical and social constructions, as embodiments of social forms that always bear a relationship to the wider society. A fundamental task of the discourse of production is to alert teachers to the primacy of identifying practices and interests that legitimate specific public representations and ways of life. To attempt to understand the process of schooling without taking into consideration how these wider forms of production are constructed, manifested, and contested both in and out of schools is inconceivable within this discourse. This becomes obvious, for instance, if we wish to analyze the ways in which state policy embodies and promotes particular practices that legitimate and render privileged some forms of knowledge over others, or some groups over others.[28] Equally significant would be an analysis of how dominant educational theory and practice are constructed, sustained, and circulated outside schools. For instance, educators need to do more than identify the language and values of corporate ideologies as they are manifested in school curricula; they also need to analyze and transform the processes through which they are produced and circulated. Another important aspect of this approach is that it points to the way in which labor is objectively constructed; that is, it provides the basis for an analysis of the conditions under which educators work and the political importance of these conditions in either limiting or enabling pedagogical practice. This is especially important for analyzing the critical possibilities that exist for public school teachers and students to act and be treated as intellectuals. Or, to put it in the words of C. W. Mills, as people who can get "in touch with the realities of themselves and their world."[29]

I would like to stress, once again, that if teachers and students work in overcrowded conditions, lack time to work collectively in a creative fashion, or are shackled by rules that disempower them, these technical and social conditions of labor have to be understood and addressed as part of the dynamics of reform and struggle.[30] The discourse of production represents an important starting point for a pedagogy of cultural politics because it evaluates the relationship between schools and wider structural forces in light of a politics of human dignity—more specifically, a politics fashioned around the ways in which human dignity can be realized in public spheres designed to provide the material conditions necessary for work, dialogue, and self-and social realization. Accordingly, these public spheres represent what Dewey, Mills, and others have called the conditions for freedom and praxis, political embodiments of a social project that takes liberation as its major goal.[31]

Critical Pedagogy and the Discourse of Textual Analysis

Another important element in the development of a critical pedagogy, which I describe as a discourse of textual analysis, refers to a form of critique capable of analyzing cultural forms as they are produced and used in specific classrooms. The purpose of this approach is to provide teachers and students with the critical tools necessary to analyze those socially constructed representations and interests that organize and emphasize particular readings of curriculum materials.

Not only does discourse of textual analysis draw attention to the ideologies out of which texts are produced, but it also allows educators to distance themselves from the text in order to uncover the layers of meanings, contradictions, and differences inscribed in the form and content of classroom materials. The political and pedagogical importance of this form of analysis is that it opens the text to deconstruction, interrogating it as part of a wider process of cultural production; in addition, by making the text an object of intellectual inquiry, such an analysis posits the reader, not as a passive consumer, but as an active producer of meanings. In this view, the text is no longer endowed with an authorial essence waiting to be translated or discovered. On the contrary, the text becomes an ensemble of discourses constituted by a play of contradictory meanings, some of which are visibly privileged and some of which, in Macherey's terms, represent "a new discourse, the articulation of a silence."[32] Critical to this perspective are the notions of critique, production, and difference, all of which provide important elements for a counterhegemonic pedagogical practice. Catherine Belsey weaves these elements together quite well in her critique of the classical realist text:

> As an alternative it was possible to recognize it [classical realist text]
> as a construct and so to treat it as available for deconstruction, that is,
> the analysis of the process and conditions of its construction out of
> the available discourses. Ideology, masquerading as coherence and
> plenitude, is in reality inconsistent, limited, contradictory, and the
> realist text as a crystallization of ideology, participates in this
> incompleteness even while it diverts attention from the fact in the
> apparent plenitude of narrative closure. The object of deconstructing
> the text is to examine the process of its production — not the private
> experience of the individual author, but the mode of production, the
> materials and their arrangement in the work. The aim is to locate the
> point of contradiction within the text, the point at which it
> transgresses the limits within which it is constructed, breaks free of
> the constraints imposed by its own realist form. Composed of
> contradictions, the text is no longer restricted to a single,
> harmonious and authoritative reading. Instead, it becomes plural,
> open to re-reading, no longer an object for passive consumption but
> an object of work by the reader to produce meaning.[33]

This mode of analysis is particularly important for educators because it argues against the idea that the means of representation in texts are merely neutral conveyors of ideas. Furthermore, such an approach points to the need for careful systematic analyses of the way in which material is used and ordered in school curricula and how its "signifiers" register particular ideological pressures and tendencies. Such an analysis allows teachers and students to deconstruct meanings that are silently built into the structuring principles of classroom meanings, thereby adding an important theoretical dimension to analyzing how the overt and hidden curricula work in schools.

At the day-to-day level of schooling, this type of textual criticism can be used to analyze how the technical conventions or images within various forms such as narrative, mode of address, and ideological reference attempt to construct a limited range of positions from which they are to be read. Richard Johnson is worth quoting on this point:

> The legitimate object of an identification of "positions" is the pressures or tendencies on the reader, the theoretical problematic which produces subjective forms, the directions in which they move in their force—once inhabited. ... If we add to this, the argument that certain kinds of text ("realism") naturalise the means by which positioning is achieved, we have a dual insight of great force. The particular promise is to render processes hitherto unconsciously suffered (and enjoyed) open to explicit analysis.[34]

Coupled with traditional forms of ideology critique directed at problematizing the subject content of school materials, text analyses also provide valuable insight into how subjectivities and cultural forms work within schools. The value of this kind of work has been exhibited in analyses arguing that the principles used in the construction of prepackaged curriculum materials utilize a mode of address that "positions" teachers merely as implementors of knowledge.[35] This is clearly at odds with treating teachers and students as critical agents who play an active role in the pedagogical process. In one illuminating display of this approach, Judith Williamson has provided an extensive study of the way in which this type of critique can be applied to mass advertising.[36] Similarly, Ariel Dorfman has applied this mode of analysis to various texts used in popular culture, including the portrayal of characters such as Donald Duck and Babar the Elephant. In his analysis of *Readers Digest* Dorfman exhibits a dazzling display of the critical value of text analysis. In one example, for instance, he analyzes how *Readers Digest* uses a mode of representation that downplays the importance of viewing knowledge in its historical and dialectical connections. He writes:

> Just as with superheroes, knowledge does not transform the reader; on the contrary, the more he [sic] reads the *Digest*, the less he needs to change. Here is where all that fragmentation returns to play the role it was always meant to play. Prior knowledge is never assumed. From month to month, the reader must purify himself, suffer from amnesia, bottle the knowledge he's acquired and put it on some out-of-the-way shelf so it doesn't interfere with the innocent pleasure of consuming more all over again. What he learned about the

Romans doesn't apply to the Etruscans. Hawaii has nothing to do with Polynesia. Knowledge is consumed for its calming effect, for 'information renewal,' for the interchange of banalities. It is useful only insofar as it can be digested anecdotally, but its potential for original sin has been washed clean along with the temptation to generate truth or movement—in other words: change.[37]

Inherent in all these positions is a call for modes of criticism that promote dialogue as the condition for social action: dialogue, in this case, informed by a number of assumptions drawn from the works of both Bakhtin and Freire as well as from the wider tradition of deconstructive criticism. These assumptions include treating the text as a social construct that is produced out of a number of available discourses; locating the contradictions and gaps within an educational text and situating them historically in terms of the interests they sustain and legitimate; recognizing in the text its internal politics of style and how this both opens up and constrains particular representations of the social world; understanding how the text actively works to silence certain voices; and, finally, discovering how it is possible to release possibilities from the text that provide new insights and critical readings regarding human understanding and social practices.

I also maintain that in order to develop a critical pedagogy as a form of cultural politics, it is essential to develop a mode of analysis that does not assume that lived experiences can be inferred automatically from structural determinations. In other words, the complexity of human behavior cannot be reduced to merely identifying the determinants in which such behavior is shaped and against which it constitutes itself, whether these be economic modes of production or systems of textual signification. The way in which individuals and groups both medi2ate and inhabit the cultural forms presented by such structural forces is in itself a form of production and needs to be analyzed through a related but different modes of analyses. In order to develop this point, I will now briefly discuss the nature and pedagogical implications of what I call the discourse of lived cultures.

Critical Pedagogy and the Discourse of Lived Cultures

Central to this view is the need to develop what Alain Touraine has called a theory of self-production.[38] In the most general sense this would demand an understanding of how teachers and students give meaning to their lives through the complex historical, cultural, and political forms that they both embody and produce. A number of issues mentioned in chapter 3 need to be developed within a critical pedagogy around this concern. First, it is necessary to acknowledge the subjective forms of political will and struggle that give meaning to the lives of the students. Second, as a mode of critique, the discourse of lived cultures should interrogate the ways in which people create stories, memories, and narratives that posit a sense of determination and agency. This is the cultural "stuff" of mediation, the conscious and unconscious material through which members of dominant and subordinate groups offer accounts of who they are in the ways in which they present their different readings of the world. It is also part of those ideologies and practices that allow us to understand the particular social locations, histories, subjective interests, and private worlds that come into play in any classroom pedagogy.

If educators treat the histories, experiences, and languages of different cultural groups as particularized forms of production, it becomes less difficult to understand the diverse readings, mediations, and behaviors that, let's say, students exhibit in response to analysis of a particular classroom text. In fact, a cultural politics necessitates that a pedagogy be developed that is attentive to the histories, dreams, and experiences that such students bring to schools. It is only by beginning with these subjective forms that critical educators can develop a language and set of practices that confirm and engage the contradictory nature of the cultural capital with which students produce meanings that legitimate particular forms of life.

Searching out the elements of self-production is not merely a pedagogical technique for confirming the experiences of those students who are often silenced or marginalized by the dominant culture of schooling. It is also part of an analysis of how power, dependence, and social inequality enable and limit students around issues of class, race, and gender. The discourse of lived cultures becomes an interrogative framework for teachers, illuminating not only how power and knowledge intersect to disconfirm the cultural capital of students from subordinate groups but also how they discover how power and knowledge can be translated into a language of possibility. The discourse of lived culture can also be used to develop a critical pedagogy of the popular, one that engages the knowledge of lived experience through the dual method of confirmation and interrogation.

The knowledge of the "other" is engaged in this instance not simply to be celebrated but also to be interrogated critically with respect to the ideologies it contains, the means of representation it utilizes, and the underlying social practices it confirms. At issue here is the need to link knowledge and power theoretically so as to give students the opportunity to understand more critically who they are as part of a wider social formation, and how they have been positioned and constituted through the social domain.

The discourse of lived cultures also points to the need for educators to view schools as cultural and political spheres actively engaged in the production and struggle for voice. In many cases, schools do not allow students from subordinate groups to authenticate their problems and lived experiences through their own individual and collective voices. As I have stressed previously, the dominant school culture generally represents and legitimates the privileged voices of the white middle and upper classes. In order for educators to demystify and make the dominant culture and to make it an object of political analysis, they will need to learn and master the language of critical understanding. If they are to understand and counter the dominant ideology at work in schools, they must attend to those voices that emerge from three different ideological spheres and settings: the school voice, the student voice, and the teacher voice. The interests that each of these voices represents have to be analyzed not so much as oppositional in the sense that they must counter and disable each other, but as an interplay of dominant and subordinate practices that shape each other in an ongoing struggle over power, meaning, and authorship. This, in turn, presupposes the necessity for analyzing schools in their historical and relational specificity, and it points to the possibility for intervening and shaping school outcomes. In order to understand the multiple and varied meanings that constitute the discourses of student voice, educators need to affirm and critically engage the polyphonic languages their students bring to schools. Educators need to learn "the collection and communicative practices associated with particular uses of both written and spoken forms among specific social groups."[39] Moreover, any adequate understanding of this language has to encompass the social and community relations that give such a language meaning and dignity.

Learning the discourse of school voice means that educators need to critically analyze the directives, imperatives, and rules that shape particular configurations of time, space, and curricula within the institutional and political settings of schools. The category of school voice, for example, points to sets of practices and ideologies that structure how classrooms are arranged, what content is taught, what general social practices teachers must follow. Moreover, it is in the interplay of the dominant school culture and the polyphonic representations and layers of meaning of student voices that dominant and oppositional ideologies define and constrain each other.

Teacher voice reflects the values, ideologies, and structuring principles that give meaning to the histories, culture, and subjectivities that define the day-to-day activities of educators. It is the voice of common and critical sense that teachers utilize to mediate between the discourses of production, texts, and lived cultures as expressed within the asymmetrical relations of power that characterize such potentially "counterpublic" spheres such as schools. In effect, it is through the mediation and action of teacher voice that the very nature of the schooling process is often either sustained or challenged; that is, the power of teacher voice to shape schooling according to the logic of emancipatory interests is inextricably related to a high degree of self-understanding regarding its own values and interests. Teacher voice moves within a contradiction that points to its pedagogical significance for both marginalizing as well as empowering students. On the one hand, teacher voice represents a basis in authority that can provide knowledge and forms of self-understanding allowing students to develop the power of critical consciousness. At the same time, regardless of how politically or ideologically correct a teacher may be, his or her "voice" may be destructive for students if it is imposed on them or if it is used to silence them.

Kathleen Weiler, in her brilliant ethnography of a group of feminist school administrators and teachers, illustrates this issue.[40] She reports on one class in which a radical teacher read a selection from *The Autobiography of Malcolm X* describing how a young Malcolm is told by one of his public school teachers that the most he can hope for in life is to get a job working with his hands. In reading this story, the teacher's aim was to illustrate a theory of socialization that is part of the discipline of sociology. John, a black student in the class, took the passage as an example of outright racism, one that he fully understood in light of his own experiences. He wasn't interested in looking at the more abstract issue of socialization. For him, the issue was naming a racist experience and condemning it outright. Molly, the teacher, saw John's questions as disruptive and chose to ignore him. In response to her actions, John dropped out of the class the next day. Defending her own position, Molly felt that students should learn how the processes of socialization work, especially if they are to understand how their own subjectivities are constructed. But in teaching this point, she failed to understand that students are multi-layered subjects with contradictory and diverse voices and as such often present different readings of the material provided in class, regardless of how important such material is politically. In this case, the culture of the teacher's voice, which is white and middle-class, comes in conflict with that of the student voice, which is black and working-class. Rather than mediating this conflict in a pedagogically progressive way, the teacher allowed her voice and authority to silence rather than give expression to the student's anger, concern, and interests.

I also want to add that the category of teacher voice points to the need for educators to unite in a collective voice as part of a wider social movement dedicated to restructuring the ideological and material conditions that work both within and outside schooling. The notion of voice in this case points to a shared tradition as well as a particular form of discourse. It is a tradition that has to organize around the issues of solidarity, struggle, and empowerment in order to provide the conditions for the particularities of teacher and student voice to gain the most emancipatory expression. Thus, the category of teacher voice needs to be understood and interrogated critically in terms of its collective political project as well as in relation to the ways it functions to mediate student voices and everyday school life.

In general terms, not only does the discourse of critical understanding represent an acknowledgement of the political and pedagogical processes at work in the construction of forms of authorship and voice within different institutional and social spheres, it also constitutes a critical attack on the vertical ordering of reality inherent in the unjust practices that are actively at work in the wider society. To redress some of the problems I have sketched out in the preceding pages, I believe that schools need to be reconceived and reconstituted as democratic public spheres, where students learn the skills and knowledge needed to live in and fight for a viable democratic society. Within this perspective, schools will have to be characterized by a pedagogy that demonstrates its commitment to engaging the views and problems that deeply concern students in their everyday lives. Equally important is the need for schools to cultivate a spirit of critique and a respect for human dignity that is capable of linking personal and social issues around the pedagogical project of helping students to become critical and active citizens.

In conclusion, each of the three major discourses introduced in this chapter represents a different view of cultural production, pedagogical analysis, and political action. And although each of these radical discourses involves a certain degree of autonomy in both form and content, it is important that a critical pedagogy be developed around the inner connections they share within the context of a cultural politics. For it is within these interconnections that a critical theory of both structure and agency can be developed that engenders an oppositional critical educational language capable of asking new questions, making new commitments and possibilities that allow educators to work and organize for the development of schools as democratic public spheres.

In the next chapter, I further develop the implications of schooling as a form of cultural politics by focusing on the more specific and related issues of literacy, voice, and critical pedagogy. In doing so, I repeat some of the assumptions that underlie the theory of voice presented in this chapter, but this is done only to the degree that it establishes the context for further unraveling and extending the specifics of a theory of critical literacy and further developing the elements at work in a theory of critical pedagogy.

5
Literacy, Critical Pedagogy, and Empowerment

Reconstructing a Radical Tradition in Literacy

Each time that in one way or another, the question of language comes to the fore, that signifies that a series of other problems is about to emerge, the formation and enlarging of the ruling class, the necessity to establish more "intimate" and sure relations between the ruling groups and the national popular masses, that is, the reorganisation of cultural hegemony.[1]

These remarks, made in the first half of the twentieth century by the Italian social theorist Antonio Gramsci, seem strangely at odds with the language and aspirations surrounding the current conservative and liberal debate on schooling and the "problem" of literacy. In fact, Gramsci's remarks appear to both politicize the notion of literacy and at the same time invest it with an ideological meaning that suggests that it may have less to do with the task of teaching people how to read and write than with producing and legitimating oppressive and exploitative social relations. Gramsci viewed literacy as both a concept and a social practice that must be linked historically to configurations of knowledge and power, on the one hand, and the political and cultural struggle over language and experience, on the other. For Gramsci, literacy was a double-edged sword; though it generally represented a signifier monopolized by the ruling classes for the perpetuation of relations of repression and domination, it could also be wielded for the purpose of self-and social empowerment. Gramsci believed that as a terrain of struggle, critical literacy had to be fought for both as an ideological construct and as a social

147

movement. As an ideology, literacy had to be viewed as a social construction that is always implicated in organizing one's view of the past, the present, and the future; furthermore, the notion of literacy needed to be grounded in an ethical and political project that dignified and extended the possibilities for human life and freedom. In other words, literacy as a radical construct had to be rooted in a spirit of critique and project of possibility that enabled people to participate in the understanding and transformation of their society. As both the mastery of specific skills and particular forms of knowledge, literacy had to become a precondition for social and cultural emancipation.

As a social movement, literacy was tied to the material and political conditions necessary to develop and organize teachers, community workers, and others both within and outside of schools. It was part of a larger struggle over the orders of knowledge, values, and social practices that must necessarily prevail if the fight for establishing democratic institutions and a democratic society were to succeed. For Gramsci, literacy became both a referent and mode of critique for developing forms of counterhegemonic education. Implicit in this view is the radical notion that forms of critical pedagogy could be developed around the political project of creating a society of intellectuals (in the widest sense of the term) who could grasp the importance of developing democratic public spheres as part of the struggle of modern life to fight against domination as well as take an active part in the struggle for creating the conditions necessary to make people literate, to give them a voice in both shaping and governing their society.

With the exception of the base communities that Freire has worked with in Brazil and throughout Latin America, it is difficult in the present historical conjuncture to identify any major prominent theoretical positions or social movements that both affirm and extend the tradition of a critical literacy that has been developed in the manner of theorists such as Gramsci, Mikhail Bakhtin, and others.[2] In the United States, a tradition of radical literacy existed among immigrants in the 1920s and in the civil rights movement of the 1960s, but at the present time the language of literacy is almost exclusively linked to popular forms of liberal and right-wing discourse. These approaches reduce literacy to either a functional perspective tied to narrowly conceived economic interests or a logic designed to initiate the poor, the underprivileged, and minorities into the ideology of a unitary, dominant cultural tradition. In the first instance, the crisis in literacy is predicated on the need to train more workers for occupational jobs that demand "functional" reading and writing skills. The conservative political interests that structure this position are evident in the influence of corporate and other groups on schools to develop curricula more closely tuned to the job market, curricula that will take on a decidedly vocational orientation and in so doing reduce the need for corporations to provide on-the-job training.[3] In the second instance, literacy becomes the ideological vehicle through which to legitimate schooling as a site for character development; in this case, literacy is associated with the transmission and mastery of a unitary Western tradition based on the virtues of hard work, industry, respect for family, institutional authority, and an unquestioning respect for the nation. In short, literacy becomes a pedagogy of chauvinism dressed up in the lingo of the Great Books.

Within this dominant discourse, *illiteracy* is not merely the inability to read and write, but also a cultural marker for naming forms of difference within the logic of cultural deprivation theory. What is important here is that the notion of cultural deprivation serves to designate in the negative sense forms of cultural currency that appear disturbingly unfamiliar and threatening when measured against the dominant culture's ideological standard regarding what is to be valorized as history, linguistic proficiency, lived experience, and standards of community life.[4] The importance of developing a politics of difference in this view is seldom a positive virtue and attribute of public life; in fact, difference is often constituted as deficiency and is part of the same logic that defines "the other" within the discourse of cultural deprivation. Both ideological tendencies strip literacy from the ethical and political obligations of speculative reason and radical democracy and subjugate it to the political and pedagogical imperatives of social conformity and domination. In both cases, literacy represents a retreat from critical thought and emancipatory politics. Stanley Aronowitz has captured both the interests at work in shaping the current discourse on literacy and the problems it reproduces. He writes:

> When America is in trouble it turns to its schools. . . . Employers want
> an educational system closely tuned to the job market, a system that

will adjust its curriculum to their changing needs and save them
money on training. Humanists insist on the holy obligation of schools
to reproduce "civilization as we know it"—Western values, literary
culture, and the skepticism of the scientific ethos. ... At the moment,
the neoconservatives have appropriated the concept of excellence
and defined it as basic skills, technical training and classroom
discipline. Schools are cuddling up to business and replacing any
sensible notion of literacy with something called "computer literacy."
In existing adult literacy programs, the materials and methods used
reflect an "end of ideology" approach that fails to inspire students—
and together with the stresses of everyday life—usually results in
massive dropout rates "proving" once again that most illiterates won't
learn even when government money is "thrown" at them. ... Few
are prepared to speak the traditional language of educational
humanism or fight for the idea that a general education is the basis
of critical literacy. Since the collapse of the '60s movements,
progressives have me-tooed the conservatives while radicals, with few
exceptions, remain silent.[5]

Although literacy has been seen as a major terrain of struggle for
conservatives and liberals, it has been only marginally embraced by
critical educational theorists.[6] When it has been incorporated as an
essential aspect of a radical pedagogy, it is gravely undertheorized,
and, though displaying the best of intentions, its pedagogical applications are often patronizing and theoretically misleading. Literacy in
this case often aims at providing working-class and minority children
with reading and writing skills necessary for economic and social
survival as well as personal affirmation and growth. In this perspective, literacy is more often than not tied to a deficit theory of learning.
The accusation is that schools unevenly distribute particular skills
and forms of knowledge so as to benefit middle-class over working-
class and minority students. At stake here is a view of literacy steeped
in a notion of equity. Literacy becomes a form of privileged cultural
capital, and subordinate groups, it is argued, deserve their distribu-
tional share of such cultural currency. The pedagogies that often
accompany this view of literacy stress the need for working-class children to learn the reading and writing skills they will need in order to
succeed in schools; moreover, their own cultures and experiences
are often seen as strengths rather than deficits to be used in devel-

oping a critical pedagogy of literacy. Unfortunately, the pedagogies that are developed within this assumption generally provide a cataloglike approach of ways of using working-class culture to develop meaningful forms of instruction.

This particular approach to radical literacy is theoretically flawed for a number of reasons. First, it fails to view working-class culture as a terrain of struggle and contradiction. Second, it suggests that those educators working with subordinate groups need only to familiarize themselves with the histories and experiences of *their* students. There is no indication here that the culture that such students bring to the schools may be in dire need of critical interrogation and analysis. Third, this approach fails to focus on the wider implications of the relationship between knowledge and power. It fails to understand that literacy is not just related to the poor or to the inability of subordinate groups to read and write adequately; it is also fundamentally related to forms of political and ideological ignorance that function as a refusal to know the limits and political consequences of one's view of the world. Viewed in this way, literacy as a process is as disempowering as it is oppressive. What is important to recognize here is the need to reconstitute a radical view of literacy that revolves around the importance of naming and transforming those ideological and social conditions that undermine the possibility for forms of community and public life organized around the imperatives of a critical democracy. This is not merely a problem associated with the poor or minority groups; it is also a problem for those members of the middle and upper classes who have withdrawn from public life into a world of privatization, pessimism, and greed. In addition, a radically reconstituted view of literacy would need to do more than illuminate the scope and nature of the meaning of illiteracy; it would also be essential to develop a programmatic discourse for literacy as part of a political project and pedagogical practice that provides a language of hope and transformation for those struggling in the present for a better future.[7]

In my view, the issue of developing an emancipatory theory of literacy along with a corresponding transformative pedagogy has taken on a new dimension and added significance in the present Cold War era. Developing a cultural politics of literacy and pedagogy becomes an important starting point for enabling those who have been silenced or marginalized by the schools, mass media, cultural industry, and video culture to reclaim the authorship of their own lives. An emancipatory theory of literacy points to the need to develop an alternative discourse and critical reading of how ideology, culture, and power work within late capitalist societies to limit, disorganize, and marginalize the more critical and radical everyday experiences and commonsense perceptions of individuals. At issue here is the recognition that the political and moral gains that teachers and others have made should be held onto and fought for with a new intellectual and political rigor. For this to happen, critical educators and workers at all levels of society need to assign the issue of political and cultural literacy the highest priority. Put another way, for a movement for radical literacy to come about, educators and others must struggle to find ways in which the pedagogical can be made more political and the political made more pedagogical. In other words, there is a dire need to develop pedagogical practices, in the first instance, that bring teachers, parents, and students together around new and more emancipatory visions of community. On the other hand, we must recognize that all aspects of politics outside the schools also represent a particular type of pedagogy; knowledge is always linked to power; social practices are always embodiments of concrete relations between diverse human beings and traditions; and all interaction contains implicit visions about the role of the citizen and the purpose of community.

Literacy in this wider view can serve to empower people through a combination of pedagogical skills and critical analysis and also function as a vehicle for examining how cultural definitions of gender, race, class, and subjectivity are constituted as both historical and social constructs. Moreover, literacy in this case becomes the central pedagogical and political mechanism through which to establish the ideological conditions and social practices necessary to develop social movements that recognize and fight for the imperatives of a radical democracy.

The Freirian Model of Emancipatory Literacy

It is against the above considerations that Paulo Freire's previous work on literacy and pedagogy has assumed increasingly important theoretical and political significance. Paulo Freire has provided one of the few practical models upon which to develop a radical philosophy of literacy and pedagogy. He has concerned himself for the past twenty years with the issue of literacy as an emancipatory political project, and he has combined the emancipatory content of his ideas with a concrete, practical pedagogy. His work has exercised a significant role in developing literacy programs not only in Brazil and Latin America, but also in Africa and in isolated programs in Europe, North America, and Australia. Central to Freire's approach to literacy is a dialectical relationship between human beings and the world, on the one hand, and language and transformative agency, on the other. Within this perspective, literacy is not approached, as it is in the dominant model, primarily as a technical skill to be acquired, but as a necessary foundation for cultural action for freedom, a central aspect of what it means to be a self-and socially constituted agent. In opposition to mainstream approaches to literacy, which often emphasize learning how to follow words across a page and understand what is there only superficially, Freire teaches people how to read so that they can decode and demythologize both their own cultural traditions as well as those that structure and legitimate the wider social order. Most dramatically, literacy for Freire is inherently a political project in which men and women assert their right and responsibility not only to read, understand, and transform their own experiences, but also to reconstitute their relationship within the wider society. In this sense, literacy is fundamental to aggressively constructing one's voice as part of a wider project of possibility and empowerment. Moreover, the issue of literacy and power does not begin and end with the process of learning how to read and write critically; instead, it begins with the fact of one's existence as part of a historically constructed practice within specific relations of power. That is, human beings (as both teachers *and* students) within particular social and cultural formations become the starting point for analyzing how they actively construct their own experiences within ongoing relations of power. The social construction of such experiences provides them with the opportunity to give meaning and expression to their own needs and voices as part of a project of self-and social empowerment. Thus, literacy for Freire is a process of becoming self-critical about the historically constructed nature of one's experience. To be able to name one's experience means to "read" the world and to begin to understand the political nature of the limits *and* possibilities that make up the larger society.[8]

As I mentioned in the previous chapter, language and power for Freire are inextricably intertwined and provide a fundamental dimension of human agency and social transformation. According to Freire, language, as shaped by the specificity of one's own historical and cultural formation, plays an active role in constructing experience and in organizing and legitimating the social practices available to various groups in society. Language is the "real stuff" of culture and constitutes both a terrain of domination and field of possibility. Language, in Gramsci's terms, is both hegemonic and counterhegemonic, instrumental in both silencing the voices of the oppressed and in legitimating oppressive social relations.[9] In universalizing particular ideologies, it attempts to subordinate the world of human agency and struggle to the interests of dominant groups. But at the same time, language is also viewed as the terrain upon which radical desires, aspirations, dreams, and hopes are given meaning through a merging of the discourse of critique and possibility.

In the most immediate sense, the political nature of literacy is a fundamental theme in Freire's early writings. This is clear in his graphic portrayals of movements designed to provide Third-World people with the conditions for criticism and social action either for overthrowing fascist dictatorships or for use in postrevolutionary situations where people are engaged in the process of social reconstruction. In each case, literacy becomes a hallmark of liberation and transformation designed to throw off the colonial voice and further develop the collective voice of suffering and affirmation silenced beneath the terror and brutality of despotic regimes.

In the following pages, I situate Freire's work on literacy in a theoretical framework that allows us to further understand the dialectical meaning/connection that it has to the contradictory reality of teaching and pedagogy. More specifically, I analyze the importance of extending literacy as a historical and social construct for engaging the discourse of domination and for defining critical pedagogy as a form of cultural politics. I then suggest some of the implications Freire's view of literacy has for developing a radical pedagogy of voice and experience.

Critical Literacy as a Precondition for
Self- and Social Empowerment

In the broadest political sense, literacy is a myriad of discursive forms and cultural competencies that construct and make available the various relations and experiences that exist between learners and the world. In a more specific sense, critical literacy is both a narrative for agency as well as a referent for critique. As a narrative for agency, literacy becomes synonymous with an attempt to rescue history, experience, and vision from conventional discourse and dominant social relations. It means developing the theoretical and practical conditions through which human beings can locate themselves in their own histories and in doing so make themselves present as actors in the struggle to expand the possibilities of human life and freedom. Literacy in these terms is not the equivalent of emancipation; it is in a more limited but essential way the precondition for engaging in struggles around both relations of meaning and relations of power. To be literate is *not* to be free; it is to be present and active in the struggle for reclaiming one's voice, history, and future. Just as *illiteracy* does not explain the causes of massive unemployment, bureaucracy, or the growing racism in major cities in the United States, South Africa, and elsewhere, literacy neither automatically reveals nor guarantees social, political, and economic freedom.[10] As a narrative for agency and as a referent for critique, literacy provides an essential precondition for organizing and understanding the socially constructed nature of subjectivity and experience and for assessing how knowledge, power, and social practice can be collectively forged in the service of making decisions instrumental to a democratic society rather than merely consenting to the wishes of the rich and the powerful.[11]

If a critical theory of literacy is to encompass human agency and critique as part of the narrative of liberation, it must reject the reductionist pedagogical practice of limiting critique to the analyses of cultural products such as texts, books, films, and other commodities.[12] The more narrowly defined theories of literacy tied to this form of ideology critique obscure the *relational* nature of how meaning is produced, i.e., the intersection of subjectivities, objects, and social practices within specific relations of power. Pedagogical practice in this more limited version of critical literacy is tied to a notion of criticism that exists at the expense of developing an adequate theory of how meaning, experience, and power are inscribed as part of a theory of human agency. Thus, central to a critical theory of literacy would be a view of human agency in which the production of meaning is not limited to analyzing how ideologies are inscribed in particular texts. In this case, a critical theory of literacy needs to incorporate a notion of ideology critique that includes a view of human agency in which the production of meaning takes place in the dialogue and interaction that mutually constitutes the dialectical relationship between human subjectivities and the objective world. As part of a more definitive political project, a radical theory of literacy needs to produce a view of human agency reconstructed through forms of narrative that operate as part of "a pedagogy of empowerment . . . centered within a social project aimed at the enhancement of human possibility."[13]

Within this perspective, the notion of literacy is reworked through a view of narrative that is not restricted to telling a story based simply on the dominant conventions of realism. The concept of narrative is extended in this case to include issues of representation that include the relationship of the reader to the text, the role of language and imagery within various cultural forms, and the positioning of the social "subject" through diverse modes of address, closure, and identifications. In other words, literacy as a form of narrative and agency provides the basis for examining cultural forms both for their ideological content and for their conventions of representation. The production of meaning is now analyzed as part of the interface of the pedagogical practices embodied in both the form and content of the relational exchange between readers and various cultural texts and objects.

Central to the notion of critical literacy developed in Freire's work are a number of crucial insights regarding the politics of illiteracy. As a social construction, literacy not only names experiences considered important to a given society, but also sets off and defines through the concept "illiterate" what can be termed the "experience of the other." The concept "illiterate" in this sense often provides an ideological cover for powerful groups simply to silence the poor, minority groups, women, or people of color. Consequently, naming "illiteracy" as part of the definition of what it means to be literate represents an ideological construction informed by particular political interests. While Freire's analysis of the concept illiteracy attempts to uncover these dominant ideological interests, it also provides a theoretical basis for understanding the political nature of illiteracy as a social practice linked to the logic of cultural hegemony and to particular forms of resistance. Implicit in this analysis is the notion that illiteracy as a social problem cuts across class lines and does not limit itself to the failure of minorities to master functional competencies in reading and writing. Illiteracy signifies on one level a form of political and intellectual ignorance and on another a possible instance of class, gender, racial, or cultural resistance. As part of the larger and more pervasive issue of cultural hegemony, illiteracy refers to the functional inability or refusal of middle-and upper-class persons to read the world and their lives in a critical and historically relational way. Stanley Aronowitz suggests a view of illiteracy as a form of cultural hegemony in his own discussion of what it should mean to be "functionally" literate.

> The real issue for the "functionally" literate is whether they can
> decode the messages of media culture, counter official
> interpretations of social, economic, and political reality; whether they
> feel capable of critically evaluating events, or, indeed, of intervening
> in them. If we understand literacy as the ability of individuals and
> groups to locate themselves in history, to see themselves as social
> actors able to debate their collective futures, then the key obstacle to
> literacy is the sweeping privatization and pessimism that has come to
> pervade public life.[14]

Aronowitz's points to the failure of most radical and critical educators to understand illiteracy as a form of cultural hegemony. Again, illiteracy as used here embodies a language and a set of social practices that underscore the need for developing a theory of literacy that takes seriously the task of uncovering how particular forms of social and moral regulation produce a culture of ignorance and categorical stupidity crucial to the silencing of all potentially critical voices.

It is also important to stress once again that as an act of resistance, the refusal to be literate may constitute less an act of ignorance on the part of subordinate groups than an act of resistance. That is, members of the working class and other oppressed groups may consciously or unconsciously refuse to learn the specific cultural codes and competencies authorized by the dominant culture's view of literacy. Such resistance should be seen as an opportunity to investigate the political and cultural conditions that warrant such resistance, not as unqualified acts of conscious political refusal. Simply put, the interests that inform such acts never speak for themselves, and they have to be analyzed within a more interpretative and contextual framework, one that links the wider context of schooling with the interpretation that students bring to the act of refusal. The refusal to be literate in such cases provides the pedagogical basis for engaging in a critical dialogue with those groups whose traditions and cultures are often the object of a massive assault and attempt by the dominant culture to delegitimate and disorganize the knowledge and traditions such groups use to define themselves and their view of the world.

For teachers, the central issue that needs to be investigated is the manner in which the social curriculum of schooling, as Philip Corrigan puts it, constructs social practices around the literate/illiterate differentiation so as to contribute to the

> regulated social construction of differential silencing and of
> categorized stupidity, within the vortices of sexuality, race, gender,
> class, language, and regionality. . . . [This] raises the centrality of the
> functionality of ignorance, the importance of declaring most people
> most of the time as unworthy, stupid, in a singular and exact
> guillotining and classifying word: bad. And making them "take on"
> this identification as if it were their only usable, exchangeable,
> "I.D."[15]

For Corrigan and others, the social construction of meaning within schooling is often structured through a dominating social grammar that limits the possibility for critical teaching and learning in schools. Dominant language in this case structures and regulates not only what *is* to be taught, but *how* it is to be taught and evaluated. This is evident in the ways in which the dominant language of technical rationality legitimates and shapes the distinction between forms of high-and low status subjects, with math and science, for instance, often given the most prestige in the school curriculum. It is also evident in the dominant culture's use of the language of accountability, which places enormous restrictions on the way school subjects can be taught and evaluated, with a major emphasis on structuring both knowledge and pedagogy around interests grounded in that which is measurable, efficient, and standardized. In this analysis, ideology combines with social practice to produce a school voice—the voice of unquestioned authority which attempts to locate and regulate the specific ways in which students learn, speak, act, and present themselves. In this sense, Corrigan is correct to argue that teaching and learning within public schooling are not merely about the reproduction of the dominant logic and ideology of capitalism. Nor are they primarily about ongoing acts of resistance waged by subordinate groups fighting for a voice and sense of dignity in the schools. Both of these social practices exist, but they are part of a much broader set of social relations in which experience and subjectivity become constructed within a variety of voices, conditions, and narratives that suggest that school represents more than compliance or rejection.

In the most general sense, schooling is about the regulation of time, space, textuality, experience, knowledge, and power amid conflicting interests and histories that simply cannot be pinned down in simple theories of reproduction and resistance.[16] Schools must be seen in their historical and relational contexts. As institutions, they exhibit contradictory positions in the wider culture and also represent a terrain of complex struggle regarding what it means to be literate and empowered in ways that would allow teachers and students to think and act in a manner commensurate with the imperatives and reality of a radical democracy.

The task of a theory of critical literacy is to broaden our conception of how teachers actively produce, sustain, and legitimate meaning and experience in classrooms. That is, how do their own values and experiences modify, alter, or reproduce dominant school codes and practices? Moreover, a theory of critical literacy necessitates a more profound understanding of how the wider conditions of the state and society produce, negotiate, transform, and bear down on the conditions of teaching so as to either enable or disable teachers from acting in a critical and transformative way. Equally important is the need to assert as a central assumption of critical literacy that knowledge is not merely produced in the heads of experts, curriculum specialists, school administrators, and teachers. The production of knowledge, as mentioned earlier, is a relational act. For teachers, this means being sensitive to the actual historical, social, and cultural conditions that contribute to the forms of knowledge and meaning that students bring to school.

If the concept of critical literacy is to be advanced in conjunction with the theoretical notions of narrative and agency, then the knowledge, values, and social practices that constitute the story/narrative of schooling embody particular interests and relations of power regarding how one should think, live, and act with regard to the past, present, and future. At its best, a theory of critical literacy argues for pedagogical practices in which the battle to make sense of one's life reaffirms and furthers the project for teachers and students to recover their own voices so they can retell their own histories and in so doing "check and criticize the history [they] are told against the one [they] have lived."[17] This means more, however, than simply the retelling and comparison of stories. As part of the dialectic of resistance, renewal, and transformation, stories invoke memories of solidarity, the rupture of the poor and oppressed into history, and serve to indict the power of self-and collective self-destruction. Toni Cade Bambara writes of stories of resistance and renewal in a way that makes clear the pedagogical value as a foundation for developing forms of historical consciousness that challenge rather than serve the interests of the powerful and the rich. She writes:

> Stories are important. They keep us alive. In the ships, in the camps,
> in the quarters, fields, prisons, on the road, on the run,
> underground, under siege, in the throes, on the verge—the
> storyteller snatches us back from the edge to hear the next chapter.
> In which we are the subjects. We, the hero of the tales. Our lives
> preserved. How it was, how it be. Passing it along in the relay. That is
> what I work to do: to produce stories that save our lives.[18]

Bambara writes of stories that save lives, stories that offer models of resistance and courage, that delineate structures of power and domination. Extrapolated from her comments is the invocation to teachers and students to recognize that stories are never neutral; they are always tied to particular memories, narratives, and histories. In order to move beyond a pedagogy of voice that suggests that all stories are innocent, we must examine such stories around the interest and principles that structure them and interrogate them as part of a political project (in the widest sense) that either undermines or enables the values and practices that provide the foundation for social justice, equality, and democratic community. In other words, it is important to construct a pedagogy of voice and difference around the recognition that some practices (voices/stories) define themselves through the suppression of other voices, support forms of human suffering, and require an explicit moral and political condemnation on the part of the teacher. Questions of racism and sexism, for example, cannot be treated merely as topics of academic interest. Such a position should not prevent a dialogue on these issues, but it should define the structure of such a discussion so as to prevent racist or sexist remarks from being made simply as an expression of one point of view among many. In its more radical sense critical literacy means making one's self present in a moral and political project that links the production of meaning to the possibility for human agency, democratic community, and transformative social action.[19]

Literacy and the Liberation of Remembrance

In his model of critical literacy, one that embodies an ongoing dialectical relationship between a critical reading of the world and the word, Freire establishes the theoretical groundwork for a new discourse in which the notion of literacy brings with it a critical attentiveness to the web of relations in which meaning is produced both as a historical construction and as part of a wider set of pedagogical practices. Literacy in this sense means more than breaking with the predefined, or as Walter Benjamin has said, "Brushing history against the grain."[20] It also means understanding the details of everyday life and the social grammar of the concrete through the larger totalities of history and social context. As part of the discourse of narrative and agency, critical literacy suggests using history as a form of liberating memory. As used here, "history" means recognizing the figural traces of untapped potentialities as well as sources of suffering that constitute one's past.[21] To reconstruct history in this sense is to situate the meaning and practice of literacy in an ethical discourse that takes as its referent those instances of suffering that need to be remembered and overcome.[22]

As a liberating element of remembrance, historical inquiry becomes more than a mere preparation for the future by means of recovering a series of past events; instead, it becomes a model for constituting the radical potential of memory. It is a sober witness to the oppression and pain endured needlessly by history's victims and a text/terrain for the exercise of critical suspicion, highlighting not only the sources of suffering that need to be remembered so as not to be repeated, but also the subjective side of human struggle and hope.[23] Put another way, liberating remembrance, along with the forms of critical literacy it supports expresses its dialectical nature in both "its demystifying critical impulse, bearing sober witness to the sufferings of the past,"[24] and in the selected and fleeting images of hope that it offers up to the present.

Literacy as a Form of Cultural Politics

Theorizing literacy as a form of cultural politics assumes that the social, cultural, political, and economic dimensions of everyday life are the primary categories for understanding contemporary schooling. School life is not conceptualized as a unitary, monolithic, and ironclad system of rules and regulations, but as a cultural terrain characterized by the production of experiences and subjectivities amid varying degrees of accommodation, contestation, and resistance. As a form of cultural politics, literacy both illuminates and interrogates school life as a place characterized by a plurality of conflicting languages and struggles, a site where dominant and subordinate cultures collide and where teachers, students, parents, and school administrators often differ as to how school experiences and practices are to be defined and understood.[25] In this type of analysis, literacy provides an important focus for understanding the political and ideological interests and principles at work in the pedagogical encounters and exchanges between the teacher, the learner, and the forms of meaning and knowledge they produce together.

At stake here is a notion of literacy that connects relations of power and knowledge not simply to *what* teachers teach but also to the productive meanings that students, in all their cultural and social differences, bring to classrooms as part of the production of knowledge and the construction of personal and social identities. To define "literacy" in the Freirian sense as a critical reading of the world and the word is to lay the theoretical groundwork for more fully analyzing how knowledge is produced and subjectivities constructed within relations of interaction in which teachers and students attempt to make themselves present as active authors of their own worlds.[26]

Traditionally, radical educators have emphasized the ideological nature of knowledge (either as a form of ideology critique or as ideologically correct content to get across to students) as the primary focus for critical educational work. Central to this perspective is a view of knowledge that suggests that it is produced in the head of the educator or teacher/theorist and not in an interactional engagement expressed through the process of writing, talking, debating, and struggling over what counts as legitimate knowledge. In short, knowledge is theoretically abstracted from its own production as part of a pedagogical encounter and is also undertheorized for the way in which it is encountered in the pedagogical context in which it is taught to students. The notion that knowledge cannot be constructed outside a pedagogical encounter is lost in the misconceived assumption that the truth content of knowledge is the most essential issue to be addressed in one's teaching. In this way, the relevance of the notion of pedagogy as part of a critical theory of education is either undertheorized or merely forgotten. What has often emerged from this view is a division of labor in which theorists who produce knowledge are limited to the university, those who merely reproduce it are seen as public school teachers, and those who passively receive it in bits and clumps at all levels of schooling fulfill the role of students. This refusal to develop what David Lusted has called a pedagogy of theory *and* teaching not only misrecognizes knowledge as an isolated production of meaning but also denies the knowledge and social forms out of which students give relevance to their lives and experiences.

> Knowledge is not produced in the intentions of those who believe they hold it, whether in the pen or in the voice. It is produced in the process of interaction, between writer and reader at the moment of reading, and between teacher and learner at the moment of classroom engagement. Knowledge is not the matter that is offered so much as the matter that is understood. To think of fields of bodies of knowledge as if they are the property of academics and teachers is wrong. It denies an equality in the relations at moments of interaction and falsely privileges one side of the exchange, and what that side "knows," over the other. Moreover, for critical cultural producers to hold this view of knowledge carries its own pedagogy,

an autocratic and elite pedagogy. It's not just that it denies the value of what learners know, which it does, but that it misrecognizes the conditions necessary for the kind of learning—critical, engaged, personal, social—called for by the knowledge itself.[27]

At the theoretical level, it is important to modify Lusted's insight by acknowledging that knowledge is *also* produced by power and traditions that are legitimated both culturally and politically. At a more practical level, the problems that arise when teachers ignore how *students* produce meaning are exemplified by teachers who define the success of their teaching exclusively through the ideological correctness of the subject matter they teach. The classic example might be the middle-class teacher who is rightly horrified at the sexism exhibited by male students in her classroom. The teacher responds by presenting students with a variety of feminist articles, films, and other curriculum materials. Rather than responding with gratitude for being politically enlightened, the students respond with scorn and resistance. The teacher is baffled as the students' sexism appears to become even further entrenched. In this encounter a number of pedagogical and political errors emerge. First, rather than give any attention to how the students produce meaning, the feminist teacher falsely assumes the self-evident nature of the political and ideological correctness of her position. In doing so, she assumes an authoritative discourse which disallows the possibility for the students to "tell" their own stories, and to present and then question the experiences they bring into play. Then, by denying students the opportunity to question and investigate the ideology of sexism as a problematic experience, the teacher not only undermines the voices of these students, but she displays what in their eyes is just another example of institutional/middle class authority telling them what to think. Consequently, what appears at first to be the legitimate pedagogical intervention of a radical teacher voice ends up undermining its own ideological convictions by ignoring the complex and fundamental relation among teaching, learning, and student culture. The teacher's best intentions are thereby subverted by employing a pedagogy that is part of the very dominant logic she seeks to challenge and dismantle. What is important to recognize here is that a democratic theory of literacy needs to be constructed around a dialectical theory of voice and empowerment. This means connecting theories of teaching and learning with wider theories of ideology and subjectivity. More specifically, this means developing an understanding of how cultural processes are produced and transformed through the discourses of production, text analysis, and lived cultures analyzed in the last chapter. Most important, how teachers and students read the world is inextricably linked to forms of pedagogy that can function either to silence and marginalize students or to legitimate their voices in an effort to empower them as critical and active citizens.[28]

A critical pedagogy consistent with an emancipatory view of literacy and voice also involves rethinking the very nature of curriculum discourse. At the outset this demands understanding curriculum as representative of a set of underlying interests that structure how a particular story is told through the organization of knowledge, social relations, values, and forms of assessment. Curriculum itself represents a narrative or voice, one that is multilayered and often contradictory but also situated within relations of power that more often than not favor white, male, middle-class, English-speaking students. What this suggests for a theory of critical literacy and pedagogy is that curriculum in the most fundamental sense is a terrain of contestation over whose forms of knowledge, history, visions, language, culture, and authority will prevail as a legitimate object of learning and analysis.[29] Curriculum is another instance of a cultural politics whose signifying practices contain not only the logic of legitimation and domination, but also the possibility for transformative and empowering forms of pedagogy.

In addition to treating curriculum as a narrative whose interests must be uncovered and critically interrogated, teachers must promote pedagogical conditions in their classrooms that provide spaces for different student voices. The critical pedagogy being proposed here is fundamentally concerned with student experience; it takes the problems and needs of the students themselves as its starting point. This suggests both confirming and legitimating the knowledge and experience through which students give meaning to their lives. Most obviously, this entails replacing the authoritative discourse of imposition and recitation with a voice capable of speaking in one's own terms, a voice capable of listening, retelling, and challenging the very grounds of knowledge and power.[30] As I have tried to portray repeatedly in this text, a critical pedagogy of literacy and voice must be attentive to the contradictory nature of student experience and voice and therefore establish the grounds whereby such experience can be interrogated and analyzed with respect to both their strengths and weaknesses. Voice in this case provides not only a theoretical framework for recognizing the cultural logic that anchors subjectivity and learning, but also a referent for criticizing the kind of romantic celebration of student experience that characterized much of the radical pedagogy of the early 1960s. At issue here is linking the pedagogy of student voice to a project of possibility that allows students to affirm the interplay of different voices and experience while recognizing that such voices must always be interrogated for the various social, intellectual, ethical, and political interests they represent. As a form of historical, textual, political, and sexual production, student voice must be rooted in a pedagogy that allows students to speak and to appreciate the nature of difference as part of both a democratic tolerance and a fundamental condition for critical dialogue and the development of forms of solidarity rooted in the principles of trust, sharing, and a commitment to improving the quality of human life. In the first instance, a pedagogy of critical literacy and voice needs to be developed around a politics of difference and community that is not simply grounded in a celebration of plurality. Such a pedagogy must be derived from a particular form of human community in which plurality becomes dignified through the construction of classroom social relations in which all voices in their differences become unified both in their efforts to identify and recall moments of human suffering and in their attempts to overcome the conditions that perpetuate such suffering.[31]

Second, a critical pedagogy must take seriously the articulation of a morality that posits a language of public life, emancipatory community, and individual and social commitment. Students need to be introduced to a language of empowerment and radical ethics that permits them to think about how community life should be constructed around a project of possibility. Roger Simon has clearly expressed this position:

> An education that empowers for possibility must raise questions of how we can work for the re-construction of social imagination in the service of human freedom. What notions of knowing and what forms of learning will support this? I think the project of possibility requires an education rooted in a view of human freedom as the understanding of necessity and the transformation of necessity. This is the pedagogy we require, one whose standards and achievement

objectives are determined in relation to goals of critique and the enhancement of social imagination. Teaching and learning must be linked to the goal of educating students to take risks, to struggle with ongoing relations of power, to critically appropriate forms of knowledge that exist outside of their immediate experience, and to envisage versions of a world which (in the Blochian sense) is "not-yet"—in order to be able to alter the grounds on which life is lived.[32]

Third, teachers should provide students with the opportunity to interrogate different languages or ideological discourses as they are developed in an assortment of texts and curriculum materials. That is, a critical pedagogy needs to analyze the conditions that make it possible for students to understand how different readings can be made of a text.[33] In doing so, students are encouraged to engage in the theoretical and practical task of interrogating their own theoretical and political positions. Furthermore, such a pedagogy should create the classroom conditions necessary for identifying and making problematic the contradictory and multiple ways of viewing the world that students use in constructing their worldview. The point here is to then further interrogate how students perform particular ideological operations to challenge or adopt certain positions offered in the texts and contexts available to them both in school and in the wider society. Following this, and crucial to developing a critical and dialectical understanding of voice, is the necessity for teachers to recognize that the meanings and ideologies in the text are not the only positions that can be appropriated by students. Since student subjectivity and cultural identity are themselves contradictory, it is important to link how students produce meaning to the various discourses and social formations outside schools that actively construct their contradictory experiences and subjectivities.

Fourth, it is especially important that teachers critically engage how ideological interests structure their ability *both* to teach and to learn with others. A radical theory of literacy and voice must remain attentive to Freire's claim that all critical educators are also learners. This is not merely a matter of learning about what students might know; it is more importantly a matter of learning how to renew a form of self-knowledge through an understanding of the community and culture that actively constitute the lives of one's students. Dieter Misgeld makes this point:

Social transformation includes and requires self-formation. . . . The identity of learners and teachers is just as much at issue and to be discovered through the pedagogy they cooperate in as the content of what they learn. . . . Freire's pedagogues (teacher-students or initiators of activities in culture circles) can therefore allow themselves to learn, and they must learn from their students. The learning we speak of is not merely incidental. It is not a question of merely monitoring student performance so that a learning task can be presented with greater teaching efficiency. Rather the purpose of the educational enterprise is learned and relearned from and with the students. The students remind the teachers of the essential learning task: that learning and teaching are meant to bring about self-knowledge with knowledge of one's culture (and "the world" as Freire . . . says). One learns to understand, appreciate, and affirm membership in the culture. One is one of those for whom culture is there. One learns about oneself as a "being of decision," an "active subject of the historical process."[34]

Along with the implication that educators need to engage con-stantly both the word and the world is the less obvious assumption that teachers adopt pedagogies that provide the space for a dialogue to emerge in which both classroom teachers and students can engage each other as agents of different/similar cultures. This indi-cates how important are pedagogies that allow teachers to assert their own voices while still being able to encourage students to affirm, tell, and retell their personal narratives. Moreover, this peda-gogical principle calls into question any form of privileged teacher authority that refuses students the opportunity to question its most basic assumptions. This is not an argument for undermining or elim-inating teacher authority and voice as much as it is for providing the pedagogical basis for understanding how and why such authority is constructed and what purpose it serves. It is also important that teachers recognize how they often silence students, even when they act out of the best of intentions.[35] This suggests being critically atten-tive not only to the immediacy of one's voice as part of the estab-lished apparatus of power, but also to the fears, resistance, and skep-ticism that students from subordinate groups bring with them to the school setting.

Fifth, the different voices that characterize school life have often been falsely theorized by radical educators as part of an unbridge-able antagonism between the voice of the teacher and the school, on the one hand, and the voices of subordinate groups of students, on the other. Trapped within a polarizing logic of reproduction versus resistance, this discourse provides an inadequate understanding of how meaning is negotiated and transformed in schools; it also leaves little or no room for developing a programmatic discourse of transformation and possibility. It is essential that educators provide an alternative reading of what goes on in schools around the production and transformation of meaning. While the official discourse of the school and the subordinate voice of the students may be forged out of different needs, there exists a frequent interplay between the two which results in a process of mutual definition and constraint.[36] This suggests a much more subtle interaction between the dominant ideology of the school and the ideologies of the various students who inhabit them. It should be recognized that this position advances far beyond the reproductive model of schooling developed by such different theorists as Paul Willis in England and Sam Bowles and Herb Gintis in the United States.[37] The characteristic nature of the shifting forms of accommodation, resistance, and interrogation that define the particular quality of the complex interaction between teacher and student voices cannot be overlooked, especially since it is precisely this type of critical exchange and understanding that allows both teachers and students to analyze dominant school culture as part of a specific historical, social, and pedagogical context.

This view of voice and pedagogy also provides the basis for developing possible alliances and projects around which teachers and students could dialogue and struggle together in order to make their respective positions heard outside their classrooms and in the larger community. This further suggests that teachers work with parents and community people in order to make schools places that establish an organic link to the communities they serve. More specifically, teachers could work with parents and others to address issues of central importance both in getting parents more actively involved in the schools and in improving the quality of school life. On the one hand, teachers could work with parents around issues such as language use in the schools, budget allocations and cuts, differential access to school resources, curriculum policy, school governance, and educational reform. On the other hand, teachers could work with parents and community people to extend the specific links that schools have to the community. Youth advocacy groups could be used to help educators and parents deal with issues such as drugs, violence, teen pregnancy, and so on. Moreover, schools could open themselves up to serve as a resource for the community itself, whether this took the form of adult education or ongoing recreational and cultural programs. In all these cases, the school bridges the gap not only between teachers and parents, but also between its own institutional (dominant) culture and the traditions and experiences that make up community life, and, not unimportantly, the voices of the students who live in those communities and attend their public schools.

It bears repeating that a critical approach to literacy and the pedagogy of voice is not simply about empowering students. It also speaks to the empowerment of teachers as part of the wider project of social and political reconstruction. Stanley Aronowitz and I have argued that critical literacy is a precondition for engaging in progressive pedagogical work and social action.[38] As I pointed out in chapter 3, fundamental to this struggle is the need to redefine the nature of teachers' work and the role of teachers as transformative intellectuals. The category of intellectual is important here for analyzing both the particular ideological and material practices that structure the pedagogical relations in which teachers engage and for identifying the ideological nature of the interests that teachers produce and legitimate as part of the wider culture. The notion of intellectual provides a referent for criticizing those forms of management pedagogies, accountability schemes, and teacher-proof curricula that would define teachers merely as technicians. Moreover, it provides the theoretical and political basis for teachers to engage in a critical dialogue among themselves and others in order to fight for the conditions they need to reflect, read, share their work with others, and produce curriculum materials.

At the present time not only are teachers in the United States under attack by the New Right and the federal government, they also labor under conditions overwhelmingly replete with organizational constraints and ideological conditions that leave them little room for collective work and critical pursuits. Their teaching hours are too long; they are generally isolated in their classrooms; they are not given adequate time for planning; and they have few opportunities to work collectively with their peers. Moreover, they are prevented from exercising their own knowledge with respect to the selection, organization, and distribution of teaching materials. Furthermore, teachers often operate under working conditions that are both demeaning and oppressive. This is powerfully illustrated in a recent study of Boston area elementary school teachers by Sara Freedman, Jane Jackson, and Katherine Boles. They found that the rhetoric often associated with the public's view of schooling was decidedly at odds with the functions teachers were asked to perform in their jobs. For example, schools are entrusted to prepare children for adulthood, but the teachers themselves were treated as if they were incapable of making mature judgments; schools are given the responsibility to encourage a sense of autonomy and trust in students, but teachers in this study were constantly monitored within a network of administrative surveillance suggesting that they could neither be trusted nor work independently; schools are asked to create citizens capable of weighing the implications of their actions in a democratic society, yet these teachers performed this imperative within a network of work relations that was both rigidly hierarchical and sexist; even worse, they were asked to teach children how to take risks, weigh alternatives, and exercise independent judgment while being restricted to teaching practices that emphasized the rote, mechanical, and technical aspects of learning and evaluation.[39]

Teachers cannot assume the role of transformative intellectuals dedicated to a pedagogy of literacy and voice unless the proper ideological and material conditions exist to support such a role. Such a battle must be fought not only around the issue of what and how to teach, but also around the material conditions that enable and constrain pedagogical labor. This is both a theoretical and practical consideration that radical teachers have to address as part of a theory of critical literacy and voice. Moreover, it is a consideration that inextricably links school reform to wider forms of social, political, and economic transformation. The point being that radical school reform is generally temporary, short-lived, and incomplete unless it is seen as part of a struggle to reform the basic structures and ideology of the wider, dominant society. The political enormity of such a task is not meant to drive teachers to despair but to suggest that by fighting for conditions that support joint teaching, collective writing and research, and democratic planning teachers will be able to make the necessary inroads into opening new spaces for creative and reflective discourse and action. The importance of creating such a critical discourse and the conditions that support it cannot be overemphasized. For it is only within such a discourse and such practical conditions necessary to realize its interests that an emancipatory pedagogy can be developed, one that relates language and power, takes popular experiences seriously as part of the learning process, combats mystification, and helps students reorder the raw experience of their lives through the perspectives opened up by approaches to learning based on the critical literacy model proposed in this chapter.

Of course, before schools can be constructed in ways that can empower both teachers and students, educators need to understand the present ideological and political crisis surrounding the purpose of public schooling. As part of the existing political assault on public services and social justice in general, schools are increasingly being subordinated to the imperatives of neoconservative and right-wing interests that would make them adjuncts of the workplace or the church or convert them into pulpits for preaching and reproducing the cultural uniformity of the classical canon. In a democratic society, schools can never be reduced to company stores, training grounds for Christian fundamentalists, or institutional replacements for an ancient Greek museum. In this age in which democracy often seems in retreat, schools need to be recovered and fought for as democratic public spheres. More specifically, progressive educators must join with each other, parents, the wider community, and with members of progressive social movements to fight for the importance and practice of educational reform as part of the indispensable process of self-and social formation necessary to creating forms of public life essential to the development and maintenance of a radical democracy. This suggests not only a new agenda around which to develop public school reform but also an agenda for linking divergent progressive political groups. Literacy is indispensable to all aspects of critical theory and radical praxis and should provide the basis for injecting the pedagogical back into the meaning of politics. This means developing a view of literacy and voice that both demonstrates and affirms the importance of schooling as part of the struggle for expanding human possibilities within a discourse that asks new questions, reveals the importance of democratic solidarity, and advances the priority of a logic that dignifies radical democracy and social justice.

172

6

Teacher Education
and Democratic Schooling

As far back as 1890, a New England teacher named Horace Willard cogently argued that in contrast to members of other professions, teachers lived "lives of mechanical routine, and were subjected to a machine of supervision, organization, classification, grading, percentages, uniformity, promotions, tests, examination."[1] Nowhere, Willard decried, was there room in the school culture for "individuality, ideas, independence, originality, study, investigation."[2] Forty years later, Henry W. Holmes, dean of Harvard University's new Graduate School of Education, echoed these sentiments in his criticism of the National Survey of the Education of Teachers in 1930. According to Holmes, the survey failed to support teachers as independent critical thinkers. Instead, it endorsed a view of the teacher that George Counts termed a "routine worker under the expert direction of principals, supervisors, and superintendents."[3] Holmes was convinced that if teachers' work continued to be defined in such a narrow fashion, schools of education would eventually respond by limiting themselves to forms of training that virtually undermined the development of teachers as critically minded intellectuals.

At different times both of these noteworthy critics of American education recognized that any viable attempt at educational reform must address the issue of teacher education. Most important was their conviction that teachers should function professionally as intellectuals, and that teacher education should be inextricably linked to critically transforming the school setting and, by extension, the wider social setting.

In the early part of the twentieth century, a number of experimental teacher education programs managed to shift the terrain of struggle for democratic schooling from a largely rhetorical platform to the program site itself. One such program was organized around New College, an experimental teacher training venture affiliated with Teachers College at Columbia University between 1927 and 1953. Spokespersons from New College proclaimed "that a sound teacher education program must lie in a proper integration of rich scholarship, educational theory, and professional practice."[4] Furthermore, New College embarked on a training program based on the principle that "it is the peculiar privilege of the teacher to play a large part in the development of the social order of the next generation."[5] New College's first announcement claimed that if teachers were to escape from the usual "academic lock step ... [they] required contact with life in its various phases and understanding of it—an understanding of the intellectual, moral, social, and economic life of the people."[6]

The idea that teacher education programs should center their academic and moral objectives on the education of teachers as critical intellectuals, while advancing democratic interests, has invariably influenced the debates on the various "crises" in education over the last fifty years.[7] Moreover, it has been precisely because of the presence of such an idea that a rationale eventually could be constructed which linked schooling to the imperatives of democracy and classroom pedagogy to the dynamics of citizenship. This is not to suggest, however, that either public education or teacher training programs were overburdened by a concern for democracy and citizenship.[8] Nevertheless, as I have argued throughout this book, the historical precedent for educating teachers as intellectuals and making schools into democratic sites for social transformation might begin to define the way in which public education and the education of teachers could be appropriately perceived today. I wish, in other words, to build on this precedent in order to argue for the education of teachers as transformative intellectuals. As I have pointed out previously, the term "transformative intellectual" refers to one who exercises forms of intellectual and pedagogical practice that attempt to insert teaching and learning directly into the political sphere by arguing that schooling represents both a struggle for meaning and a struggle over power relations. I am also referring to one whose intellectual practices are necessarily grounded in forms of moral and ethical discourse exhibiting a preferential concern for the suffering and struggles of the disadvantaged and oppressed. Here I extend the traditional view of the intellectual as someone who is able to analyze various interests and contradictions within society to someone capable of articulating emancipatory possibilities and working toward their realization. Teachers who assume the role of transformative intellectuals treat students as critical agents, question how knowledge is produced and distributed, utilize dialogue, and make knowledge meaningful, critical, and ultimately emancipatory.[9]

I further develop in this chapter a theme that has permeated this book; that is, within the current discourse on educational reform[10] there exists, with few exceptions,[11] an ominous silence regarding the role that both teacher education and public schooling should play in advancing democratic practices, critical citizenship, and the role of the teacher as intellectual. Given the legacy of democracy and social reform bequeathed to us by our educational forebears, such as John Dewey and George Counts, not only does this silence suggest that some of the current reformers are suffering from political and historical amnesia; it also points to the ideological interests that underlie their proposals. Regrettably, such interests tell us less about the ills of schooling than they do about the nature of the real crisis facing this nation—a crisis which, in my view, not only augurs poorly for the future of American education, but underscores the need to reclaim a democratic tradition presently in retreat. Bluntly stated, much of the current literature on educational reform points to a crisis in American democracy itself.

The discourse of recent educational reform characteristically excludes certain proposals from consideration. For instance, missing from the various privileged discourses that have fashioned the recent reform movement, and absent from the practices of public school teachers whose participation in the current debate on education has been less than vigorous, are concerted attempts at democratizing schools and empowering students to become critical, active citizens. This reluctance of teachers has had a particularly deleterious effect, since the absence of proposals for rethinking the purpose of schools of education around democratic concerns has further strengthened the ideological and political pressures that define teachers as technicians and structure teachers' work in a demeaning and overburdening manner. Kenneth Zeichner underscores this concern when he writes:

> It is hoped that future debate in teacher education will be more concerned with the question of which educational, moral and political commitments ought to guide our work in the field rather than with the practice of merely dwelling on which procedures and organizational arrangements will most effectively help us realize tacit and often unexamined ends. Only after we have begun to resolve some of these necessarily prior questions related to ends should we concentrate on the resolution of more instrumental issues related to effectively accomplishing our goals.[12]

The current debate provides an opportunity to critically analyze the ideological and material conditions—both in and out of schools—that contribute to teachers' passivity and powerlessness. I also believe that recognition of the failure to link the purposes of public schooling to the imperatives of economic and social reform provides a starting point for examining the ideological shift in education that has taken place in the 1980s and for developing a new language of democracy, empowerment, and possibility in which teacher education programs and classroom practices can be defined. My central concern is to develop a view of teacher education that defines teachers as transformative intellectuals and schooling as part of an ongoing struggle for democracy. In developing my argument, I will focus on four considerations. First, I will analyze the dominant new conservative positions that have generated current educational reforms in terms of the implications these viewpoints hold for the reorganization of teacher education programs. Second, I will develop a rationale for organizing teacher education programs around a critical view of teachers' work and authority, one that I believe is consistent with the principles and practices of democracy. Third, I will present some programmatic suggestions for analyzing teacher education as a form of cultural politics. Finally, I will argue for a critical pedagogy that draws upon the many-sided conversations and voices that make up community life.

Education Reform and the Retreat From Democracy

Underlying the educational reforms proposed by the recent coalition of conservatives and liberals, conveniently labeled "the new conservatives," is a discourse that both edifies and mystifies their proposals. Capitalizing upon the waning confidence of the general public and a growing number of teachers in the effectiveness of public schools, the new conservatives argue for educational reform by faulting schools for a series of crises that include everything from a growing trade deficit to the breakdown of family morality.[13] The new conservatives have seized the initiative by framing their arguments in a terse rhetoric that resonates with a growing public concern about downward mobility in hard economic times, that appeals to a resurgence of chauvinistic patriotism, and that reformulates educational goals along elitist lines. Such a discourse is dangerous not only because it misconstrues the responsibility schools have for wider economic and social problems—a position that has been convincingly refuted and need not be argued against here[14]—but also because it reflects an alarming ideological shift regarding the role schools should play in society. The effect of this shift, launched by the New Right's full-fledged attack on the educational and social reforms of the 1960s, has been to redefine the purpose of education so as to eliminate its citizenship function in favor of a narrowly defined labor market perspective. The essence and implications of this position have been well documented by Barbara Finkelstein.

> Contemporary reformers seem to be recalling public education from its traditional utopian mission—to nurture a critical and committed citizenry that would stimulate the processes of political and cultural transformation and refine and extend the workings of political democracy. ... Reformers seem to imagine public schools as economic rather than political instrumentalities. They forge no new visions of political and social possibilities. Instead, they call public schools to industrial and cultural service exclusively. ... Reformers have disjoined their calls for educational reform from calls for a redistribution of power and authority, and the cultivation of cultural forms celebrating pluralism and diversity. As if they have had enough of political democracy, Americans, for the first time in a one hundred and fifty-year history, seem ready to do ideological surgery on their public schools—cutting them away from the fate of social justice andpolitical democracy completely and grafting them onto elite corporate, industrial, military, and cultural interests.[15]

It is important to recognize that the new conservative attack on the reforms of the last decade has resulted in a shift away from defining schools as agencies of equity and justice. There is little concern with how public education could better serve the interests of diverse groups of students by enabling them to understand and gain some control over the sociopolitical forces that influence their destinies. Rather, through this new discourse, and its preoccupation with accountability schemes, testing, accreditation, and credentializing, educational reform has become synonymous with turning schools into testing centers. It now defines school life primarily by measuring its utility against its contribution to economic growth and cultural uniformity. Similarly, at the heart of the present ideological shift is an attempt to reformulate the purpose of public education around a set of interests and social relations that define academic success almost exclusively in terms of the accumulation of capital and the logic of the marketplace. This represents a shift away from teacher control of the curriculum and toward a fundamentally technicist form of education that is more directly tied to economic modes of production. Moreover, the new conservatives provide a view of society in which authority derives from technical expertise and culture embodies an idealized tradition that glorifies hard work, industrial discipline, domesticated desire, and cheerful obedience. Edward Berman has deftly captured the political nature of this ideological shift.

> Architects of the current reform have, to their credit, dropped the rhetoric about the school as a vehicle for personal betterment. There is little pretense in today's reports of the resultant programs that individual improvement and social mobility are important concerns of a reconstituted school system. The former rhetoric about individual mobility has given way to exhortations to build educational structures that will allow individual students to make a greater contribution to the economic output of the corporate state. There are few rhetorical flourishes to obfuscate this overriding objective.[16]

The ideological shift that characterized the current reform period is also evident in the ways in which teacher preparation and classroom pedagogy are currently being defined. The rash of reform proposals for reorganizing schools points to a definition of teachers' work that seriously exacerbates conditions that are presently eroding the authority and intellectual integrity of teachers. In fact, the most compelling aspect of the influential reports, especially the widely publicized *A Nation at Risk, Action for Excellence,* and *A Nation Prepared: Teachers for the 21st Century,* is their studious refusal to address the ideological, social, and economic conditions underlying poor teacher and student performance.[17] For example, as Marilyn Frankenstein and Louis Kampf point out, public school teachers constantly confront conditions "such as the overwhelming emphasis on quantification (both in scoring children and keeping records), the growing lack of control over curriculum (separating conception from execution) and over other aspects of their work, the isolation from their peers, the condescending treatment by administrators, and the massive layoffs of veteran teachers."[18]

Instead of addressing these issues, many of the reforms taking place at the state level further consolidate administrative structures and prevent teachers from collectively and creatively shaping the conditions under which they work. For instance, at both the local and federal levels, the new educational discourse has influenced a number of policy recommendations, such as competency-based testing for teachers, a lockstep sequencing of materials, mastery learning techniques, systematized evaluation schemes, standardized curricula, and the implementation of mandated "basics."[19] The consequences are evident not only in the substantively narrow view of the purposes of education, but also in the definitions of teaching, learning, and literacy that are championed by the new management-oriented policymakers. In place of developing critical understanding, engaging student experience, and fostering active and critical citizenship, schools are redefined through a language and policies that emphasize standardization, competency, and narrowly defined performance skills.

Within this paradigm, the development of curricula is increasingly left to administrative experts or simply adopted from publishers, with few, if any, contributions from teachers who are expected to implement the new programs. In its most ideologically offensive form, this prepackaged curriculum is rationalized as teacher-proof and is designed to be applied to any classroom context regardless of the historical, cultural, and socioeconomic differences that characterize various schools and students.[20] What is important to note is that the deskilling of teachers appears to go hand in hand with the increasing adoption of management-type pedagogies.

Viewing teachers as semiskilled, low-paid workers in the mass production of education, policymakers have sought to change education, to improve it, by "teacher-proofing" it. Over the past decade we have seen the proliferation of elaborate accountability schemes that go by acronyms like MBO (management by objectives), PBBS (performance-based budgeting systems), CBE (competency-based education), CBTE (competency-based teacher education), and MCT (minimum competency testing).[21]

The growing removal of curriculum development and analysis from the hands of teachers is related to the ways technocratic rationality is used to redefine teachers' work. This type of rationality increasingly takes place within a social division of labor in which thinking is removed from implementation and the model of the teacher becomes that of the technician or white-collar clerk. Likewise, learning is reduced to the memorization of narrowly defined facts and isolated pieces of information that can easily be measured and evaluated. The significance of the overall effects of this type of rationalization and bureaucratic control on teachers' work and morale has been forcefully articulated by Linda Darling-Hammond. She writes:

In a Rand study of teachers' views of the effect of educational policies on their classroom practices, we learned from teachers that in response to policies that prescribe teaching practices and outcomes, they spend less time on untested subjects, such as science and social studies; they use less writing in their classrooms in order to gear assignments to the format of standardized tests; they resort to lectures rather than classroom discussions in order to cover the prescribed behavioral objectives without getting "off the track"; they are precluded from using teaching materials that are not on prescribed textbook lists, even when they think these materials are essential to meet the needs of some of their students; and they feel constrained from following up on expressed student interests that lie outside of the bounds of mandated curricula. . . . And 45 percent of the teachers in this study told us that the single thing that would make them leave teaching was the increased prescriptiveness of teaching content and methods — in short, the continuing deprofessionalization of teaching.[22]

As previously stated, the ideological interests that inform the new conservative proposals are based on a view of morality and politics that is legitimated through an appeal to national unity and tradition.

Within this discourse, democracy loses its dynamic character and is reduced to a set of inherited principles and institutional arrangements that teach students how to adapt rather than to question the basic precepts of society. What is left in the new reform proposals is a view of authority constructed around a mandate to follow and implement predetermined rules, to transmit an unquestioned cultural tradition, and to sanctify industrial discipline. Couple these problems with large classes, excessive paperwork, fragmented work periods, and low salaries, and it comes as no surprise that teachers are increasingly leaving the field.[23]

In effect, the ideological shift at work here points to a restricted definition of schooling, one that almost completely strips public education of a democratic vision where citizenship and the politics of possibility are given serious consideration. When I argue that the recent conservative or "blue-ribbon" reform recommendations lack a politics of possibility and citizenship, I mean that primacy is given to education as economic investment, that is, to pedagogical practices designed to create a school-business partnership and make the American economic system more competitive in world markets. Of course, there is a less influential but equally anti-utopian and pedestrian conservative approach to school reform that I analyzed in chapter 4. In this view, critical learning and citizenship are reduced to an elitist, Platonic notion of pedagogy in which the complexity of the knowledge/power relation is held hostage by a claim to the virtues of a reductionist notion of cultural literacy. In this case, culture and knowledge are treated statically as a warehouse of either great books or a list of information that need only be transmitted to willing and grateful students. A politics of possibility and citizenship, by contrast, refers to a conception of schooling in which classrooms are seen as active sites of public intervention and social struggle. Moreover, this view maintains that possibilities exist for teachers and students to redefine the nature of critical learning and practice outside the imperatives of the corporate marketplace. The idea of a politics and project of possibility is grounded in Ernst Bloch's idea of "natural law" wherein "the standpoint of the victims of any society ought to always provide the starting point for the critique of that society."[24] Such a politics defines schools as sites around which struggles should be waged in the name of developing a more just, humane, and equitable social order both within and outside schools.

181

I have spent some time reemphasizing the new conservative discourse and the ideological shift it represents because in my view the current reforms, with few exceptions, pose a grave threat to both public schooling and the nature of democracy itself. The definition to teaching and learning provided by this discourse ignores, as I have pointed out, the imperative of viewing schools as sites of social transformation where students are educated to become informed, active, and critical citizens. The gravity of this ideological shift is hardly ameliorated by the fact that even public schooling's more liberal spokespersons have failed to develop a critical discourse that challenges the hegemony of dominant ideologies. For example, the highly publicized reports by John Goodlad, Theodore Sizer, Ernest Boyer, and others neither acknowledge nor utilize the radical tradition of educational scholarship.[25] Although the liberal position does take the concepts of "equality of opportunity" and "citizenship" seriously, we are, nevertheless, left with analyses of schooling that lack a sufficiently critical understanding of the ways in which power has been used to favor select groups of students over others. In addition, we are given only a cursory treatment of the political economy of schooling, with its scattered history of dishonorable linkages to corporate interests and ideology. Furthermore, we are provided with little understanding of how the hidden curriculum in schools works in a subtly discriminating way to discredit the dreams, experiences, and knowledges associated with students from specific class, racial, and gender groupings.[26]

In the absence of any competing critical agenda for reform, the new conservative discourse encourages institutions for teacher education to define themselves primarily as training sites that provide students with the technical expertise required to find a place within the corporate hierarchy. Thomas Popkewitz and Allan Pitman have characterized the ideology underlying the current reform proposals, moreover, as betraying a fundamental elitism since it basically adopts a perspective of society that is undifferentiated by class, race, or gender. The logic endemic to these reports, the authors argue, demonstrates an attachment to possessive individualism and instrumental rationality. In other words: "Quantity is seen as quality. Procedural concerns are made objects of value and moral domains. The teacher is a facilitator ... or a counselor.... Individualization is pacing through a common curriculum.... Flexibility in instruction is to begin 'where the student is ready to begin.'. . . There is no discussion of what is to be facilitated or the conceptions of curriculum to guide procedures."[27]

Furthermore, Popkewitz and Pitman see a distinctive shift from a concern with equity to a slavish regard for a restricted notion of excellence. That is, the concept of excellence that informs these new reports "ignores the social differentiations while providing political symbols to give credibility to education which only a few can appreciate."[28] What is rightly being stressed is that the concept of excellence fashioned in the reports is designed to benefit "those who have already access to positions of status and privilege through accidents of birth."[29]

Given the context in which teaching and learning are currently being defined, it becomes all the more necessary to insist on an alternative view of teacher education, one which, in refusing to passively serve the existing ideological and institutional arrangements of the public schools, is aimed at challenging and reforming them.

Teacher Education: Democracy and the Imperative of Social Reform

I want to return to the idea that the fundamental concerns of democracy and critical citizenship should be central to any discussion of the purpose of teacher education. In doing so, I will organize my discussion around an initial effort to develop a critical language with which to reconstruct the relationship between teacher education programs and the public schools, on the one hand, and public education and society, on the other.

If teacher education programs are to provide the basis for democratic struggle and renewal in our schools, they will have to redefine their current relationship to such institutions. As it presently stands, schools of education rarely encourage their students to take seriously the imperatives of social critique and social change as part of a wider emancipatory vision. If and when education students begin to grapple with these concerns at the classroom level, it is invariably years after graduation. My own experience in teacher education institutions—both as a student and as an instructor—has confirmed for me what is generally agreed to be commonplace in most schools and colleges of education throughout the United States: that these institutions continue to define themselves essentially as service institutions which are generally mandated to provide the requisite technical expertise to carry out whatever pedagogical functions are deemed necessary by the various school communities in which students undertake their practicum experiences.[30] In order to escape this political posture, teacher education programs need to reorient their focus to the critical transformation of public schools rather than to the simple reproduction of existing institutions and ideologies.[31]

One starting point would be to recognize the importance of educating students in the languages of critique and possibility; that is, providing teachers with the critical terminology and conceptual apparatus that will allow them not only to critically analyze the democratic and political shortcomings of schools, but also to develop the knowledge and skills that will advance the possibilities for generating curricula, classroom social practices, and organizational arrangements based on and cultivating a deep respect for a democratic and ethically based community. In effect, this means that the relationship of teacher education programs to public schooling would be self-consciously guided by political and moral considerations. Dewey expressed well the need for educators to make political and moral considerations a central aspect of their education and work when he distinguished between "education as a function of society" and "society as a function of education."[32] In simple terms, Dewey's distinction reminds us that education can function either to create passive, risk-free citizens or to create a politicized citizenry educated to fight for various forms of public life informed by a concern for justice, happiness, and equality. At issue here is whether schools of education are to serve and reproduce the existing society or to adopt the more critical role of challenging the social order so as to develop and advance its democratic imperatives. Also at issue is developing a rationale for defining teacher education programs in political terms that make explicit a particular view of the relationship between public schools and the social order, a view based on defending the imperatives of a democratic society.

Public Schools as Democratic Public Spheres

My second concern is directed to the broader question of how educators should view the purpose of public schooling. My position echoes Dewey's in that I believe public schools need to be defined as democratic public spheres. This means regarding schools as democratic sites dedicated to self-and social empowerment. Understood in these terms, schools can be public places where students learn the knowledge and skills necessary to create in a critical democracy. Contrary to the view that schools are extensions of the workplace or frontline institutions in the corporate battle for international markets, schools viewed as democratic public spheres center their activities on critical inquiry and meaningful dialogue. In this case, students are given the opportunity to learn the discourse of public association and civic responsibility. Such a discourse seeks to recapture the idea of a critical democracy that commands respect for individual freedom and social justice. Moreover, viewing schools as democratic public spheres provides a rationale for defending them, along with progressive forms of pedagogy and teachers' work, as agencies of social reform. When defined in these terms, schools can be defended as institutions that provide the knowledge, skills, social relations, and vision necessary to educate a citizenry capable of building a critical democracy. That is, school practice can be rationalized in a political language that recovers and emphasizes the transformative role that schools can play in advancing the democratic possibilities inherent in the existing society.[33]

Rethinking the Nature of Teacher Education

I would like to bring the foregoing discussion to bear on the more practical mission of reconstructing teacher education programs around a new vision of democratic schooling and teaching for critical citizenship. Consequently, I will devote the remainder of my discussion to outlining, in detailed and programmatic terms, what I believe are some essential components and categories for a teacher education curriculum and a critical pedagogy for the schools. But before discussing this issue, I want to argue against some of the more recent calls for the abolition of schools of education. I maintain that many schools of education as they are currently organized need to be drastically reformed; the issue for me is reform not abolition. The proposal to retain schools of education rests on a number of considerations. The nature of public schooling demands that prospective teachers be introduced to a notion of theory and practice that is forged outside the disciplinary boundaries that primarily characterize undergraduate liberal arts programs. In other words, the education of teachers cannot be reduced to forms of learning in which students are required merely to master the cognate disciplines. The nature of public schooling requires that students know more than the subject matter they will be teaching. They also need a fundamental understanding of issues specific to the economic, political, and cultural nature of schooling itself. That is, they need to learn an interdisciplinary language that focuses on the history, sociology, philosophy, political economy, and political science of schooling. Students need to be able to theorize in a language that includes but goes far beyond the limits of traditional disciplines; they need to understand the sociology of school cultures, the meaning of the hidden curriculum, a politics of knowledge and power, a philosophy of school/state relations, and a sociology of teaching. They also need to develop approaches to research, methods of inquiry, and theory that are directly tied to the problems and possibilities of schooling. It is also important to stress that if the education of teachers is left to liberal arts programs, the wedge between the university and schools will widen. Liberal arts programs take as their first concern a view of learning organized around the disciplines; they do not focus on public school problems; they contain no mechanisms for developing school-community relations; and they have no reason to reform the theory and practice relation so as to allow teachers to work as reflective researchers in collaboration with university teachers and students. These concerns can only be taught within a school of education, one that embraces the notion of educating teachers as transformative intellectuals around the demands of a critical pedagogy and a cultural politics. To abolish schools of education is to undermine the possibility of developing them as centers for democratic learning and as public spheres that can work organically with the communities in which they are located.

Of course, most teacher education programs have been, and continue to be, entirely removed from a vision and a set of practices dedicated to the fostering of critical democracy and social justice. A repeated criticism made by educators working within the radical tradition has been that, as it currently exists, teacher education rarely addresses either the moral implications of societal inequalities within our present form of industrial capitalism or the ways in which schools function to reproduce and legitimate these inequalities.[34]

When classroom life is discussed in teacher education programs, it is usually presented as a fundamentally one-dimensional set of rules and regulative practices, rather than as a cultural terrain where a variety of interests and practices collide in a constant and often chaotic struggle for dominance. Thus, prospective teachers frequently receive the impression that classroom culture is essentially free from ambiguity and contradiction. According to this view, schools are supposedly devoid of all vestiges of contestation, struggle, and cultural politics.[35] Furthermore, classroom reality is rarely presented as if it were socially constructed, historically determined, and reproduced through institutionalized relationships of class, gender, race, and power. Unfortunately, this dominant conception of schooling vastly contradicts what the student teacher often experiences during his or her practicum of fieldsite work, especially if the student is placed in a school largely populated by economically disadvantaged and disenfranchised students. Yet student teachers are nevertheless instructed to view schooling as a neutral terrain devoid of power and politics. It is against this transparent depiction of schooling that prospective teachers, more often than not, view their own ideologies and experiences through a dominant theoretical and cultural perspective that remains largely unquestioned. Most important, teachers in this situation have no grounds upon which to question the dominant cultural assumptions that shape and structure the ways in which they respond to and influence student behavior.

Consequently, many student teachers who find themselves teaching working-class or minority students lack a well-articulated framework for understanding the class, cultural, ideological, and gender dimensions that inform classroom life. As a result, cultural differences among students often are viewed uncritically as deficiencies rather than as strengths, and what passes for teaching is in actuality an assault on the specific histories, experiences, and knowledges that such students use both to define their own identities and to make sense of their larger world. I use the term "assault" not because such knowledge is openly attacked—but because it is devalued through a process that is at once subtle and debilitating. What happens is that within the dominant school culture, subordinate knowledge is generally ignored, marginalized, or treated in a disorganized fashion. Such knowledge is often treated as if it did not exist, or treated in ways that disconfirm it. Conversely, ideologies that do not aid subordinate groups in interpreting the reality they actually experience often pass for objective forms of knowledge. In this process prospective teachers lose an understanding of the relationship between culture and power as well as a sense of how to develop pedagogical possibilities for their students from the cultural differences that often characterize school and classroom life. In the next section, I discuss the elements that, in my view, should constitute a new model of teacher education, one that addresses the above issue more specifically.

Teacher Education as Cultural Politics

My concern here is with reconstituting the grounds upon which teacher education programs are built. This means implementing an alternative form of teacher education that conceptualizes schooling as taking place within a political and cultural arena where forms of student experience and subjectivity are actively produced and mediated. In other words, I wish to state once again the idea that schools do not merely teach academic subjects, but also, in part, produce student subjectivities or particular sets of experiences that are in themselves part of an ideological process. Conceptualizing schooling as the construction and transmission of subjectivities permits us to understand more clearly the idea that the curriculum is more than just an introduction of students to particular subject disciplines and teaching methodologies; it also serves as an introduction to a particular way of life.[36]

Here, I must forego a detailed specification of teaching practices and instead attempt to briefly sketch out particular areas of study crucial to the development of a reconceptualized teacher education curriculum. I assign the term "cultural politics" to my curriculum agenda because I believe that this term permits me to capture the significance of the sociocultural dimension of the schooling process. Furthermore, the term allows me to highlight the political consequences of interaction between teachers and students who come from dominant and subordinate cultures. A teacher education curriculum as a form of cultural politics assumes that the social, cultural, political, and economic dimensions are the primary categories for understanding contemporary schooling.[37] Within this context, school life is conceptualized not as a unitary, monolithic, and iron-clad system of rules and regulations, but as a cultural terrain characterized by varying degrees of accommodation, contestation, and resistance. Furthermore, school life is understood as a plurality of conflicting languages and struggles, a place where classroom and street-corner cultures collide and where teachers, students, and school administrators often differ as to how school experiences and practices are to be defined and understood.

The imperative of this curriculum is to create conditions for student self-empowerment and self-constitution as an active political and moral subject. By "empowerment" I mean the process whereby students acquire the means to critically appropriate knowledge existing outside their immediate experience in order to broaden their understanding of themselves, the world, and the possibilities for transforming the taken-for-granted assumptions about the way we live. Stanley Aronowitz has described one aspect of empowerment as "the process of appreciating and loving oneself."[38] In this sense, empowerment is gained from knowledge and social relations that dignify one's own history, language, and cultural traditions. But empowerment means more than self-confirmation. It also refers to the process by which students are able to interrogate and selectively appropriate those aspects of the dominant culture that will provide them with the basis for defining and transforming, rather than merely serving, the wider social order.

The project of "doing" a teacher education curriculum based on cultural politics consists of linking critical social theory to a set of stipulated practices through which student teachers are able to dismantle and critically examine preferred educational and cultural traditions, many of which have fallen prey to an instrumental rationality that either limits or ignores democratic ideals and principles. One of my main concerns focuses on developing a language of critique and demystification that is capable of analyzing the latent interests and ideologies that work to socialize students in a manner compatible with the dominant culture. I am equally concerned, however, with creating alternative teaching practices capable of helping to empower students both inside and outside schools. Although it is impossible to provide a detailed outline of the courses of a curriculum for cultural politics, I want to comment on some important areas of analysis that are central to such a program. These include the critical study of power, language, history, and culture.

Power

A pivotal concern of a teacher education curriculum that subscribes to a cultural politics approach is to assist student teachers in understanding the relationship between power and knowledge. Within the dominant curriculum, knowledge is often removed from the issue of power and is generally treated in a technical manner; that is, it is seen in instrumental terms as something to be mastered. That such knowledge is always an ideological construction linked to particular interests and social relations generally receives little consideration in teacher education programs. An understanding of the knowledge/power relationship raises important issues regarding what kinds of knowledge educators can provide to empower students to understand and engage the world around them as well as to exercise the kind of courage needed to change the social order where necessary. Of considerable concern, then, is the need for student teachers to recognize that power relations correspond to forms of school knowledge that both distort the truth and produce it. That is, knowledge should be examined both for the way in which it might misrepresent or mediate social reality and for the way in which it actually reflects peoples' experiences and, as such, influences their lives. Understood in this way, knowledge not only reproduces reality by distorting or illuminating the social world, but also has the more concrete function of shaping the day-to-day lives of people through their felt, relatively unmediated world of commonsense assumptions. This suggests that a curriculum for democratic empowerment must examine the conditions of school knowledge in terms of how it is produced and what particular interests it might represent; in addition, it should scrutinize the effects of such knowledge at the level of everyday life. In short, prospective teachers need to understand that knowledge does more than distort; it also produces particular forms of life. Finally, knowledge contains hopes, desires, and needs that resonate positively with the subjective experience of a particular

audience, and such knowledge needs to be analyzed to find the utopian promises often implicit in its claims.[39]

Language

In traditional approaches to reading, writing, and second-language
learning, language issues are primarily defined by technical and
developmental concerns. Although such concerns are indeed important, what is often ignored in mainstream language courses in
teacher education programs is how language is actively implicated in
power relations that generally support the dominant culture. An
alternative starting point to the study of language recognizes the significance of Antonio Gramsci's notion that every language contains
elements of a conception of the world. It is through language that we
come to consciousness and negotiate a sense of identity, since language does not merely reflect reality but plays an active role in constructing it. As language constructs meaning, it shapes our world,
informs our identities, and provides the cultural codes for perceiving
and classifying the world. This implies, of course, that within the
available discourses of the school or the society, language plays a
powerful role because it serves to "mark the boundaries of permis-
sible discourse, discourage the clarification of social alternatives, and
makes it difficult for the dispossessed to locate the source of their
unease, let alone remedy it."[40] Through the study of language within
the perspective of a cultural politics, prospective teachers can gain an
understanding of how language functions to "position" people in the
world, to shape the range of possible meanings surrounding an
issue, and to actively construct reality rather than merely reflect it. As
part of language studies, student teachers would become more
knowledgeable about and sensitive to the omnipresence and power
of language as constitutive of their own experiences and those of
their potential students.[41] Student teachers would also benefit from
an introductory understanding of European traditions of discourse
theory and the textual strategies that characterize their methods of
inquiry.[42] Furthermore, through an exposure to the semiotics of
mass and popular cultures, students could at least learn the rudimen-
tary methods of examining the various codes and meanings that are
constitutive of both their own personal constructions of self and soci-

ety and those of the students they work with during their practicum or on-site sessions.[43]

History

The study of history should play a more expansive role in teacher education programs.[44] A critical approach to history would attempt to provide student teachers with an understanding of how cultural traditions are formed; it would also be designed to bring to light the various ways in which curricula and discipline-based texts have been constructed and read throughout different historical periods. Furthermore, such an approach would be self-consciously critical of the problems surrounding the teaching of history as a school subject, since what is conventionally taught overwhelmingly reflects the perspectives and values of white, middle-class males. Too often excluded are the histories of women, minority groups, and indigenous peoples. This exclusion is not politically innocent when we consider how existing social arrangements are partly constitutive of and dependent on the subjugation and elimination of the histories and voices of those groups marginalized and disempowered by the dominant culture. In addition, the concept of history can also help illuminate what kinds of knowledge are deemed legitimate and promulgated through the school curriculum. Conventional emphasis on chronological history "which traditionally saw its object as somehow unalterably 'there,' given, waiting only to be discovered,"[45] would be supplanted by a focus on how specific educational practices can be understood as historical constructions related to the economic, social, and political events of a particular time and place. It is primarily through this form of historical analysis that students can recover what I referred to in chapter 3 as "subjugated knowledges."[46] My use of this term directs us to those aspects of history in which criticism and struggle have played a significant role in defining the nature and meaning of educational theory and practice. For example, students will have the opportunity to examine critically the historical contexts and interests at work in defining what forms of school knowledge become privileged over others, how specific forms of school authority are sustained, and how particular patterns of learning become institutionalized.

Within the format of a curriculum as a form of cultural politics, it is also necessary that the study of history be theoretically connected to both language and reading. In this context, language can be subsequently studied as "the bearer of history" and history can be analyzed as a social construction open to critical examination. The important linkage between reading and history can be made by emphasizing that "reading occurs within history and that the point of integration is always the reader."[47] In analyzing this relationship, teachers can focus on the cultural meanings that students use to understand a text. Such a focus will better equip student teachers to understand how the process of reading occurs within a particular student's cultural history and in the context of his or her own concerns and beliefs. This will also assist student teachers to become more critically aware of how students from subordinate cultures bring their own sets of experiences, as well as their own dreams, desires, and voices to the reading act. In other words, student teachers must develop a critical theory of learning that includes an analysis of how students produce rather than just receive knowledge. This entails understanding how students bring their own categories of meaning into play in the exchange between school knowledge and their own subjectivities and histories.

Culture

The concept of culture, varied though it may be, is essential to any teacher education curriculum aspiring to be critical. I am using the term "culture" here to signify the particular ways in which a social group lives out and makes sense of its "given" circumstances and conditions of life.[48] In addition to defining "culture" as a set of practices and ideologies from which different groups draw to make sense of the world, I want to refashion the ways in which cultural questions become the starting point for understanding the issue of who has power and how it is reproduced and manifested in the social relations that link schooling to the wider social order. The link between culture and power has been extensively analyzed in critical social theory over the past ten years. It is therefore possible to offer four insights from that literature that are particularly relevant for illuminating the political logic that underlies various cultural/power relations. First, the concept of culture has been intimately connected with the question of how *social relations are structured* within class, gender, and age formations that produce forms of oppression and dependency. Second, culture has been analyzed within the radical perspective not simply as a way of life, but as a *form of production* through which different groups in either their dominant or subordinate social relations define and realize their aspirations through asymmetrical relations of power. Third, culture has been viewed as a *field of struggle* in which the production, legitimation, and circulation of particular forms of knowledge and experience are central areas of conflict. Fourth, the production of culture has been analyzed primarily through analysis of language as the constitutive and expressive signifier of meaning. What is important here is that each of these insights raises fundamental questions about the ways in which inequalities are maintained and challenged in the sphere of culture.

The study of cultures—or, more specifically, what has come to be known as "cultural studies"—should become the touchstone of a teacher education curriculum. Because it can provide student teachers with the critical categories necessary for examining school and classroom relations as social and political practices inextricably related to the construction and maintenance of specific relations of power. Moreover, by recognizing that school life is often mediated through the clash of dominant and subordinate cultures, prospective teachers can gain some insight into the ways in which classroom experiences are necessarily intertwined with their students' home life and street-corner culture. This point is meant to be more than a rallying cry for relevance; rather, it asserts the need for prospective teachers to understand the systems of meaning that students employ in their encounters with forms of dominant school knowledge and social relations. It is important, therefore, that student teachers learn to analyze expressions of mass and popular culture, such as music videos, television, and film. In this way, a successful cultural studies approach would provide an important theoretical avenue for teachers to comprehend how ideologies become inscribed through representations of everyday life.

More specifically, a cultural studies program can be organized around a variety of core courses in which the issues of power, history, language, and culture can be approached in an interdisciplinary context. Cultural studies would provide a more interdisciplinary foundation in order to analyze the limits of the traditional disciplines in addressing educational problems as well as to reconstruct relationships among faculty and students. The potential a cultural studies program has for reshaping relationships among faculty as well as between faculty and students is enormous. Generally, schools of education are divided into a number of departments that have few programmatic links to each other. Programs are usually organized around areas such as educational psychology, educational administration, foundations of education, curriculum and instruction, and guidance and counseling and often function in an insular fashion with little or no opportunities for faculty or students from these different programs to work together.

A cultural studies program would offer a number of mandatory courses to be taken by students in the various departments. Such courses would work in conjunction with disciplinary specialists in order to provide students with a language and a method of inquiry that allows them to understand both the limits and the strengths of the disciplinary matrix. In addition, the program would utilize faculty from the different departments to teach interdisciplinary courses and to engage in collaborative research. For example, courses offered could be developed around themes like language and power in educational administration, reading educational psychology as historical texts, analyzing diverse curricula languages as a form of cultural production, analyzing pedagogy as an ethical discourse, and so on. Such a program could also be used to engage faculty and students in shared research projects that could not ordinarily take place within mainstream disciplines and methods of inquiry.

A cultural studies program could also become a site for initiating new relations between public schools and the community at large. For example, productive relations could be developed between public school teachers and the faculty and students of the cultural studies program around some of the concrete problems facing public schools. This could be particularly productive around race, gender, ethnic, language, and class considerations as they present themselves in various aspects of the schooling process. Similarly, teachers and staff members could participate in study groups and seminars designed to further the groups' collective knowledge and possibilities for working together around common problems. A cultural studies program could also provide the basis for establishing organic links with surrounding communities. The histories, resources, public services, and voices of the community could be researched and brought together through the cultural studies program in order to develop curriculum projects, elements of a critical pedagogy, and policy initiatives. Such projects developed in relation with community groups could serve as an ongoing vehicle for mutual dialogue, learning, and collective action. Although these suggestions are general and schematic, they do provide a glimpse of the theoretical and practical possibilities that could be developed in rethinking the nature of a teacher education program in which cultural studies is viewed as one of its major programmatic concerns.

Toward a Critical Pedagogy for the Classroom

In the previous sections I highlighted the importance of viewing schools as social and political sites involved in the struggle for democracy. In addition, I reconsidered the relationship between authority and teachers' work and attempted to develop the theoretical rudiments of a program in which teacher education would be viewed as a form of cultural politics. In this final section, I shift the focus from questions of institutional purpose and teacher definition to the issues of critical pedagogy and student learning. In so doing, I restate some of the fundamental theoretical elements I have pointed to in previous chapters that I believe can be used to construct a critical pedagogy in which the issue of student interests or motivation is linked to the dynamics of self-and social empowerment. I wish to underscore here that the public schools shape and reinforce the attitudes that prospective teachers bring to their clinical experiences. By focusing on some of the theoretical elements that constitute a critical pedagogy, I attempt to clarify the link between our notion of a teacher education curriculum as a form of cultural politics and the actual dynamics of classroom pedagogy. With this in mind, I will now sketch out the rudiments of a critical discourse that defines classroom pedagogy within the parameters of a political project centering on the primacy of student experience, the concept of voice, and the importance of transforming schools and communities into democratic public spheres.

The Primacy of Student Experience

The type of critical pedagogy I am proposing is fundamentally concerned with student experience insofar as it takes the problems and needs of the students themselves as its starting point. As a historical construction and lived practice that is produced and legitimated within particular social forms, student experience becomes an object of inquiry rather than an unproblematic given. As part of a pedagogy of possibility, student experience provides the basis for analyzing the social forms that reconstruct the subjective character of the stories, memories, and meanings that are in place when students come to schools. A critical pedagogy in this instance encourages a critique of dominant forms of knowledge and social practices that semantically and emotionally organize meanings and experiences that give students a sense of voice and identity; similarly, it attempts to provide students with the critical knowledge and skills necessary for them to examine their own particular lived experiences and cultural resources. As I have mentioned previously, this means assisting students to draw on their own voices and histories as a basis for engaging and interrogating the multiple and often contradictory experiences that provide them with a sense of identity, worth, and presence. In this form of pedagogy, knowledge is being made for these students inside their language and histories and not outside history. The historicity of knowledge and experience provides the basis for helping students to develop a respect for their own experiences so they can be legitimate and reclaim their own language and histories. The important pedagogical principle at work here is to validate students' experience in order to empower them and not merely to please them.

Student experience must be given preeminence in an emancipatory curriculum. But learning how to understand, affirm, and analyze such experience means not only understanding the cultural and social forms through which students learn how to define themselves, but also learning how to engage student experience in a way that neither unqualifiedly endorses nor delegitimates it. In part, this suggests that teachers learn how to create an affirmative and critical continuity between how students view the world and those forms of analyses that provide the basis for both analyzing and enriching such perspectives. To do so is to acknowledge, as I have argued throughout this book, that at the heart of any critical pedagogy is the necessity for teachers to work with the knowledges that students actually have. Although this may seem risky and in some cases dangerous, it provides the basis for validating the way in which students read the world as well as for giving them the intellectual content for putting knowledge and meaning into their own categories of meaning and cultural capital. This suggests that school knowledge as produced and modified through the voice of the teacher has to be made meaningful to students before it can be made critical. School knowledge never speaks for itself; rather, it is constantly filtered through the ideological and cultural experiences that students bring to the classroom. To ignore the ideological dimensions of student experience is to deny the ground on which students learn, speak, and imagine.

The important pedagogical implications for student teachers is that they should be educated to understand how student experience produced in the various domains and layers of everyday life gives rise to the often contradictory *and* different voices students employ to give meaning to their own existence in relation to both the communities in which they live and the wider society. What should be recognized is that in the multiple experience, meanings, and voices that students inhabit there are tensions and contradictory beliefs that need to be analyzed regarding the interests and values they celebrate and legitimate. It is crucial, therefore, that educators address the question of how aspects of the social world are experienced, mediated, and produced by students in often contradictory ways and how the forms of meaning that arise out of these contradictions collectively disable or enable the possibilities open to students within the existing society. Failure to do so not only will prevent teachers from tapping into the drives, emotions, and interests that give students their own unique voice, but also will make it equally difficult to provide the momentum for learning itself.

While the concept of student experience is being offered as central to a critical pedagogy, it should also be recognized as a central category of teacher education programs. This suggests that student practicums should be seen as sites where the question of how experience is produced, legitimated, and accomplished becomes an object of study for teachers and students alike. Unfortunately, most student practicums are viewed as either a rite of passage into the profession or merely a formal culminating experience in the teacher education program.

Student Voice and the Public Sphere

The concept of voice, as I indicated in chapters 4 and 5, constitutes the focal point for a theory of teaching and learning that generates new forms of sociality as well as new and challenging ways of confronting and engaging everyday life. Voice, quite simply, refers to the various measures by which students and teachers actively participate in dialogue. It is related to the discursive means whereby teachers and students attempt to make themselves "heard" and to define themselves as active authors of their worlds. Displaying a voice means, to cite Mikhail Bakhtin, "retelling a story in one's own words."[49] More specifically, the term "voice" refers to the principles of dialogue as they are enunciated and enacted within particular social settings. The concept of voice represents the unique instances of self-expression through which students affirm their own class, cultural, racial, and gender identities. A student's voice is necessarily shaped by personal history and distinctive lived engagement with the surrounding culture. The category of voice, then, refers to the means at our disposal—the discourses available to use—to make ourselves understood and listened to, and to define ourselves as active participants in the world. However, as I have stressed previously, the dominant school culture generally represents and legitimates the voices of white males from the middle and upper classes to the exclusion of economically disadvantaged students, most especially females from minority backgrounds.[50] A critical pedagogy takes into account the various ways in which the voices that teachers use to communicate with students can either silence or legitimate them.

The concept of voice is crucial to the development of a critical classroom pedagogy because it provides an important basis for constructing and demonstrating the fundamental imperatives of a critical democracy. Such a pedagogy attempts to organize classroom relationships so that students can draw on and confirm those dimensions of their own histories and experiences that are deeply rooted in the surrounding community. In addition, by creating active links with the community, teachers can open up their classrooms to its diverse resources and traditions. This presupposes that teachers familiarize themselves with the culture, economy, and historical traditions that belong to the communities in which they teach. In other words, teachers must assume a pedagogical responsibility for attempting to understand the relationships and forces that influence their students outside the immediate context of the classroom. This responsibility requires teachers to develop their curricula and pedagogical practices around those community traditions, histories, and forms of knowledge that are often ignored within the dominant school culture. This can, of course, lead to a deeper understanding by both teachers and students of how both "local" and "official" knowledges get produced, sustained, and legitimated.

Teachers need to develop pedagogical practices that link student experiences with those aspects of community life that inform and sustain such experiences. For example, student teachers could compile oral histories of the communities in which they teach, which could then be used as a school and curricula resource—particularly in reading programs. In addition, they could work in and analyze how different community social agencies function so as to produce, distribute, and legitimate particular forms of knowledge and social relations. This would broaden their notions of pedagogical practices and help them understand the relevance of their own work for institutions other than schools. Similarly, prospective teachers could develop organic links with active community agencies such as business, religious organizations, and other public spheres in an attempt to develop a more meaningful connection between the school curriculum and the experiences that define and characterize the local community. The concept of voice can thus provide a basic organizing principle for the development of a relationship between knowledge and student experiences and, at the same time, create a forum for examining broader school and community issues. In other words, teachers must become aware of both the transformative strengths and structures of oppression of the community-at-large and develop this awareness into curriculum strategies designed to empower students toward creating a more liberating and humane society. In short, teachers should be attentive to what it means to construct forms of learning in their classrooms that enable students to affirm their voices within areas of community life, that is, within democratic public spheres needing constant criticism, safeguarding, and renewal.

Steve Tozer has written on this issue:

> The process of fitting students for community life, then, is an effort

to prepare students both for the existing community and to bring them to understand and to appreciate the historical values and ideas which point to a more ideal community than the one that exists . . . the teacher's duty is to recognize the historical ideals which make community life worth living, ideals upon which the larger society is founded: ideals of human dignity and equality, freedom, and mutual concern of one person for another. . . . This is not to say that teachers should prepare students for some nonexistent utopia. Rather, teachers must develop an understanding of the community as it exists and an understanding of what kind of people will be required to make it better. They can try to develop for themselves an ideal of the community their students should strive for, and they should help their students with the knowledge, the values and the skills they will need if they are to be resilient enough to maintain high standards of belief and conduct in an imperfect society.[51]

It is an unfortunate truism that when communities are ignored by teachers, students often find themselves trapped in institutions that not only deny them a voice, but also deprive them of a relational or contextual understanding of how the knowledge they acquire in the classroom can be used to influence and transform the public sphere. Implicit in the concept of linking classroom experiences to the wider community is the idea that the school is best understood as a polity, as a locus of citizenship. Within this locus, students and teachers can engage in a process of deliberation and discussion aimed at advancing the public welfare in accordance with fundamental moral judgments and principles. To bring schools closer to the concept of polity, it is necessary to define them as public spaces that seek to recapture the idea of critical democracy and community. In effect, I want to define teachers as active community participants whose function is to establish public spaces where students can debate, appropriate, and learn the knowledge and skills necessary to live in a critical democracy.

By "public space" I mean, as Hannah Arendt did, a concrete set of learning conditions where people come together to speak, to engage in dialogue, to share their stories, and to struggle together within social relations that strengthen rather than weaken possibilities for active citizenship.[52] School and classroom practices should in some manner be organized around forms of learning that serve to prepare students for responsible roles as transformative intellectuals, as community members, and as critically active citizens outside schools.[53]

I began this chapter by arguing that teacher education should be seriously rethought along the lines of the critical democratic tradition, a tradition which, regrettably, has been all but excluded from the current debates on American schooling. I have argued that this tradition provides the basis for rethinking the relationship of schooling to the social order and for restructuring the education of prospective teachers so as to prepare them for the role of transformative intellectual. Moreover, I have argued that teacher education programs must assume a central role in reforming public education and, in so doing, must assert the primacy of a democratic tradition in order to restructure school-community relations.

In my view, the search for a creative democracy undertaken at the beginning of the century by Dewey and others is presently in retreat, having been abandoned by liberals and radicals alike. This situation presents a dual challenge to critical educators: there is now an urgent need not only to resurrect the tradition of liberal democracy, but to develop a theoretical perspective that goes beyond it. In the current age of conservatism, public education must analyze its strengths and weaknesses against an ideal of critical democracy rather than the current corporate referent of the capitalist marketplace. Similarly, public education must fulfill the task of educating citizens to take risks, to struggle for institutional and social change, and to fight for democracy and against oppression both inside and outside schools. Pedagogical empowerment necessarily goes hand in hand with social and political transformation.

My position is indebted to Dewey but attempts to extend his democratic project. My position accentuates the idea that schools represent only one important site in the struggle for democracy. But it is different from Dewey's view because it perceives the self-and social empowerment of students as involving not just the politics of classroom culture, but also political and social struggle that occurs outside school sites. Such an approach acknowledges that critical pedagogy is but one intervention—albeit a crucial one—in the struggle to restructure the ideological and material conditions of everyday life. I am convinced that teacher education institutions and public schools can and should play an active and productive role in broadening the possibilities for the democratic promise of American schooling, politics, and society.

7
Conclusion
Beyond the Politics of
Anti-Utopianism in Education

During the time between the end of the First World War and the rise of the culture industry in the industrialized West in the 1940s and 1950s, a number of Marxist thinkers struggled to keep alive a redemptive and radically utopian spirit as a basis for linking radical thought and action. One such thinker, George Lukács, analyzed the possibilities of radicalizing the working class through a redefined notion of cultural politics.[1] Another, Walter Benjamin, pointed to a radical discourse that went beyond the technocratic instrumentality of the new age.[2] Most important, Ernst Bloch created an entire political philosophy on what he was to later call *The Principle of Hope*.[3] Bloch found it inconceivable to speak of a radical discourse outside a radical utopianism and steadfastly refused to engage in what Benjamin had labeled "left melancholy," or a tendency among some leftists in the 1930s to substitute a "fatalistic for an interventionist attitude toward the world."[4] Bloch formulated the discourse of possibility into a political project and argued that "only thinking directed towards changing the world and informing the desire to change it does not confront the future . . . as embarrassment and the past as spell."[5] Even Theodor Adorno, the consummate negative dialectician, argued against the assumption that a radical project need only commit itself to the discourse of critique and despair. Endorsing Benjamin's emphasis on messianic forms of thought, Adorno wrote:

> The only philosophy which can be responsibly practiced in the face
> of despair is to contemplate all things as they would present
> themselves from the standpoint of redemption. Knowledge has no
> light but that shed on the world by redemption: all else is

Conclusion

reconstruction, mere technique. Perspectives must be fashioned that
displace and estrange the world; reveal it to be, with its rifts and
crevices, as it will appear one day in the messianic light. To gain
such perspectives without velleity or violence, entirely from felt
contact with object—this alone is the task of thought.[6]

This legacy of hope as a precondition for radical thought and
struggle is not generally characteristic of either radical social theory
or prevailing forms of radical educational theory in North America.
Within the discourse of critique that informs much of the new radical
social theory, one often finds the denial of all first principles upon
which to reconstruct a social vision, historical analyses replaced by a
fetish for structuralist discourses, and the abandonment of political
struggles for ideological and textual readings. Attempting to give
their discourse legitimacy within the academy, many radical theorists
solemnly battle over the indeterminacy of textual meanings and in
doing so produce a catalog of empirically based distinctions and
technical methods to be used in analyzing different levels of signifi-
cations. Lost in an ever-deepening quagmire of theoretical obfusca-
tion, these attempts too often redefine social crises in purely technical and academic terms. Meanwhile, as the web of human suffering
widens, radical intellectuals engage in journal exchanges over the
inescapability of language or the prison-house of signification, or the
inscription of subjectivity in the dominant discourse. Consequently,
the battleground for social and political struggle is no longer the fac-
tory, the public school, the churches, the unions, or mass culture; on
the contrary, the new terrain is increasingly becoming the "radical
conference," the symposium at which academics can read their
papers and cash in their political currency.

In spite of its own radical intent, much of the new social theory
exhibits elements of scientism, functionalism, and ahistoricism
which to a large degree undermine the possibility for a viable political project while producing work quite acceptable to the universities. Put another way, the failure of these critics to articulate a well-
developed political and public project built on concrete principles of
solidarity, resistance, and struggle make their work hospitable to the
status quo. What could be more promising than "radicals" who fuel
the universities with a discourse of critique that is simultaneously a
practice of political impotence. In short, much of what is currently
produced within the tradition of new radical social theory, with the

exception of feminist theory and liberation theology, represents a language of critique, devoid of any language of possibility, which, in turn, threatens to undermine the very notion of radical theory and politics.[7]

While critical educational theory does not reproduce all the problems of dominant forms of radical social theory, it does share a profoundly anti-utopian spirit. That is, there is a growing tendency, especially among a second generation of educational theorists, to eschew a logic of hope and possibility as the basis for theoretical and political engagement.[8] Whereas the larger sphere of radical social theory draws on various sophisticated theoretical currents in order to define its project, radical educational theory still appears tied to a legacy of "scienticism" and ideological reductionism that tends to manifest itself either as a variant of vulgar Marxism or as simply bad scholarship. One of the most striking aspects of much of radical educational theorizing is its increasing celebration of "theory" as method and verification. Radical educational theorists now speak of the importance of theory being empirically secure, or of its value as a coherent structure of assertions. Some radical educators argue in Popperian fashion for radical educational theory to stand up to the test of being either empirically confirmed or falsified.[9] In other cases, theory is simply relegated to an afterthought of experience. The particular form of anti-intellectualism at work here suggests that one's own experience legitimates or delegitimates one's theoretical framework. The notion that theory is constitutive of the meaning of experience or that the discourse of theory can be read like a text is lost in this position. In opposition to the reductionist nature of such a position, educators need to support the position that critical theory in its first instance should be valued for its political project, its estranging quality, and the nature of its criticism as a part of a project of democratic possibility and hope. In other words, it should be valued for the extent to which it can provide potentially liberating forms of critique and the theoretical basis for new forms of social relations. The underlying value of critical educational theory cannot be reduced to the deadening issue of consistency and reliability, a peculiar obsession of dominant social theory; on the contrary, its value should be assessed against the ability of educational theory to confront the discourse and social practices of oppression with what Benjamin once called "potentially liberating images of freedom."

Conclusion

Theory should be seen as abstract and anticipatory: abstract in that it makes the self-evident problematic; anticipatory in that it points to a language and project of possibility.

In part, the profoundly anti-utopian nature of much of contemporary radical educational theory is due to the isolation of radical theorists from larger social movements and sources of social criticism as well as to the pessimism of those academics who distrust any form of struggle or theorizing that might emerge in public spheres outside the university. In some cases, this takes the form of an outright refusal to grant any hope or possibility that teachers and others might be able to wage counterhegemonic struggles in the schools. We have the exaggerated claims, for example, by some theorists that any form of struggle for democratic reform and student empowerment within schools leads only to a kind of "false consciousness." Focusing primarily on a discourse that stresses the overwhelming logic of domination or the failure of teachers to be able to act in the face of domination, these theorists appear to merely recycle the ethos of reproduction theory without acknowledging how its ideological assumptions shape their own pronouncements.[10] This is the language of noncommitment buttressed as ideological critique—a language that lacks even the slightest glimmer of political engagement. Similarly, another group of radical theorists perform the paradoxical feat of calling for educational change by celebrating reform from the "bottom up," at the same time displaying little faith or understanding in either the efforts of teachers or the power of social theory to contribute to such change.[11]

The despair and reductionism are such approaches is also manifest in the refusal of many radical educators to consider the possibility of developing political strategies in which schools can be linked to other social movements and counterpublic spheres. Brandishing their orthodox Marxist credentials in good classical fashion, some radical educators go so far as to argue that radical educational theory has given too much attention to issues of race, gender, and age considerations; and that if one wants to be "really" radical, it is important to get down to business by emphasizing the primacy of class as *the* universal and major determination in the struggle for freedom.[12] This is more than dull theorizing since it is frequently accompanied by unconscionable forms of academic discourse which substitute the imperatives of critical analyses for sweeping, stylistic insults. Radical

traditions are perfunctorily dismissed as mere "inspirational inter-
ludes," complex radical analyses are blithely termed "preachy exaggerations and . . . didactic simplifications."[13] In addition to a casual
dismissal of certain radical educational traditions and schools of
thought, there has emerged a certain meanness of spirit that abstracts
and reifies the pain and suffering that takes place in schools. That is,
amid "scientific" analyses regarding the labor conditions of teachers
and the perils of the political economy of schooling, little attention is
given to a discourse of events, to a politics of the body, to concrete
human suffering, or to forms of collective empowerment among
teachers and/or students as they emerge out of various struggles
against domination inside schools. In fact, the disappearance of a discourse of ethics and the body, one that illuminates and points to concrete instances of suffering and opposition, is a crucial theoretical
absence because it points to the disappearance of the discourse of
politics and engagement. Instead of developing a political project
and discourse of ethics that embody a language of critique and hope,
that connect schools and other institutions to forms of ongoing struggle, these newly emerging strains of radical educational theory
appear to be suffocating in a form of ideological narcissism that is
tied more closely to the self-serving tenets of vanguardism and
despair than to empowering students.

It is clear that critical educational theory itself needs to be resus-
citated and deepened so as to provide a more critical and comprehensive basis for teachers and other educators to rethink the underlying nature of their political and ethical project. That is, educational
theory must develop the theoretical foundation necessary for teachers to understand and critically engage their role as social activists
whose work is both supported and informed by wider social movements and struggles to change the existing society. Amid the deep-
ening crisis in democracy facing the industrialized nations of the
West, it is becoming increasingly important that the relationship
between intellectuals and emancipatory social movements be given
serious consideration by educators. As I pointed out earlier, the
teacher education programs rarely encourage the discourse of moral
leadership and social criticism. Consequently, the call for the development of democratic public spheres outside colleges of education
points to the need to reconstruct a cultural politics in which educators and other intellectuals develop a public voice and become part

of any one of a number of social movements in which they can put
their theoretical and pedagogical skills to use in building historical
blocs capable of emancipatory social change. On one level, this suggests that such intellectuals can work to analyze specific historical
struggles waged by various social movements around the political
importance of education in the battle for economic and social justice.
Not only does this type of analysis illuminate the activities of social
movements outside established schooling, it also provides the basis
for considering what types of public spheres might be useful politically in the current historical juncture.

This is an important concern because it provides the theoretical
grounds for developing democratic public spheres as a defense and
transformation of public education itself. By expanding the notion of
education and extending the possibilities for pedagogical activity
within a variety of social sites, educators can open the policies, discourses, and practices of schooling to criticism and thus make them
available to a greater number of people who otherwise are generally
excluded from such a discourse. It is important for educators to consider how social institutions such as the neighborhood church, and
local political groups may be understood and developed as part of a
wider political and educational struggle; moreover, by combining
the language of critique with a language of possibility such educators
can develop a political project that broadens the social and political
contexts in which pedagogical activity can function as part of a strategy of resistance and transformation. In part, this means writing for a
public culture around issues that emerge out of daily life. Essential to
this project is the question of how specific forms of democratic practice can be supported by a particular version of justice and morality.
As I have tried to portray repeatedly in this text, educators must be
clear about the moral referents for justifying how particular forms of
experience can be legitimated and accomplished as part of both the
development of democratic public spheres and radical social change
in general. Clearly, the discourse of social change needs to develop a
radical conception of democracy as a condition of possibility that
gives it meaning as a social practice rooted in a specific set of moral
principles and political interests. In short, educators must explore
the meaning and purpose of public schooling as part of a discourse
of democracy grounded in a utopian project of possibility. The con-

cept of "utopia" is an important one for developing an emancipatory theory of schooling and it is to this issue that I now want to turn.

Writing in the 1920s, Ernst Bloch attempted to counter the nineteenth-century Enlightenment perspective in which the concept of utopia was dismissed because it could not be legitimated through reason and grounded in an immediate empirical reality. Bloch argued that utopia was a form of "cultural surplus" in the world, but not of it: "it contains the spark that reaches out beyond the surrounding emptiness."[14] Bloch's language of hope and analysis of the traces of possibility in everyday life has been given expression by a number of feminist theologians who through their critiques of traditional Christianity reject universal abstractions about the goodness of humanity, at the same time positing a notion of hope that focuses on concrete instances of suffering, the acts of resistance they often engender, and the "alternative visions of society, humanity, institutional structures, orders of knowing [that] ... are brought into play."[15] In this case, hope is both a referent for social change and pedagogical struggle. It is also the basis for reconstructing a critical theory of education, one that combines the vision of liberation theology, with its focus on the oppressed, with the radical feminist goal of reconstructing social identities and subjectivities within new forms of democratic community.

Central to this project is the important task of developing a language that gives central expression to the primacy of experience, power, and ethics. The goal is to move beyond the "hollow space" of Enlightenment rationality which limits experience to perception in order to forge a discourse that provides historical and social understanding of how experience is shaped, legitimated, and accomplished within particular social forms as these are organized within particular relations of power. In this view, experience is seen as both historical construction and lived practice. It connects the need to understand how social forms position and produce experience with the further imperative of interrogating how experience in its contradictory and often less than coherent moments is felt and inhabited. Educators must understand language as a social construction linked to apparatuses of power and particular definitions of the truth. One of the major strengths of this position resides in the insight that language has to be seen in its historical and socially formative dimensions as part of a politics of identity, ethics, and struggle. I have argued that educators should give serious consideration to developing a view of theory defined, in part, through its ability to recall and legitimate standards of ethical practice that best serve human needs and hopes. As part of this task pedagogical practice should be constructed around a particular view of human suffering, solidarity, and human community. This relationship is worth elaborating. In the first instance, educational practice can begin with an identification of the needs and desires of dominated groups and their ongoing attempts to end their suffering and oppression. This is not merely a reflection on human suffering as much as it is a moral referent for political action rooted in an affirmation of the importance of human life and the necessity to address injustices caused by class discrimination, sexism, racism, and other forms of exploitation. Essential to this view is a double-sided notion of critique. First, there is the need to develop forms of critical analyses that illuminate how the concrete mechanisms of power work within different ideological and institutional relations of domination. Second, there is the emphasis on analyzing critique itself as a particular type of practice in which men and women challenge oppressive and dominating institutions. Critique in this view is linked to acknowledging as part of any radical project the historical and cultural specifics that constitute the nature of particular types of resistance.

As I have previously indicated, the category of solidarity can provide a major organizing principle for developing a critical theory of schooling. As a participatory act, solidarity can provide the theoretical basis for critically developing new forms of sociality based on a respect for human freedom and life itself. As such, solidarity as a lived experience and form of critical discourse can serve both as a referent for criticizing oppressive social institutions and as an ideal for developing the material and ideological conditions necessary for creating communities in which humanity is affirmed rather than denied. Inherent in the notion of solidarity are principles of political and pedagogical practice that highlight a specific view of the relationship between power, knowledge, and cultural struggle. Sharon Welch is instructive on this issue.

> To challenge the truth of oppression is not to point to its intellectual
> or conceptual frailties, but to expose its frailties of practice, to
> disclose and nurture alternate forms of human community that

challenge it on the level of daily operations of power/knowledge. To challenge oppression effectively is to point to its failure to determine the nature of human existence and to seek to extend the sphere of influence of alternate structures. . . . The temptation to define others' hopes for liberation must be avoided. The cultural genocide of an imperialistic Christianity is not accidental, but is grounded in such an arrogant approach to liberation. It is oppressive to "free" people if their own history and culture do not serve as the primary sources of the definition of their freedom.[16]

The radical imperative to articulate a notion and politics of truth resonates with the empowering spirit found in the writings of Ernst Bloch and Michel Foucault. For instance, Bloch argues against a transcendental grounding of truth since it is the logic of such a priori rationalizations that is often used to legitimate the status quo. For Bloch, truth should be directed *against* the world and located in the ongoing dialectics of human interaction and community. As Bloch notes,

> There exists a second concept of truth . . . which is instead suffused with value (Wertgeladen) — as, for example, in the concept 'a true friend,' or in Juvenal's expression Tempestas poetica — that is, the kind of storm one finds in a book, a poetic storm, the kind that reality has never witnessed, a storm carried to the extreme, a radical storm and therefore a true storm.[17]

This formulation of the concept "truth" as rooted in the most fundamental aspects of experience and solidarity clearly rejects, along with Bloch, the Enlightenment notion of truth as a universal way of knowing and ordering experience. But whereas Bloch provides a notion of truth as radical critique, Foucault links truth with the most fundamental workings of power and knowledge and in doing so provides a radically new way to conceptualize the role of the intellectual and intellectual practice.

In Foucault's terms, truth cannot be viewed as existing outside power; nor is it a product and reward of those intellectuals who have freed themselves from ignorance. On the contrary, truth is part of a political economy of power. In Foucault's own words,

> Truth is a thing of this world: it is produced only by virtue of multiple forms of constraint. And it induces regular effects of power. Each society has its regime of truth, its 'general politics' of truth: that is, the types of discourse which it accepts and makes function as true;

the mechanisms and instances which enable one to distinguish true and false statements, the means by which each is sanctioned; the techniques and procedures accorded value in the acquisition of truth; the status of those who are charged with saying what counts as true. ... It seems to me that what must now be taken into account in the intellectual is not the 'bearer of universal values.' Rather, it's the person occupying a specific position — but whose specificity is linked, in a society like ours, to the general functioning of an apparatus of truth.[18]

Foucault's analysis of the political economy of truth and his study of the discursive and institutional ways that "regimes of truth" are organized and legitimated can provide educators with a theoretical basis upon which to develop the category of intellectual practice as a form of cultural politics. As I have observed at numerous points, teachers' work has to be analyzed in terms of its social and political function within particular "regimes of truth." That is, teachers can no longer deceive themselves into believing they are serving on behalf of truth, when, in fact, they are deeply involved in battles "about the status of truth and the economic and political role it plays."[19]

In developing this view, I have further argued that if intellectual practice is to be tied to creating an alternative and emancipatory politics of truth, it needs to be grounded in forms of moral and ethical discourse and action that address the suffering and struggles of the oppressed. This is one of the most important formulations developed throughout this book, particularly as it developed through an analysis and critical appropriation of the discourses of democracy, memory, solidarity, and hope as they are developed through a number of traditions of protest. For educators, it is important to recognize youth as an oppressed social category. That is, it is important to link the purpose of schooling, teaching, and pedagogy to analysis and struggles that attempt to rectify those conditions that deprive children of food, clothing, housing, medical care, and education. Educators need to understand the ideological and material conditions that place children at risk both in our schools and in the wider community. Within this context, schools can be better understood as sites of struggle that address the suffering and struggles of the oppressed, and teaching can be linked directly with a political and moral discourse that takes as one of its first consideration the issue of

212

how schools contribute to the oppression of youth and how such conditions can be changed.

Another major pedagogical formulation presented in this book emerges from the conviction that teachers need to reconsider the relationship between knowledge and power. This is an important issue that needs to be stressed and I want to clarify it further through an analysis of the shortcomings of the traditional Marxist view of ideology.[20] In the classical Marxist view, power relates to knowledge primarily through the ways in which it serves to distort or mystify the truth. Consequently, ideology critique mainly serves to examine the underlying economic and social conditions of knowledge or the ways in which knowledge can be analyzed for its distortions and mystifications. What is lost in this formulation is any understanding of the productive role that power plays in generating forms of knowledge that produce and legitimate particular forms of life, resonate with people's desires and needs, and serve to construct particular forms of experience. The point here is that the knowledge/power relation produces dangerous "positive" effects in the way it creates particular needs, desires, and truths. Within this type of analysis, educators can begin to establish the theoretical edifice for reconstructing a critical social theory that links pedagogy to forms of critique and possibility. By illuminating the productive effects of power, it becomes possible for teachers as intellectuals to develop forms of practice that take seriously how subjectivities are constructed within particular "regimes of truth"; the discourse of power and knowledge also highlights the importance of developing a theory of experience as a central aspect of critical pedagogy. As I pointed out in Chapter 3, this view of the knowledge/power relationship also points to the role that educators can play as bearers of dangerous memory. That is, as transformative intellectuals, educators can serve to uncover and excavate those forms of historical and subjugated knowledges that point to experiences of suffering, conflict, and collective struggle. In this way, teachers as intellectuals can begin to link the notion of historical understanding to elements of critique and hope. Such memories keep alive the horror of needless exploitation as well as the need to constantly intervene and collectively struggle to eliminate the conditions that produce it.

One of the central messages of this book is that educators must struggle collectively in order to transform schools into democratic public spheres. Such a formulation requires that teachers think not in terms of civility, professionalism, and tenure promotions, but redefine their role within the specificity of political, economic, and cultural sites where "regimes of truth" are produced, legitimated, and distributed. Within such contexts teachers can confront the microphysics of power and work to build alternative public spheres that have an ongoing organic connection to the dynamics of everyday life.

All those concerned with the issue of how schools can empower both teachers and students must reestablish a concern for the purpose of education. Educators need to fight against those who would simply make schools an adjunct of the corporation or local church. Schools need to be defended as an important public service that educates students to be critical citizens who can think, challenge, take risks, and believe that their actions will make a difference in the larger society. This means that public schools should become places that provide the opportunity for literate occasions, that is, that provide opportunities for students to share their experiences, to work in social relations that emphasize care and concern for others, and to be introduced to forms of knowledge that provide them with the conviction and opportunity to fight for a quality of life in which all human beings benefit.

In short, let me reemphasize that teachers should concern themselves with the business of moral and political education and not be party to the ideologically transparent argument that they work to become curriculum or policy experts or highly specialized classroom technicians. Educators need to take as their first concern the issue of empowerment, and the route to that goal is not through definitions of professionalism based on the testing of teachers or other empirically driven forms of accountability. Empowerment, in this case, depends on the ability of teachers in the future to struggle collectively in order to create those ideological and material conditions of work that enable them to share power, to shape policy, and to play an active role in structuring school/community relations. Similarly, teachers and other critical educators need to create a language in order to reclaim the notions of struggle, solidarity, and hope around forms of pedagogy and social action that expand rather than restrict the forms and practices of authentic democracy and public life. If we are to prevent democracy from collapsing into a new form of barbarism, we will have to fight hard to rescue the language of tradition, morality, and possibility from the ravages and power of the dominant ideology. At stake here is the willingness of educators at all levels of schooling to struggle collectively as transformative intellectuals, that is, as educators who have a social vision and commitment to make public schools democratic public spheres, where all children, regardless of race, class, gender, and age can learn what it means to be able to participate fully in a society that affirms and sustains the principles of equality, freedom, and social justice. To be a teacher who can make a difference in both the lives of students and in the quality of life in general necessitates more than acquiring a language of critique and possibility. It also means having the courage to take risks, to look into the future, and to imagine a world that could be as opposed to simply what is. This book commends those teachers everywhere who are struggling to embody such qualities and who do make a *difference* in the lives of the children they teach.

Notes

Notes

1. INTRODUCTION: SCHOOLING, CITIZENSHIP, AND THE STRUGGLE FOR DEMOCRACY

1. Quoted in Marshall Blonsky, "Introduction: The Agony of Semiotics: Reassessing the Discipline," in *On Signs*, ed. Marshall Blonsky (Baltimore, Md.: The Johns Hopkins University Press, 1985), p. xxxii.

2. Gregory Kealey, "Herbert Gutman, 1928-1985, and the Writing of Working Class History," *Monthly Review* (May 1968), p. 30.

3. I am using the term "discourse" in the manner described by Richard Terdiman as "the complexes of signs and practices which organize social existence and social reproduction. In their structured, material persistence, discourses are what give differential substance to membership of a social group or class or formation, which mediate an internal sense of belonging, and outward sense of otherness." Richard Terdiman, *Discourse-Counter-Discourse* (New York: Cornell University Press, 1985), p. 54.

4. This is not meant to suggest that a radical discourse on democracy does not exist. It simply means that it is insufficient theoretically, and it has not been at the heart of a Left politics. David Held provides an important comment on the limitations of a Left discourse of democracy. He writes:

> Poulantzas, Macpherson and Pateman have all sought to combine and
> refashion insights from both the liberal and the Marxist traditions. While their
> efforts move political debate away from the seemingly endless and fruitless
> juxtaposition of liberalism with Marxism, they say very little about fundamental
> factors such as how, for instance, the economy is actually to be organized and
> related to the political apparatus, how institutions of representative democracy
> are to be combined with those of direct democracy, how the scope and power
> of administrative organizations are to be checked, how households and
> childcare facilities are to be related to work, how those who wish to "opt out"
> of the political system might do so, or how the problems posed by the ever
> changing international system of states could be dealt with. . . . Furthermore,
> they tend to assume that people in general want to extend the sphere of
> control over their lives. What if they do not want to do so? What if they do not
> really want to participate in the management of social and economic affairs?
> What if they do not wish to become creatures of democratic reason? Or, what

if they wield democratic power "undemocratically"—to limit or end democracy? (David Held, *Models of Democracy* [Stanford, Calif.: Stanford University Press, 1987], pp. 262-63.)

Some recent radical efforts to redevelop a conception of radical democracy can be found in: Martin Carnoy and Derek Shearer, *Economic Democracy: the Challenge of the 1980s* (New York: M. Sharpe, Inc., 1980); Joshua Cohen and Joel Rogers, *On Democracy: Toward a Transformation of American Society* (New York: Penguin, 1983); Andrew Levine, *Arguing for Socialism* (New York: Routledge and Kegan Paul, 1984); Adam Przeworski, *Capitalism and Social Democracy* (New York: Cambridge University Press, 1985); Carole Pateman, *The Problem of Political Obligation: A Critique of Liberal Theory* (Cambridge: Polity Press, 1985); Ernesto Laclau and Chantal Mouffe, *Hegemony and Socialist Strategy* (London: Verso Books, 1985); Samuel Bowles and Herbert Gintis, *Democracy and Capitalism* (New York: Basic Books, 1986); Harry C. Boyte and Frank Riessman, eds., *The New Populism: The Politics of Empowerment* (Philadelphia: Temple University Press, 1986); Held, *Models of Democracy*. Some recent examples of attempts to take up the issue of schooling and democracy include Harold Berlak's Public Information Network (Washington University) and George Wood's (Ohio University) Institute for Democratic Education. It is necessary to see these efforts as a response to the absence of any major discussion of democracy and schooling in the United States. These groups represent important interventions by the Left, but, unfortunately, they represent a marginal force in the overall context of how education is being defined and analyzed as part of the current educational reform movement. Of course, this serves primarily as a commentary on the power of the capitalist state to limit the range of oppositional discourses around the issue of critical democracy.

5. Michel Crozier, Samuel P. Huntington, and Joji Watanuki, *The Crisis of Democracy* (New York: New York University Press, 1975), p. 113.

6. Noam Chomsky, *Turning the Tide* (Boston, Mass.: South End Press, 1985), p. 225.

7. Ernst Bloch quoted in Anson Rabinach, "Unclaimed Heritage: Ernst Bloch's *Heritage of Our Times* and the Theory of Fascism," *New German Critique*, 11 (Spring 1977), p. 8. At various times throughout this book I use the term "New Right," which refers to two distinct political-ideological tendencies that have united in the 1980s. On the one hand, the term refers to a merging of neoliberalism, with its emphasis on the economic freedom of the market economy as a prerequisite to political freedom, with a brand of neoconservativism that argues for a nineteenth-century version of social order in which the ideas, values, and social relations of the past provide a basis for restructuring contemporary social and political life. On the other hand, the New Right represents a marriage of its traditional elitist libertarian ideology with a strain of popularist ideology that focuses on social issues such as abortion, school prayer, taxes, and other concerns that resonate with the daily experiences of working people and other groups generally ignored by the old conservatives. Combining an elitist view of economics (upholding the economic interests of the wealthy), a populist focus (a form of moral authoritarianism) on social issues, and a mythic view of the past, the New Right represents both a new alliance of traditionally disparate political factions and a new political resurgency aimed at reversing many of the political, social, and cultural changes that emerged out of the New Deal of the 1930s, the Great Society programs of

the 1960s, and the various social and political policies put into place by progressive groups in the last twenty years. For an in-depth analysis of the character and emergence of the New Right, see the various essays in Fred Block, Richard A. Cloward, Barbara Ehrenreich, and Frances Fox Piven, *The Mean Season: The Attack on the Welfare State* (New York: Pantheon, 1987) and Harvey J. Kaye, "The Use and Abuse of the Past: The New Right and the Crisis of History," in *The Socialist Register 1987*, ed. Ralph Miliband, Leo Panitch, and John Saville (London: Merlin Press, 1987), pp. 332-64.

8. Two important qualifications must be made here. First, by Left critics I mean Left in the generic sense to refer to an amalgam of progressive, liberals, social democrats and radical populists who struggle for social and economic justice within the wider goal of furthering a radical democratic society. Second, at the heart of the "crisis of democracy" in America and elsewhere are not only ideological issues, but also the question of who controls economic resources, wealth, and has the power to set economic and social priorities within the wider society. Capitalist exploitation rooted in economic inequalities is not something for which the Left is directly responsible. It is simply not an actor on this terrain. Moreover, operating within asymmetrical relations of power, the Left does not have an equal footing in shaping the agendas that constitute the cultural terrain. But at the same time, it has failed in its various public spheres to attract and mobilize a following precisely because of the limited nature of its ideological appeal. For a serious debate on this issue, see the exchange among Lillian Rubin and Richard Lichtman, on the one hand, and Christopher Lasch, on the other, in *Tikkun*, 1:2 (1986), pp. 85-93. Also see Stanley Aronowitz and Henry A. Giroux, *Education under Siege: The Conservative, Liberal, and Radical Debate over Schooling* (South Hadley, Mass.: Bergin and Garvey, 1985). It is also worth noting as Jost Halfmann has pointed out that the New Right has taken some central concepts concerning democracy and capitalism and assimilated them into their own ideological framework. He writes:

> The neo conservatives have seized an idea which the Left has largely given up, namely, that bourgeois democracy and the capitalist mode of production stand in a precarious and immanently immutable relation of tension to each other. The difference made by the conservatives is that they hold the welfare state and mass democracy rather than the productive relations responsible for the evils of modern societies. (Jost Halfmann, "The German Left and Democracy," *New German Critique*, 33 [Spring 1985], p. 174.)

9. Richard Hanson, *The Democratic Imagination* (Princeton: Princeton University Press, 1985), p. 418.

10. Douglas Kellner and Harry O'Hara, "Utopia and Marxism in Ernst Bloch," *New German Critique*, 9 (Fall 1976), p. 22.

11. Murray Bookchin, *The Modern Crisis* (Philadelphia: New Society Publishers, 1986), p. 33.

12. "Orientation," *The Social Frontier*, 1 (October 1934), pp. 3-4; see also James M. Giarelli, "The Social Frontier, 1934-1943: Retrospect and Prospect," unpublished paper presented at the American Educational Studies Association Annual Meeting, Colorado Springs, Colorado, November 1980, 20 pp.

13. Needless to say, a number of theoretical differences existed among the social reconstructionists, but their criticism found a common ground in the attempt to link schooling to the imperatives of a reconstructed democratic tradition. See W. B. Stanley, "The Philosophy of Social Reconstructionism and Contemporary Curriculum

Rationales in Social Education," unpublished doctoral dissertation, Rutgers University (1979). See James M. Giarelli, "The Social Frontier 1934-1943"; C. A. Bowers, *The Progressive Educator and the Depression* (New York: Random House, 1969).

14. Harold Rugg, "The School Curriculum and the Drama of American Life," in *Curriculum Making: Past and Present*, 22nd Yearbook, ed. Harold Rugg (Chicago: National Society for the Study of Education, 1927), p. 7.

15. Theodore Brameld, "Philosophies of Education in an Age of Crisis," *School and Society*, 65 (Winter 1947), p. 452.

16. John Childs, "Should the School Seek Actively to Reconstruct Society?" *Annals of the American Academy of Political and Social Science*, CLXXXII (November, 1935), pp. 8-9. Of course, Childs's emphasis on linking education to the dictates and assumptions of social democracy should not be mistaken for a more radical position which would argue not only for a transformation of the control and ownership of the means of production but also for a transformation in the wider terrain of culture and everyday life. George Counts later recognized that in his earlier work he had overemphasized the issue of economic reform, but instead of extending his radical critique of the economy to everyday life, he, like many other social reconstructionists, adopted a more liberal position in which the emphasis on economic issues was almost completely dropped as a result of their increasing distrust of any form of Marxist and radical theory. See George S. Counts, "A Liberal Looks at Life," *Frontiers of Democracy*, 7:2 (1950), pp. 242-3.

17. Herbert M. Kliebard, *The Struggle for the American Curriculum, 1893-1958* (New York: Routledge and Kegan Paul, 1986), p. 468.

18. For an insightful commentary on the social reconstructionist movement and its relevance for radical educational theory, see William B. Stanley, "The Radical Reconstructionist Rationale for Social Education," *Theory and Research in Social Education*, 8 (Winter 1981), pp. 55-77.

19. See especially, C. Wright Mills, *White Collar: The American Middle Classes* (New York: Oxford University Press, 1951); *The Power Elite* (New York: Oxford University Press, 1956); *The Sociological Imagination* (New York: Oxford University Press, 1959); *Power, Politics, and People: The Collected Essays of C. Wright Mills*, ed. Irving Horowitz (New York: Oxford University Press, 1963).

20. Classic examples include Herbert Marcuse, *One-Dimensional Man* (Boston, Mass.: Beacon Press, 1964); Theodor Adorno and Max Horkheimer, *Dialectic of Enlightenment* (New York: Herder and Herder, 1972 [original edition, 1944]).

21. Fred Pfeil, "Makin' Floppy-Floppy-Boom PMC," in *The Year Left: An American Socialist Yearbook, 1985*, ed. Mark Davis, Fred Pfeil, and Michael Sprinker (London: Verso Books, 1985), p. 266.

22. Mills, *Power, Politics, and People*, p. 360.

23. I dealt with this issue in more detail in Henry A. Giroux, *Theory and Resistance in Education* (South Hadley, Mass.: Bergin and Garvey, 1983), especially in "Critical Theory and Rationality in Citizenship Education," pp. 168-204. See also the excellent history of citizenship education in the United States and Sweden by Tomas Englund, *Curriculum as a Political Problem: Changing Educational Conceptions, with Special Reference to Citizenship Education* (Sweden: Chartwelt Bratt, 1986); William Stanley, *Review of Research in Social Studies Education, 1976-1983* (Boulder, Colo.: ERIC Clearing House, 1985).

24. Tony Wagner, "Educating for Excellence on an Endangered Planet: Peace Studies Refined," unpublished paper, Boston, Mass., 1986, 6 pp.

25. Barbara Finkelstein, "Education and the Retreat from Democracy in the United States, 1979-198?," *Teachers College Record*, 86 (Winter 1984), pp. 280-281.

26. The National Commission on Excellence in Education, *A Nation at Risk: The Imperative for Educational Reform* (Washington, D.C.: United States Department of Education, 1983), p. 17.

27. Gary L. Bauer, "Teaching Virtue," Speech given before the 50th Annual Convention of the National Federation of McGuffey Societies, Miami University, Oxford, Ohio, May 11, 1986, p. 4.

28. Daniel Yankelovich, "How the Public Learns the Public's Business," *Kettering Review* (Winter 1985), p. 11.

29. Clark's education philosophy and comments have been given extensive coverage in the popular press. For a critical commentary on Clark, as well as a compendium of some of his more publicly quoted comments, see Stan Karp, "Tests and Bullhorns," *Radical Teacher* (June 1986), pp. 11-15. The Reagan Administration's support for Clark proved to be too much even for some of its most ardent supporters. For example, see Albert Shanker, "Teaching to the Tune of a Bullhorn," *The New York Times* (January 17, 1988), p. 7.

30. Cited in Marshall Blonsky, "Introduction: The Agony of Semiotics," p. xxxiii.

31. Judith Newton and Deborah Rosenfelt, "Toward a Materialist-Feminist Criticism," in *Feminist Criticism and Social Change*, ed. J. Newton and D. Rosenfelt (New York: Methuen, 1985), p. xix.

32. Teresa De Lauretis, *Alice Doesn't: Feminism, Semiotics and Cinema* (Bloomington: Indiana University Press, 1984), p. 37.

33. De Lauretis argues that the images produced in films are productive of contradictions in both social processes and subjectivities. She then raises a series of important questions that provide a pedagogical starting point for exploring these issues:

> By what processes do images on the screen produce imaging on and off the screen, articulate meaning and desire, for the spectators? How are images perceived? How do we see? How do we attribute meaning to what we see? And do those meanings remail linked to images? What about language? Or sound? What relations do language and sound bear to images? Do we image as well as imagine, or are they the same thing? And then again we must ask: what historical factors intervene in imaging? (Historical factors might include social discourses, genre codification, audience expectations, but also unconscious production, memory, and fantasy.) Finally, what are the "productive relations" of imaging in filmmaking and filmviewing, or spectatorship—productive of what? productive how? (Ibid., p. 39.)

34. Peter J. Boyer, "TV Turns to the Hard Boiled Male," *The New York Times*, February 16, 1986, p. 1.

35. Ernesto Laclau and Chantal Mouffe, *Hegemony and Socialist Strategy* (London: Verso Books, 1985), pp. 186-187.

36. Ibid., p. 76.

37. Benjamin Barber, "A New Language for the Left," *Harper's Magazine* (November 1986), p. 50.

38. Noam Chomsky, *Turning the Tide* (Boston: South End Press, 1985), p. 223.

39. Cited in ibid., p. 222.

40. Christopher Lasch, "Fraternalist Manifesto," *Harper's Magazine* (April 1987), pp. 17-20.

41. Ernst Bloch, *The Philosophy of the Future* (New York: Herder and Herder, 1970), pp. 86-87.

42. Barbara Finkelstein, "Thinking Publicly About Civic Learning: An Agenda for Education Reform in the '80s," in *Civic Learning for Teachers: Capstone for Educational Reform*, ed. Alan H. Jones (Ann Arbor: Prakken Publishers, 1984), p. 16.

2. SCHOOLING AND THE POLITICS OF ETHICS: BEYOND CONSERVATIVE AND LIBERAL DISCOURSES

1. The "paradox of morality" to which I refer can be seen in what Steven Lukes calls the paradoxical stance of Marxism toward morality. Kate Soper is instructive on this issue.

On the one hand, it presents morality as nothing more than bourgeois prejudice, a form of ideology that is social in origin, illusory in content, and serving class interests; on the other hand, Marxism continually implies and often explicitly invokes moral concepts and categories in its critique of capitalism and advocacy of communism. ... And yet Marx just as constantly suggests that all moralizing and moral vocabulary must be expunged as unscientific and prejudicial to proletarian revolution. Nor is such inconsistency simply a quirk of Marx; it is equally to be found in the position of Engels, of Lenin, of Trotsky, and indeed of the Marxist tradition in general, where passionate denunciation of the evils of capitalism has always combined with equally fiery polemics against all ethical standpoints. (Kate Soper, *New Left Review*, 163 [May/June 1987], p. 103.)

I am using the terms "moral" and "ethical" in the manner defined by Michel Foucault. "Moral" refers to the prescriptive code or rule one follows to live in a particular society and culture. Of course, these codes are not only externally enforced, mediated, and modified, but also often internalized as well. The category of moral code is not meant to suggest that the latter is homogeneous; an individual's moral code is often a composite of contradictory, fractured, and layered experiences and discourses. "Ethical" refers to the kind of person and life one aspires to attain. For a discussion of this distinction, see John Rajchman, "Ethics after Foucault," *Social Text*, 13/14 (Winter/Spring 1986), p. 172; moreover, it is important to recognize that I am not supporting a position that Marx rightly argued against; namely, that to acknowledge the importance of developing a discourse of ethics and morality is not to be equated with the idealist notion that all struggles, conflicts, and forms of oppression represent no more than the clash of moral concepts and can be resolved merely in the realm of ideas.

2. It is important to stress that the notion of democratic public sphere that I refer to in this chapter is not of the Walter Lippmann variety. Rather, it derives its meaning from Gramsci's notion of civil society, Habermas's discussion of the public sphere, and from the work done on the public sphere by John Dewey, Stanley Aronowitz, and others. For a review of this work, see Henry A. Giroux, *Theory and Resistance in Education* (South Hadley, Mass.: Bergin and Garvey, 1983), especially the last chapter.

3. Stanley Aronowitz and Henry A. Giroux, *Education under Siege: The Conservative, Liberal, and Radical Debate over Schooling* (South Hadley, Mass.: Bergin and Garvey, 1983).

4. Cornel West, "Fredric Jameson's Marxist Hermeneutics," *Boundary 2*, 11:2 (Fall/Winter 1982-83), p. 191.

5. James Giarelli, "Review of *Education under Siege*," *Harvard Educational Review*, 56:3 (August 1986), p. 323.

6. Murray Bookchin, *The Modern Crisis* (Philadelphia: New Society Publishers, 1986), p. 8.

7. I am indebted to Stanley Aronowitz for this insight.

8. Walter Benjamin, "Thesis on the Philosophy of History," in *Illuminations*, ed. Hannah Arendt (New York: Schocken Books, 1969).

9. See Christopher Lasch, "What's Wrong with the Right?" *Tikkun*, 1:1 (1986), pp. 23-29; Michael Lerner, "A New Paradigm for Liberals: The Primacy of Ethics and Emotions," *Tikkun*, 2:1 (1987), pp. 22-28, 132-36; Henry A. Giroux, "Public Philosophy and the Struggle for Democracy," *Educational Theory*, 37:2 (1987), pp. 104-20.

10. The most recent example of this is a ruling by U.S. District Judge W. Brevard Hand, the controversial right-winger, who ordered the banning of forty-four textbooks from use in the Alabama public schools on the grounds that they promote a religious belief system of secular humanism.

11. For an example of this position, see Franklin Parker, "Moral Education in the United States," *The College Board Review*, 137 (Fall 1985), pp. 10-15, 30; this position is also sponsored by the former Secretary of Education, William Bennett, and John Silber, the president of Boston University. Bennett and Silber are leading right-wing spokespersons on educational issues as well as other political concerns. In fact, what is notable about the Right, exemplified in the discourse of Bennett and Silber, is that they often publicly link their views of education to a number of other issues. For example, it comes as no surprise to find Bennett endorsing the notorious Cold War-inspired documentary *Amerika* in one breath and arguing about educational issues in the next sentence. Nor is it surprising to find Silber debating a particular education issue one minute and then immediately switching gears to defend, for instance, his creation of a program in the Boston University communications department designed to train Afghan rebels in the journalistic skills necessary to wage a propaganda war against the Soviets, or to mount a defense of his developing a Disinformation Documentation Center headed by a former Czech spy. These broader concerns make clear what the right-wing view of the world is about as well as the ideological interests that underlie its view of education.

12. Edward A. Wynne, "The Great Tradition in Education: Transmitting Moral Values," *Educational Leadership* (December 1986/January 1987), pp. 8-9.

13. Ibid., p. 6.

14. Kevin Ryan, "The New Moral Education," *Phi Delta Kappan* (November 1986), p. 231.

15. William Bennett spells out the Reagan Administration's list of desirable moral traits in Application for Grants Under the Secretary's Discretionary Program, U.S. Department of Education, CFDA no. 84.122B, 1985, p. B2. In one of his recent speeches on the teaching of values in the public schools, President Reagan argued that teaching values was part of getting back to basics, and to legitimate his point suggested that educators "turn to the Judeo-Christian ethic, specifically the Ten Commandments." See Blake Rodman, "President Hits Road to Spread Message On School Agenda," *Education Week*, 6:27 (April 1, 1987), p. 53. For a discussion of this issue, see

Robert Nash and Robert Griffen, "Balancing the Private and Public," *Harvard Educational Review*, 56:2 (1986), pp. 171-82, especially page 180.

16. Ryan, "The New Moral Education," p. 231.

17. Parker, "Moral Education in the United States," p. 171.

18. Wynne, "The Great Tradition in Education," p. 4. In many ways, Wynne is simply reaffirming what former White House Presidential Adviser (former Undersecretary of Education) Gary L. Bauer has been saying for the last five years. Bauer's diatribe's against the 1960s reached a new level of ideological and political ignorance in a report on the American family released to President Reagan in October 1986. In it, the task force under Bauer's guidance, as reported in *Education Week*, states:

> "The social damage of America's youthful fling with self-indulgence" during the 1960s and 1970s "has not been mended," the group asserts. "Now we face the unfinished agenda: turning back to the households of this land the autonomy that was once theirs, in a society stable and secure, where the family can generate and nurture what no government can ever produce— Americans who will responsibly exercise their freedom and, if necessary, defend it." (Tom Mirga, "Restore Family Stability, Panel Urges," *Education Week* [November 19, 1986], pp. 14, 17.)

These are indeed chilling words coming from spokespersons for a government that is performing terrorists acts against Nicaragua, eroding civil liberties, trading with Iranian terrorists, and undermining the viability of American public schools.

19. Ryan, "The New Moral Education," p. 231. For a more recent lament on how the sixties, feminism, and rock music undermined the right-wing version of order and authority, see Allan Bloom, *The Closing of the American Mind* (New York: Simon and Schuster, 1987).

20. Ira Shor, "Equality Is Excellence: Transforming Teacher Education and the Learning Process," *Harvard Educational Review*, 56:4 (November 1986), p. 408.

21. For example, at the Federal level, see U.S. Department of Education, *What Works: Research about Teaching and Learning* (Washington, D.C.: GPO, 1986); for a statement on this issue from right-wing intellectuals who have served the Reagan government in a predictable way, see Edward A. Wynne and Herbert J. Walberg, eds., *Developing Character: Transmitting Knowledge* (Posen, Ill.: ARL Services, 1984); for a representative view from the corporate interests, see Research and Policy Committee of the Committee for Economic Development, *Investing in Our Children* (New York: Committee for Economic Development, 1985).

22. Ann Bastian, Norm Fruchter, Marilyn Gittell, Colin Greer, and Kenneth Haskins, "Choosing Equality: The Case for Democratic Schooling," *Social Policy*, 15:4 (Spring 1985), p. 35.

23. Louis Raths, Merrill Harmin, and Sidney Simon, *Values and Teaching*, 2nd ed. (Columbus, Ohio: Charles E. Merrill, 1978). An applied example of this work can be found in Sidney B. Simon, Robert C. Hawley, and David D. Bretton, *Composition for Personal Growth* (New York: Hart Publishing, 1973).

24. Christina Hoff Sommers, "Ethics without Virtue," *The American Scholar*, 53 (Summer 1984), p. 382.

25. Lawrence Kohlberg, *The Philosophy of Moral Development* (New York: Harper and Row, 1981). A review of the literature on values clarification and moral development can be found in Barry Chazan, *Contemporary Approaches to Moral Education* (New York: Teachers College Press, 1985); John Martin Rich and Joseph L. Devitis, *The-*

ories of Moral Development (Springfield, Ill.: Charles C. Thomas, 1985). For a critical reader on the different theoretical positions in moral education, see Henry A. Giroux and David Purpel, *The Hidden Curriculum and Moral Education* (Berkeley, Calif.: McCutchan Publishing, 1983).

26. Lawrence Kohlberg, "Moral Development and the New Social Studies," *Social Education* (May 1973), p. 37.

27. Sommers, "Ethics without Virtue," p. 386.

28. Ibid., p. 387.

29. John Weiss, quoted in Robert Marquand, "Moral Education: Has 'Values Neutrality' Left Students Adrift?" *The Christian Science Monitor*, Friday, January 30, 1987, B2.

30. Sommers, "Ethics without Virtue," p. 387.

31. Lerner, "A New Paradigm for Liberals."

32. This point is developed theoretically and historically in Philip Corrigan and Derek Sayer, *The Great Arch: English State Formation as Cultural Revolution* (New York: Basil Blackwell, 1985).

33. Roger Simon, "Empowerment as Pedagogy," *Language Arts*, 64:4 (1987), p. 373.

34. Philip Corrigan, "The Politics of Feeling Good: Reflections on Marxism and Cultural Relations," unpublished paper, 1984, pp. 5-6.

35. For an excellent discussion of this issue, see Edward T. Silva and Sheila A. Slaughter, *Serving Power: The Making of the Academic Social Science Expert* (Westport, Conn.: Greenwood Press, 1984); Thomas S. Popkewitz, *Paradigm & Ideology in Educational Research* (Philadelphia: Falmer Press, 1984); Thomas Popkewitz, "Professionalization of Knowledge and Policy Legitimation: Social Science During the Formative Years of Schooling," unpublished paper, 1987.

36. Giarelli, "Review of *Education under Siege*," pp. 319-20.

37. Kenneth A. Strike, *Educational Policy and the Just Society* (Urbana: University of Illinois Press, 1982); John Rawls, *A Theory of Justice* (Cambridge, Mass.: Harvard University Press, 1971); see also Ronald Dworkin, *Taking Rights Seriously* (Cambridge, Mass.: Harvard University Press, 1977).

38. Strike, *Educational Policy and the Just Society*, p. 248.

39. Seyla Benhabib, "The Utopian Dimension in Communicative Ethics," *New German Critique*, 35 (Spring 1985), p. 84.

40. Fred Siegel, "Is Archie Bunker Fit to Rule? Or: How Immanuel Kant Became One of the Founding Fathers," *Telos*, 69 (Fall 1986), p. 27.

41. Lawrence Kohlberg, *The Philosophy of Moral Development* (New York: Harper and Row, 1981). A representative collection of this literature can be found in Ralph Mosher, ed., *Adolescents' Development and Education: A Janus Knot* (Berkeley: McCutchan Publishing, 1979). See also Barry Chazan, *Contemporary Approaches to Moral Education* (New York: Teachers College Press, 1985) and John Martin Rich and Joseph L. Devitis, *Theories of Moral Development* (Springfield, Ill.: Charles C. Thomas, 1985); Jürgen Habermas, *The Theory of Communicative Action* (Boston: Beacon Press, l983).

42. A particular example of this approach can be found in Ronald E. Galbraith and Thomas M. Jones, *Moral Reasoning: A Teaching Handbook for Adapting Kohlberg to the Classroom* (Minneapolis: Greenhaven Press, 1976).

43. Max Horkheimer, "Ethics and Critical Theory," *Telos*, 69 (Fall 1986), pp. 85-118. Horkheimer's insistence that we develop an ethical discourse that stares into history in order to bear witness to the legacy of suffering and struggle, to reveal the objective

conditions of evil, is powerfully exemplified in what Terrence Des Pres calls the literature of the *survivor-as-witness*. But for Des Pres, the importance of this literature rests not only in its revelation of the unspeakable and unthinkable horrors of history, but also in the placing of the "screams" and voices of the survivors in a collective consciousness that testifies to the fact of both survival and hope and struggle. Des Pres provides a powerful commentary on the importance of resurrecting those voices that have survived a history for which the scream of pain is translated into the struggle for emancipatory possibilities. He writes:

> And like any witness, the survivor gives testimony in situations where moral judgment depends on knowledge of what took place. Through him [sic] the events in question are verified and their reality made binding in the eyes of others. The survivor-as-witness, therefore, embodies a socio-historical process founded not upon the desire for justice (what can justice mean when genocide is the issue?), but upon the involvement of all human beings in common care for life and the future. "I want the world to read and to resolve that this must never, never be permitted to happen again" so concludes one survivor of Auschwitz. "I believe it is my duty," says another, "to let the world know on the basis of first-hand experience what can happen, what does happen, what must happen when human dignity is treated with cynical contempt." This is an attitude expressed often indeed by survivors. The assumption is that good and evil are only clear in retrospect; that moral vision depends on assimilation of the past; that man as man cannot dispense with memory. Wisdom depends on knowledge and it comes at a terrible price. It comes from consciousness of, and then response to, the deeds and events through which men have already passed. Conscience, as Schopenhauer puts it, is "man's knowledge concerning what he has done." (Terrence Des Pres, *the Survivor: An Anatomy of Life in the Death Camps* [New York: Washington Square Press], pp. 51-52).

44. Benhabib, "The Utopian Dimension in Communicative Ethics," pp. 93-94.

45. Agnes Heller, "The Basic Question of Moral Philosophy," *Philosophy and Social Criticism*, 1:11 (Summer 1985), p. 57.

46. Michael Lerner, "A New Paradigm for Liberals: The Primacy of Ethics and Emotions," *Tikkun*, 2:1 (1987), p. 136.

47. Heller, "The Basic Question of Moral Philosophy," p. 57.

48. Fredric Jameson, "Postmodernism, or the Cultural Logic of State Capitalism," *New Left Review*, 146 (July-August, 1984), p. 61.

49. Perry Anderson, *In the Tracks of Historical Materialism* (Chicago: University of Chicago Press, 1984); also see Ibid.

50. Terry Eagleton, "Marxism, Structuralism, and Post-Structuralism," *Diacritics* (Winter 1985), p. 5. For a well-balanced analysis of postmodernism, see Mas'ud Zavarzadeh and Donald Morton, "The Nostalgia for Law and Order and the Policing of Knowledge," *Syracuse Scholar* (Spring 1987), pp.25-71.

51. This is not true of course of the poststructuralist theorizing being done by a number of feminist theorists such as Luce Irigaray, Julia Kristeva, and Teresa de Lauretis, who have made significant gains in analyzing patriarchal discourse, female sexuality, and visual representation in the arts; moreover, the more recent work of Michel Foucault, Gilles Deleuze, Félix Guattari, Jacques Donzelot, and others begins to address the notion of the political project. See, for example, Foucault's work on the history of sexuality.

52. Critics remain at odds as to the conceptual utility of the term "postmodernity." The term is usually associated with the work of thinkers like Nietzsche, Heidegger, De Saussure, Peirce, Frege, Wittgenstein, Lyotard, Derrida, and Foucault, to name but a few. The term "postmodern" is also frequently associated with current movements in avant-garde art and architecture. Not only do we have a postmodern "condition" referring to the crisis of contemporary mass culture, but we also have postmodern social theory to help us deconstruct and unravel the complexities of such a condition. Nevertheless, postmodern social theorists and philosophers have often been criticized for their depoliticized discourse. The disillusionment brewing around postmodern social theory is perhaps best exemplified in recent criticisms of Michel Foucault and other poststructuralist writers. For example, Peter Dews speaks of Foucault's concept of power as an ubiquitous metaphysical ether that infuses all sociocultural relations and practices. See Peter Dews, "Power and Subjectivity in Foucault," *New Left Review*, 144 (March/April 1984), p. 91; see also John Rajchman, "Foucault's Dilemma," *Social Text*, 8 (Winter 1983/84), pp. 3-24; Rajchman, "Ethics after Foucault," *Social Text* 13/14 (Winter/Spring 1986), pp. 165-83. See also Keith Gandal's "Michel Foucault: Intellectual Work and Politics," *Telos*, 67 (Spring 1986), pp. 121-34. Unlike Dews, Gandal cogently concludes that "[Foucault] does provide us with the example of activism that is tactical and ethical and an intellectual practice that uses historical analysis to set up possible strategies and to create problems that we badly need" (p. 134). I share Gandal's position and also Rajchman's view that Foucault's work, especially his more recent work, constitutes a political project.

One of the more celebrated debates surrounding the postmodern turn in social theory has been a heated exchange between Lyotard and Habermas. Habermas has gone so far as to label Foucault, Lyotard, and Deleuze as "neoconservative" because they offer no theoretical explanations for the particular social directions they take in their work. For excellent commentaries on this exchange and other controversies surrounding the concept of "postmodernity," see all the entries of Praxis International 4, 1 (April 1984), or the book based on these articles, Richard Bernstein, ed., *Habermas and Modernity* (Cambridge, Mass.: MIT Press, 1985); for another excellent collection of articles on the postmodern condition, see *New German Critique*, 33 (Fall, 1984); for a discussion of Derrida's position, see Henry Staten "Rorty's Circumvention of Derrida," *Critical Inquiry*, 12:2 (1986), pp. 453-61; and Rorty's response, "The Higher Naturalism in a Nutshell: A Reply to Henry Staten," *Critical Inquiry*, 12:2 (1986), pp. 462-466. I would recommend the following: Jackson Lears, *No Place of Grace: Antimodernism and the Transformation of American Culture, 1880-1920* ((New York: Pantheon Books, 1981); David Frisby, *Fragments of Modernity* (Cambridge, Mass.: MIT Press, 1986); Hal Foster, ed., *The Anti-Aesthetic: Essays on Postmodern Culture* (Port Townsend, Wash.: Bay Press, 1983); John Fekete, ed., *The Structural Allegory: Reconstructive Encounters with New French Thought* (Minneapolis: University of Minnesota Press, 1984); Jean-François Lyotard, *The Postmodern Condition: A Report on Knowledge* (Minneapolis: University of Minnesota Press, 1979); Arthur Kroker and David Cook, *The Postmodern Scene* (New York: St. Martin's Press, 1986). There have also been a number of special issues on the postmodern/modernist debate in *Telos, New German Critique, Theory, Culture, and Society*, and *Social Text*.

53. Jameson, "Postmodernism," p. 66.

54. See the following works by Richard Rorty: *Philosophy and the Mirror of Nature* (Princeton: Princeton University Press, 1979); *Consequences of Pragmatism: Essays,*

1972-1980 (Minneapolis: University of Minnesota Press, 1982); "The Contingency of Language," *London Review of Books*, 8:7 (April 17, 1986), pp. 3-6; "Deconstruction and Circumvention," *Critical Inquiry* (September 1984), pp. 11-15; "Habermas and Lyotard on Postmodernity," in *Habermas and Modernity*, ed. Richard Bernstein (Cambridge, Mass.: MIT Press, 1985), pp. 161-76; "The Priority of Democracy to Philosophy," unpublished manuscript, 1986; "Solidarity or Objectivity?" in *Post-Analytic Philosophy*, ed. John Rajchman and Cornel West (New York: Columbia University Press, 1985), pp. 3-19.

55. Cornel West, "The Politics of American Neo-Pragmatism," in *Post Analytic Philosophy*, p. 266.

56. Rorty, *Consequences of Pragmatism*, p. xxxix.

57. Ibid., p. x.

58. Alfonso J. Damico, "The Politics after Deconstruction: Rorty, Dewey, and Marx," unpublished manuscript, 1986, p. 14.

59. West, "The Politics of American Neo-Pragmatism," p. 268.

60. Rebecca Comay, "Interrupting the Conversation: Notes on Rorty," *Telos*, 69 (Fall 1986), p. 124.

61. Landon Beyer and George Wood, "Critical Inquiry and Moral Action in Education," *Educational Theory*, 36:1 (1986), pp. 1-14.

62. Jo Anne Pagano, "The Schools We Deserve," *Curriculum Inquiry*, 17:1 (1987), pp. 107-22.

63. The notion of a politics of emotional investment is developed in Lawrence Grossberg, "Teaching the Popular," in *Theory in the Classroom*, ed. Cary Nelson (Urbana: University of Illinois Press, 1986), pp. 177-200.

64. A typical example of this position can be found in C. A. Bowers, *The Promise of Theory* (New York: Teachers College Press, 1984); *Elements of a Post-Liberal Theory of Education* (New York: Teachers College Press, 1984).

65. "The philosophers have only interpreted the world in various ways; the point is, to change it." Eleventh thesis on Feuerbach, Notebooks of 1844-1845, in *Writings of the Young Marx on Philosophy and Society*, ed. Lloyd D. Easton and Kurt H. Guddart (Garden City, N.Y.: Doubleday, 1967), p. 402.

66. Noam Chomsky, Turning the Tide (Boston: South End Press, 1985), p. 221.

67. "Reading the World and Reading the Word: An Interview with Paulo Freire," *Language Arts*, 62:1 (1985), pp. 17-18.

3. AUTHORITY, ETHICS, AND THE POLITICS OF SCHOOLING

1. A more recent set of writings on this view can be found in Diane Ravitch and Chester E. Finn, Jr., "High Expectations and Disciplined Effort," in *Against Mediocrity*, ed. Robert Fancher and Diane Ravitch (New York: Holmes and Meier, 1984); Diane Ravitch, *The Schools We Deserve* (New York: Basic Books, 1985); Thomas Sowell, *Education: Assumptions vs. History* (Stanford: Hoover Press, 1986); Allan Bloom, *The Closing of the American Mind* (New York: Simon and Schuster, 1987).

2. Edward Wynne, "The Great Tradition in Education: Transmitting Moral Values," *Educational Leadership*, 43:4 (December 1985), p. 7. Wynne's conservatism is a far cry from the thoughtful way in which Hannah Arendt defined the "conservative" nature of education. She is worth repeating here.

Basically we are always educating for a world that is or is becoming out of joint, for this is the basic human situation, in which the world is created by mortal hands to serve mortals for a limited time as home. Because the world is made by mortals it wears out; and because it continuously changes its inhabitants it runs the risk of becoming as mortal as they. To preserve the world against the mortality of its creators and inhabitants it must be constantly set right anew. The problem is simply to educate in such a way that a setting-right remains actually possible, even though it can, of course, never be assured. Our hope always hangs on the new which every generation brings; but precisely because we can base our hope only on this, we destroy everything if we so try to control the new that we, the old, can dictate how it will look. Exactly for the sake of what is new and revolutionary in every child, education must be conservative; it must preserve this newness and introduce it as a new thing into an old world, which, however revolutionary its actions may be, is always, from the standpoint of the next generation, superannuated and close to destruction. (Hannah Arendt, "What Is Authority?" in *Between Past and Present* [New York: Penguin Books, 1977], pp. 192-93.)

3. For an exceptional critique of this position, see Barbara Finkelstein, "Education and the Retreat from Democracy in the United States, 1979-198?," *Teachers College Record*, 86:2 (Winter 1984), pp. 275-82; Maxine Greene, "Public Education and the Public Space," *Educational Researcher* (June-July 1982), pp. 4-9.

4. Agnes Heller, "Marx and the Liberation of Humankind," *Philosophy and Social Criticism*, ¾ (1982), p. 367.

5. David Nyberg and Paul Farber, "Authority in Education," *Teachers College Record*, 88:1 (Fall 1986), p. 1.

6. Critiques of this position can be found in William V. Spanos, "The Apollonian Investment of Modern Humanist Education: The Example of Mathew Arnold, Irving Babbitt, and I. A. Richards," *Cultural Critique*, 1 (Fall 1985), pp. 7-22; Henry A. Giroux, David Shumway, Paul Smith, and James Sosnoski, "The Need for Cultural Studies: Resisting Intellectuals and Oppositional Public Spheres," *Dalhousie Review*, 64:2 (Summer 1984), pp. 472-86.

7. Jerry Farber, *The Student as Nigger* (New York: Pocket, 1969), p. 121.

8. Susan Stanford Friedman, "Authority in the Feminist Classroom: A Contradiction in Terms?" in *Gendered Subjects: The Dynamics of Feminist Teaching*, ed. Margo Culley and Catherine Portuges (London: Routledge and Kegan Paul, 1985), pp. 206-07.

9. This view of radical educational theory and its various representations is comprehensively analyzed in Stanley Aronowitz and Henry A. Giroux, *Education under Siege: The Conservative, Liberal, and Radical Debate in Schooling* (South Hadley, Mass.: Bergin and Garvey, 1985).

10. Kenneth D. Benne, "Authority in Education," *Harvard Educational Review*, 40:3 (August 1970), pp. 385-410; another classic example of the liberal position can be found in Paul Nash, *Authority and Freedom in Education* (New York: Wiley, 1966).

11. Cited in Colin Gordon, "Afterword," in Michel Foucault, *Power/Knowledge: Selected Interviews and Other Writings, 1972-1977*, ed. Colin Gordon (New York: Pantheon, 1980), p. 233.

12. Nyberg and Farmer, "Authority in Education"; Steve Tozer, "Dominant Ideology and the Teacher's Authority," *Contemporary Education*, 56:3 (Spring 1985), pp. 150-53; Steve Tozer, "Civism, Democratic Empowerment, and the Social Foundations of Education," in *Philosophy of Education 1985*, ed. David Nyberg (Philosophy of

Education Society, 1986), pp. 186-200; George Wood, "Schooling in a Democracy," *Educational Theory*, 34:3 (Summer 1984), pp. 219-38. Helen Freeman, "Authority, Power, and Knowledge: Politics and Epistemology in the 'New' Sociology of Education," in *Philosophy of Education 1980: Proceedings of the Philosophy of Education Society*, ed. C. J. B. Macmillan (Normal, Ill.: Illinois State University, 1981). A classic statement has been made by Hannah Arendt in "What Is Authority?" in *Between Past and Present* (New York: Penguin, 1977).

13. John Dewey, "Creative Democracy—The Task Before Us," in *Classic American Philosophers*, ed. Max H. Fisch (New York: Appleton-Century-Crofts, 1951), p. 394.

14. John Dewey, "Outline of a Critical Theory of Ethics," in *The Early Works of John Dewey, 1882-1898*, Volume III (Carbondale: Southern Illinois University Press, 1969), p. 35.

15. John Childs, "Democracy and Educational Method," *Progressive Education*, 16:1 (February, 1939), pp. 119-20. It is important to contrast the social reconstructionist position of individualism as a referent for improving community life with the conservatives emphasis on patriotism, obedience, and adaptation to existing social arrangements.

16. Ibid., p. 119. Again, excellence in this perspective is quite at odds with the current conservative position which defines teachers' work and students' learning, not around ethical criteria designed to improve the quality of human life, but as the application of predefined goals and the mastering of "basic" techniques. The Reagan administration's sense of educational excellence can be seen in the nomination of Linus Wright, superintendent of the Dallas Independent School System, for the position of Undersecretary of Education. Wright's claim to leadership appears to rest not on his sense of democratic vision, but rather on his adeptness at developing a *computerized* merit-pay system for teachers based on student performance on standardized tests.

17. This debate generated an interesting exchange in the pages of *The Social Frontier* between John Childs and Boyd Bode, both of whom were theoretically indebted to the work of John Dewey. See Boyd Bode, "Education and Social Reconstruction," *The Social Frontier*, 1:4 (January 1935), pp. 18-22; John Childs, "Professor Bode on 'Faith in Intelligence,'" *The Social Frontier*, 1:6 (March 1935), pp. 20-21; Boyd Bode, "Dr. Childs and Education for Democracy," *The Social Frontier*, 5:39 (November 1938), pp. 40-43; John Childs, "Dr. Bode on Authentic Democracy," *The Social Frontier*, 5:39 (November 1938), pp. 40-43. Dewey responded to this debate by siding with neither Bode nor Childs; instead, he attempted to portray their respective positions as making distinct but related contributions to the overall general debate on the relationship between schooling and democracy. See John Dewey, "Education, Democracy, and Socialized Economy," *The Social Frontier*, 5:40 (December 1938), pp. 70-72. A classic statement on the issues discussed in this debate can be found in Sidney Hook, "The Importance of a Point of View," *The Social Frontier*, 1:1 (October 1934), pp. 19-22.

18. John Dewey, "The Need for a Recovery of Philosophy," reprinted in *The Philosophy of John Dewey*, ed. John McDermott (Chicago: University of Chicago Press, 1981), p. 473.

19. See John Dewey, *Democracy and Education* (New York: The Free Press, 1944, originally published in 1916); John Dewey, *The Public and Its Problems in The Later*

Works of John Dewey, Volume 2., 1925-1927, ed. Jo Ann Boydston (Carbondale: Southern Illinois University Press, 1984), pp. 235-372.

20. Jesse Newlon, "Democracy or Super-patriotism?" *The Social Frontier*, 7:59 (April 1941), p. 210

21. Claude Lefort, *The Political Forms of Modern Society* (Cambridge, Mass.: MIT Press, 1987), especially Chapter 8, "The Logic of Totalitarianism," pp. 273-91. For a criticism of classroom authority from the perspective of symbolic anthropology, see Peter McLaren, *Schooling as a Ritual Performance* (London and New York: Routledge and Kegan Paul, 1986).

22. This point is clearly expressed by Richard Bernstein and is worth quoting at length:

> Long before the current fascination with radical incommensurability, Dewey was aware of the danger of the type of degenerate pluralism that would block community and communication. He was perspicacious in seeing this not primarily as a theoretical problem, but as a practical problem—a problem that demands working toward a type of society in which we can at once respect and even celebrate differences and plurality but always strive to understand and seek a common ground with what is other and different. ... But now we are threatened by what I earlier called "wild pluralism" which has infected almost every aspect of our everyday lives and has spread to virtually every area of human culture. This is a pluralism in which we are so enclosed in our own frameworks and our own points of view that we seem to be losing the civility, desire, and even the ability to communicate and share with others. (Richard Bernstein, "The Varieties of Pluralism," in *Current Issues in Education*, ed. Chris Eisele [Normal, Ill.: The College of Education, Illinois State University for the John Dewey Society and the Study of Education and Culture, 1985], pp. 15-16.)

23. John Childs, "Democracy, Education, and the Class Struggle," *The Social Frontier*, 3:3 (June 1936), p. 277.

24. Antonio Gramsci, *Selections from the Prison Notebooks*, ed. and trans. Quinten Hoare and Geoffrey Smith (New York: International Publishers, 1971).

25. Alvin Gouldner, *The Future of Intellectuals and the Rise of the New Class* (New York: Seabury Press, 1979); Pierre Bourdieu and Jean-Claude Passeron, *Reproduction in Education, Society, and Culture*, trans. Richard Nice (Beverly Hills: Sage, 1977); Pierre Bourdieu, *Distinction: A Social Critique of the Judgment of Taste*, trans. Richard Nice (Cambridge, Mass.: Harvard University Press, 1984); André Gorz, *Farewell to the Working Class* (Boston: South End Press, 1982); Also see George Konrad and Ivan Szelenyi, *The Intellectuals on the Road to Class Power* (New York: Harcourt Brace Jovanovich, 1979); Paul A. Bove, *Intellectuals in Power* (New York: Columbia University Press, 1986); Alvin W. Gouldner, *Against Fragmentation: The Origins of Marxism and the Sociology of Intellectuals* (New York: Oxford University Press, 1985).

26. John Dewey, *Democracy and Education* (New York: Macmillan, 1916); John Dewey, "Creative Democracy—the Task Before Us," reprinted in *Classic American Philosophers*, ed. Max Fisch (New York: Appleton-Century-Crofts, 1951); George S. Counts, *Dare the Schools Build a New Social Order* (New York: Day, 1932); see also Richard J. Bernstein, "Dewey, Democracy: The Task Ahead of Us," in *Post-Analytic Philosophy*, ed. John Rajchman and Cornel West (New York: Columbia University Press, 1985).

27. Benjamin Barber, *Strong Democracy: Participating Politics for a New Age* (Berkeley: University of California Press, 1984).
28. Sheldon Wolin, "Revolutionary Action Today," in *Post-Analytic Philosophy*, p. 256.
29. For an important discussion on these concepts, see Richard Lichtman, "Socialist Freedom," in *Socialist Perspectives*, ed. Phyllis and Julius Jacobson (New York: Kary-Cohl Publishing, 1983); Landon E. Beyer and George Wood, "Critical Inquiry and Moral Action in Education," *Educational Theory*, 36:1 (Winter 1986), pp. 1-14.
30. For an excellent discussion of this issue, see Doug White, "Education; Controlling the Participants," *Arena*, 72 (1985), pp. 63-79.
31. It is impossible to cite all the important sources in feminist theory. The following books have been helpful in my own reading and are indicative of the theoretical range of some of the major contributions being made in feminist theory: Jean Grimshaw, *Philosophy and Feminist Thinking* (Minneapolis: University of Minnesota Press, 1986); Sondra Farganis, *The Social Reconstruction of the Feminine Character* (New Jersey: Rowman and Littlefield, 1986); Teresa de Lauretis, ed., *Feminist Studies, Critical Studies* (Bloomington: Indiana University Press, 1986); Carole Pateman and Elizabeth Gross, eds., *Feminist Challenges: Social and Political Theory* (Boston: Northeastern University Press, 1986); Juliet Mitchell and Ann Oakley, *What Is Feminism?* (New York: Pantheon, 1986); Lillian S. Robinson, *Sex, Class, and Culture* (New York: Methuen, 1986); Hélène Cixous and Catherine Clement, *The Newly Born Woman*, trans. Betsy Wing (Minneapolis: University of Minnesota Press, 1986); Alice A. Jardine, *Gynesis: Configurations of Woman and Modernity* (Ithaca: Cornell University Press, 1985); Luce Irigary, *Speculum of the Other Woman*, trans. Gillian Gill (Ithaca: Cornell University Press, 1985); Luce Irigary, *This Sex Which Is Not One* (Ithaca: Cornell University Press, 1985); Janice A. Radway, *Reading the Romance* (Chapel Hill: The University of North Carolina Press, 1984); Carroll Smith-Rosenberg, *Disorderly Conduct* (New York: Oxford University Press, 1984); Judith Newton and Deborah Rosenfelt, eds., *Feminist Criticism and Social Change* (New York: Methuen, 1984); Teresa de Lauretis, *Alice Doesn't: Feminism, Semiotics, Cinema* (Bloomington: Indiana University Press, 1984); Nell Noddings, *Caring: A Feminine Approach to Ethics and Moral Education* (Berkeley: University of California Press, 1984); Carole S. Vance, ed. *Pleasure and Danger: Exploring Female Sexuality* (London: Routledge and Kegan Paul, 1984); Elly Bulkin, Minnie Pratt, and Barbara Smith, *Yours in Struggle* (New York: Long Haul Press, 1984); Ann Snitow, Christine Stansell and Sharon Thompson, eds., *Powers of Desire: The Politics of Sexuality* (New York: Monthly Review Press, 1983); Annette Kuhn, *Women's Pictures* (London: Routledge and Kegan Paul, 1982); Carol Gilligan, *In a Different Voice* (Cambridge, Mass.: Harvard University Press, 1982); Michele Barrett, *Women's Oppression Today: Problems in Marxist Feminist Analysis* (London: Verso Press, 1980); Nancy Chodorow, *The Reproduction of Mothering: Psychoanalysis and the Sociology of Gender* (Berkeley: University of California Press, 1978); Juliet Mitchell, *Psychoanalysis and Feminism: Freud, Reich, Laing, and Women* (New York: Vintage Books, 1975).
32. Jurgen Moltmann, *Theology of Hope: On the Ground and the Implications of a Christian Eschatology*, trans. James W. Leitch (New York: Harper and Row, 1967); Gustavo Guitierrez, *A Theology of Liberation*, ed. and trans. Sister Caridad Inda and John Eagleson (Maryknoll, N.Y.: Orbis Books, 1973); Gustavo Guitierrez, *The Power of the Poor in History*, trans. Robert R. Barr (Maryknoll, N.Y.: Orbis Books, 1973); Jose Miguez Binino, *Doing Theology in a Revolutionary Situation* (Philadelphia: Fortress

Press, 1975); Leonardo Boff, *Christology at the Crossroads: A Latin American Approach*, trans. John Drury (Maryknoll, N.Y.: Orbis Books, 1978); Thomas F. McFadden, ed., *Liberation, Revolution and Freedom* (New York: Seabury Press, 1979); Johann Baptist Metz, *Faith in History and Society*, trans. David Smith (New York: Seabury Press, 1980); Dorothee Soelle, *Choosing Life* (Philadelphia: Fortress Press, 1981); Cornel West, *Prophesy Deliverance* (Philadelphia: The Westminister Press, 1982); Juan Luis Segundo, *The Liberation of Theology* (Maryknoll, N.Y.: Orbis Books, 1982); Mathew Lamb, *Solidarity with Victims: Toward a Theology of Social Transformation* (New York: Crossroad Publishing, Co., 1982); Enrique Dussel, *Philosophy of Liberation* (Maryknoll, New York: Orbis Books, 1985); Franz J. Hinkelammert, *The Ideological Weapons of Death: A Theological Critique of Capitalism* (Maryknoll, N.Y.: Orbis Books, 1986); Philip Berryman, *Liberation Theology* (New York: Pantheon Books, 1986); Rebecca S. Chopp, *The Praxis of Suffering* (Maryknoll, N.Y.: Orbis Books, 1986).

33. Sharon Welch, *A Feminist Ethic of Risk and Resistance* (Philadelphia: Fortress Press, forthcoming). I am theoretically indebted to Sharon Welch for both the use and development of the category "feminist ethic of risk and resistance." The work of the feminist theologians I am referring to in this section includes: Beverly Wildung Harrison, *Making the Connections: Essays in Feminist Social Ethics*, ed. Carol S. Robb (Boston: Beacon Press, 1985); Sharon Welch, *Communities of Resistance and Solidarity* (Maryknoll, N.Y.: Orbis Books, 1985); Rosemary Radford Ruether, *Sexism and God-Talk: Toward a Feminist Theology* (Boston: Beacon Press, 1983); Margaret A. Farley, *Personal Commitments* (New York: Harper and Row, 1986).

34. Harrison, *Making the Connections*, pp. 249-50.

35. Noddings, *Caring*; Grimshaw, *Philosophy and Feminist Thinking*.

36. Metz, *Faith in History and Society*, p. 172.

37. Grimshaw, *Philosophy and Feminist Thinking*, pp. 197-98.

38. Noddings, *Caring*; Farley, *Personal Commitments*.

39. Harrison, *Making the Connections*, p. 21.

40. Ibid., p. 20.

41. Carol Robb, "Introduction," in Beverly Harrison, *Making the Connections*, p. xix. Another feature of the dominant ideology that structures the mind/body duality is that it often functions either to ignore or denigrate the importance of the formation of desire and pleasure as a fundamental aspect of individual and social identity. This issue is developed in Valerie Walkerdine, "Video Replay: Families, Films, and Fantasy," in *Formations of Fantasy*, ed. Victor Burgin, James Donald, and Cora Kaplan (New York: Methuen, 1986), pp. 167-99.

42. Metz, *Faith in History and Society*, p. 66.

43. Chopp, *The Praxis of Suffering*, p. 28.

44. Sharon Welch, *Communities of Resistance and Solidarity* (New York: Orbis Press, 1985), p. 31.

45. Ibid., p. 31.

46. Ibid., p. 36.

47. Michel Foucault, "Two Lectures," in *Power/Knowledge: Selected Interviews and Other Writings*, ed. C. Gordon (New York: Pantheon, 1980), pp. 82-83.

48. Hannah Arendt, *The Human Condition* (Chicago: The University of Chicago Press, 1958).

49. Maxine Greene, "Excellence, Meanings and Multiplicity," *Teachers College Record*, 86:2 (Winter 1984), p. 296.

50. James Donald, "Troublesome Texts: On Subjectivity and Schooling," *British Journal of Sociology of Education*, 6:3 (1985), p. 342; Roger Simon, "Work Experience as the Production of Subjectivity," in *Pedagogy and Cultural Power*, ed. David Livingstone (South Hadley, Mass.: Bergin and Garvey, 1986).

51. For an critical analysis of these issues and how progressive educators can deal with them, see Ann Bastian, Norm Fruchter, Marilyn Gittell, Colin Greer, and Kenneth Haskins, *Choosing Equality: The Case for Democratic Schooling* (New York: New World Foundation, 1985).

52. Michel Foucault, "The Subject of Power," in *Beyond Structuralism and Hermeneutics* by Hubert Dreyfus and Paul Rabinow (Chicago: University of Chicago Press, 1982), p. 221. For an interesting analysis of why power should be a central category in educational discourse, see David Nyberg, *Power over Power* (New York: Cornell University Press, 1981).

53. Aronowitz and Giroux, *Education under Siege*.

54. Michel Foucault, "The Subject of Power."

55. Colin Fletcher, Maxine Caron and Wyn Williams, *Schools on Trials* (Philadelphia: Open University Press, 1985).

56. Nyberg rightly argues that educators need to develop a theory and pedagogy about power as a central aspect of the curriculum, see David Nyberg, *Power over Power*.

57. R. W. Connell, D. J. Ashenden, S. Kessler, G. W. Dowsett, *Making the Difference* (Sydney, Australia: Allen and Unwin, 1982), p. 199.

58. Michelle Gibbs Russell, "Black Eyed Blues Connections: From the Inside Out," in *Learning Our Way: Essays in Feminist Education*, eds. Charlotte Bunch and Sandra Pollack (New York: The Crossing Press, 1983), p. 272.

59. Ibid., p. 273.

60. Judith Williamson, "Is There Anyone Here From a Classroom?" *Screen*, 26:1 (January-February 1985), p. 94.

61. Ann Bastian, Norm Fruchter, Marilyn Gittell, Colin Greer and Kenneth Haskins, "Choosing Equality: The Case for Democratic Schooling," *Social Policy*, 15:4 (Spring 1985), p. 47.

62. Timothy Sieber, "The Politics of Middle-Class Success in an Inner-City Public School," *Boston University Journal of Education*, 164:137 (Winter 1982), pp. 30-47.

63. Martin Carnoy, "Education, Democracy and Social Conflict," *Harvard Educational Review*, 53:4 (November 1983), pp. 401-2.

4. SCHOOLING AND THE POLITICS OF STUDENT VOICE

1. This position has a long history in American public education and is reviewed in Raymond Callahan, *The Cult of Efficiency* (Chicago: University of Chicago Press, 1962); Joel Spring, *Education and the Rise of the Corporate Order* (Boston: Beacon Press, 1972); Henry A. Giroux, "Public Philosophy and the Crisis in Education," *Harvard Educational Review*, 54:2 (1984), pp. 186-94.

2. The most celebrated example of this position can be found in Sam Bowles and Herbert Gintis, *Schooling in Capitalist America* (New York: Basic Books, 1976). The literature on schooling and the reproductive thesis is critically reviewed in Stanley Aronowitz and Henry A. Giroux, *Education under Siege: The Conservative, Liberal, and Radical Debate over Schooling* (South Hadley, Mass.: Bergin and Garvey, 1985).

3. Mikhail Bakhtin, *The Dialogic Imagination*, trans. Caryl Emerson and Michael Holquist (Austin: University of Texas Press, 1981), p. 294.

4. Mortimer J. Adler, *The Paideia Proposal* (New York: Macmillan, 1982). E. D. Hirsch Jr., *Cultural Literacy: What Every American Needs to Know* (Boston: Houghton Mifflin, 1987); Allan Bloom, *The Closing of the American Mind* (Chicago: University of Chicago, 1987).

5. Bloom, *The Closing of the American Mind*, p. 75.

6. Ibid, p. 74.

7. Adler, *The Paideia Proposal*, p. 42.

8. Philip Cusick, *The Egalitarian Ideal and the American School* (New York: Longman, 1983), pp. 25, 71.

9. Ibid., p. 108.

10. Philip Corrigan, "Race, Ethnicity, Gender, Culture: Embodying Differences Educationally—An Argument," unpublished Paper, Ontario Institute for Studies in Education, 1985, p. 7.

11. Robert Jeffcoate, *Positive Image: Towards a Multicultural Curriculum* (London: Writers and Readers Cooperative, 1979), p. 122.

12. Nathan Glazer, "Cultural Pluralism: The Social Aspect," in *Pluralism in a Democratic Society*, ed. M. Tumen and W. Plotch (New York: Prager, 1977), p. 51.

13. I want to make clear that there is a major distinction between the work of John Dewey, especially *Democracy and Education* (New York: The Free Press, 1916), and the hybrid discourses of progressive, educational reform that characterized the late 1960s and 1970s in the United States. The discourse of relevance and integration that I am analyzing here bears little resemblance to Dewey's philosophy of experience in that Dewey stressed the relationship among student experience, critical reflection, and learning. In contrast, the call for relevance that has characterized the dominant quarters of progressive education generally surrenders the concept of systematic knowledge acquisition and uncritically privileges an anti-intellectual concept of student experience.

14. Cusick, "The Egalitarian Ideal and the American School," p. 55.

15. Jeanne Oakes, "Keeping Track, Part 1: The Policy and Practice of Curriculum Inequality," *Phi Delta Kappan*, (September 1986), p. 15. For a more extensive treatment of tracking, see Jeannie Oakes, *Keeping Track: How Schools Structure Inequality* (New Haven: Yale University Press, 1985). See also Henry A. Giroux and David Purpel, *The Hidden Curriculum and Moral Education* (Berkeley: McCutchan Publishing, 1983).

16. Julian Henriques, Wendy Hollway, Cathy Urwin, Couze Venn, and Valerie Walkerdine, *Changing the Subject* (New York: Methuen, 1984).

17. Carl Rogers, *Freedom to Learn* (Columbus, Ohio: Charles Merrill, 1969).

18. National Coalition of Advocates for Students, *Barriers to Excellence: Our Children at Risk* (Boston: NCAS, 1985), p. x.

19. Ibid., pp. 10, 14, 16.

20. Henry A. Giroux, *Theory and Resistance in Education* (South Hadley, Mass.: Bergin and Garvey, 1983).

21. The works from which I will be drawing for both authors include Paulo Freire, *Pedagogy of the Oppressed* (New York: Seabury Press, 1970); Paulo Freire, *Education for Critical Consciousness* (New York: Seabury Press, 1973); Paulo Freire, *The Politics of Education* (South Hadley, Mass.: Bergin and Garvey, 1985). Mikhail Bakhtin, *Rabe-*

lais and His World, trans. Helene Iswolsky (Bloomington: Indiana University Press, 1984); Mikhail Bakhtin, *Problems of Dostoevsky's Poetics*, trans. Caryl Emerson (Minneapolis: University of Minnesota Press, 1984); Mikhail Bakhtin, *The Dialogic Imagination*, trans. Caryl Emerson and Michael Holquist (Austin: University of Texas Press, 1981); V. N. Volosinov [M. M. Bakhtin] *Marxism and the Philosophy of Language*, trans. Ladislav Mateyka and I. R. Titunik, (New York: Seminar Press, 1973); V. N. Volosinov [M. M. Bakhtin], *Freudianism: A Marxist Critique*, trans. I. R. Titunik and edited in collaboration with Neal H. Bruss (New York: Academic Press, 1976).

22. Richard Johnson, "What Is Cultural Studies Anyway?" *Anglistica*, 26:1-2 (1983), p. 11.

23. Roger Simon, "Work Experience as the Production of Subjectivity," in *Critical Pedagogy and Cultural Power*, ed. David Livingstone (South Hadley, Mass.: Bergin and Garvey, 1987), pp. 176-77.

24. See Ann Shukman, ed., *Bakhtin's School Papers* (Oxford: RPT Publications, 1983); V. N. Volosinov (M. M. Bakhtin), *Marxism and the Philosophy of Language*.

25. Volosinov [Bakhtin], *Marxism and the Philosophy of Language*, pp. 85-86.

26. V. N. Volosinov (M. M. Bakhtin), "Discourse in Life and Discourse in Art," in *Freudianism: A Marxist Critique*, p. 106.

27. A major analysis of these discourses and the traditions of which they are generally associated can be found in Richard Johnson, "What Is Cultural Studies Anyway?"

28. Examples of this discourse can be found in Martin Carnoy and Henry Levin, *Schooling and Work in the Democratic State* (Stanford: Stanford University Press, 1985).

29. C. W. Mills, "Mass Society and Liberal Education," in *The Collected Essays of C. W. Mills*, ed. Irving Louis Horowitz (New York: Oxford University Press, 1979), p. 370.

30. Stanley Aronowitz and Henry A. Giroux, *Education under Siege* (South Hadley, Mass.: Bergin and Garvey, 1985).

31. John Dewey, *The Public and Its Problems* (originally published in 1927) in *John Dewey, The Later Works, Volume 2: 1925-1927*, ed. Jo Ann Boydston (Carbondale, Ill.: Southern Illinois University Press, 1984); C. W. Mills, "Mass Society and Liberal Education."

32. Pierre Macherey, *A Theory of Literary Production*, trans. Geoffrey Wall (London: Routledge and Kegan Paul, 1978), p. 6.

33. Catherine Belsey, *Critical Practice* (New York: Methuen, 1980), p. 104.

34. Johnson, "What Is Cultural Studies Anyway?" pp. 64-65.

35. Michael Apple, *Education and Power* (New York: Routledge and Kegan Paul, 1983).

36. Judith Williamson, *Decoding Advertisements* (New York: Marion Boyars, 1978).

37. Ariel Dorfman, *The Empire's Old Clothes* (New York: Pantheon Press, 1983).

38. Alain Touraine, *The Self-Production of Society*, trans. Derek Coltman (Chicago: University of Chicago Press, 1977).

39. Michele Sola and Adrian Bennett, "The Struggle for Voice; Narrative, Literacy, and Consciousness in an East Harlem School," *Boston University Journal of Education*, 167:1 (1985), p. 89.

40. Kathleen Weiler, *Women Teaching for Change: Gender, Class and Power* (South Hadley, Mass: Bergin and Garvey, 1987).

5. LITERACY, CRITICAL PEDAGOGY, AND EMPOWERMENT

1. Antonio Gramsci, quoted in James Donald, "Language, Literacy, and Schooling," *The State and Popular Culture* (Milton Keynes: Open University Press, U203 Popular Culture Unit, 1982), p. 44. For Gramsci's remarks on language, see scattered remarks in Antonio Gramsci, *Selections From Prison Notebooks*, ed. and trans. Quinten Hoare and Geoffrey Smith (New York: International Publishers, 1971); *Letters from Prison* (London: Jonathan Cape, 1975).

2. See, for example, Paulo Freire, *Pedagogy of the Oppressed* (New York: Seabury Press, 1970); Paulo Freire, *Education for Critical Consciousness* (New York: Seabury Press, 1973); Paulo Freire, *The Politics of Education* (South Hadley, Mass.: Bergin and Garvey, 1985). Mikhail Bakhtin, *The Dialogic Imagination*, trans. Caryl Emerson and Michael Holquist (Austin: University of Texas Press, 1981); V. N. Volosinov [M. M. Bakhtin] *Marxism and the Philosophy of Language*, trans. Ladislav Mateyka and I. R. Titunik (New York: Seminar Press, 1973); V. N. Volosinov [M. M. Bakhtin], *Freudianism: A Marxist Critique*, trans. I. R. Titunik and edited in collaboration with Neal H. Bruss (New York: Academic Press, 1976).

3. For a classic advocacy statement of this position, see Research and Policy Committee of the Committee for Economic Development, *Investing in Our Children: Business and the Public Schools* (New York: Committee for Economic Development, 1985). A critique of this position can be found in Stanley Aronowitz and Henry A. Giroux, *Education under Siege: The Conservative, Liberal, and Radical Debate over Schooling* (South Hadley, Mass.: Bergin and Garvey, 1985).

4. This is particularly obvious not only in the discourse of cultural deprivation theorists of the New Right such as Nathan Glazer, but also in the advocacy of federal policy on education by the Reagan administration. For instance, Secretary of Education, William Bennett, an outspoken opponent of bilingualism, argues a position that is less an attack on language-minority policy per se than it is on the role that education might play in the empowerment of minorities by dignifying their culture and experience. For an interesting popular analysis of this issue, see James Crawford, "Bilingual Educators Discuss Politics of Education," *Education Week* (November 19, 1986), pp. 15-16. For a more theoretical treatment, see James Cummins, "Empowering Minority Students: A Framework for Intervention," *Harvard Educational Review* 56:1 (February 1986), pp. 18-36.

5. Stanley Aronowitz, "Why Should Johnny Read?" *The Village Voice Literary Supplement* (May 1985), p. 13.

6. For an exception to this issue, see the various articles on the politics of literacy, edited by Donald Lazere in *Humanities in Society*, 4:4 (Fall 1981). See also Richard Ohmann, *English in America* (Cambridge: Oxford University Press, 1976); Richard Ohmann, "Literacy, Technology and Monopoly Capital," *College English*, 47:(1985), pp. 675-84; Valerie Miller, *Between Struggle and Hope: The Nicaraguan Literacy Crusade* (Boulder: Westview Press, 1985); Aronowitz, "Why Should Johnny Read?"; Donald, "Language, Literature, and Schooling." For a review of the conservative, liberal, and radical literature on literacy, see Henry A. Giroux, *Theory and Resistance in Education* (South Hadley, Mass.: Bergin and Garvey, 1983); Linda Brodkey, "Tropics of Literacy," *Boston University Journal of Education*, 168:2 (1986), pp.47-54; Rita Roth, "Schooling, Literacy Acquisition and Cultural Transmission," *Boston University Journal of Education*, 166:3 (1984), pp. 291-308; Ira Shor, *Culture Wars* (New York: Rout-

ledge and Kegan Paul, 1986). For an excellent demonstration of the relationship between a radical theory of literacy and classroom practice, see Alex McLeod, "Critical Literacy: Taking Control of Our Own Lives," *Language Arts*, 63:1 (January 1986), pp. 37-50; Shirley Heath, *Way with Words* (New York: McGraw-Hill, 1983). For an excellent review of the literature on literacy and reading instruction, see Patrick Shannon, "Reading Instruction and Social Class," *Language Arts*, 62:6 (October 1985), pp. 604-11; for an important critique of the dominant approach to reading and literacy based on the use of Basal Readers, see Kenneth Goodman, "Basal Readers: A Call for Action," *Language Arts*, 63:4 (April 1986), pp. 358-63. For an analysis of the literacy crisis in the United States, see Jonothan Kozol, *Illiterate America*, (New York: New American Library, 1986).

7. For a theoretical analysis of the relationship between Freire's work and the discourse of hope and transformation, see Peter McLaren, "Postmodernity and the Death of Politics: A Brazilian Reprieve," *Educational Theory*, 36:4 (1986), pp. 389-401.

8. The most recent book on Freire's theory of literacy is Paulo Freire and Donaldo Macedo, *Literacy: Reading the World and the Word* (South Hadley, Mass.: Bergin and Garvey, 1987); For a recent view of Freire's theory of literacy and politics, see David Dillon, "Reading the World and Reading the Word: An Interview with Paulo Freire," *Language Arts*, 62:1 (January 1985), pp. 15-21.

9. Antonio Gramsci, *Selections from Prison Notebooks*, ed. and trans. Quinten Hoare and Geoffrey Smith (New York: International Publishers, 1971).

10. For an outstanding discussion of literacy and ideology, see Linda Brodkey, *Writing on Parole: Essays and Studies on Academic Discourse* (Philadelphia: Temple University Press, 1987); Kathleen Rockhill, "Gender, Language, and the Politics of Literacy," *British Journal of Sociology of Education*, 8:2 (1987), pp. 153-67; Kathleen Rockhill, "Literacy as Threat/Desire: Longing to be SOMEBODY," Ontario Institute for Studies in Education, 1987, unpublished manuscript, 33 pp.

11. Aronowitz and Giroux, *Education under Siege*.

12. Gillian Swanson, "Rethinking Representations," *Screen*, 27:5 (October 1986), pp. 16-28.

13. Roger Simon, "Empowerment as a Pedagogy of Possibility," *Language Arts*, 64:4 (April 1987), pp. 370-82.

14. Stanley Aronowitz, "Why Should Johnny Read?" p. 13.

15. Philip Corrigan, "State Formation and Classroom Practice," paper delivered at the "Ivor Goodson" Seminar, University of Western Ontario, October 2-3, 1986, pp. 5-6.

16. For a critical discussion of theories of reproduction and resistance, see Henry A. Giroux, *Theory and Resistance in Education*; also see J. C. Walker, "Romanticising Resistance, Romanticising Culture: Problems in Willis's Theory of Cultural Production," *British Journal of Sociology of Education*, 7:1 (1986), pp. 59-80.

17. Fred Inglis, *The Management of Ignorance* (London: Blackwell, 1985), p. 108.

18. Toni Cade Bambara, "Salvation is the Issue," in *Black Women Writers (1950-1980): A Critical Evaluation* (Garden City, N.Y.: Anchor Books, 1984), p. 46. This theme is brilliantly developed in Sharon Welch, *A Feminist Ethic of Risk* (New York: Fortress Press, forthcoming).

19. Harold Rosen, "The Importance of Story," *Language Arts*, 63:3 (March 1986), pp. 226-237.

20. Walter Benjamin, *Illuminations*, ed. Hannah Arendt (New York: Schocken, 1969), especially "Thesis on the Philosophy of History," pp. 253-64.

21. Ernst Bloch, *The Principle of Hope*, vol. 3 (Cambridge, Mass.: MIT Press, 1985). For a detailed discussion of the politics of anti-utopianism, hope, and struggle in radical theories of education, see chapter 7.

22. This theme is most developed in the various works and traditions of liberation theology. For an insightful overview and critical analysis of this perspective, see Rebecca S. Chopp, *The Praxis of Suffering* (Maryknoll, N.Y.: Orbis Books, 1986).

23. See Herbert Marcuse, *Eros and Civilization* (Boston: Beacon Press, 1955); Paul Ricoeur, *Freud and Philosophy: An Essay on Interpretation*, trans. Denis Savage (New Haven: Yale University Press, 1970).

24. Martin Jay, "Anamnestic Totalization," *Theory and Society*, 11 (1982), p. 13.

25. Peter McLaren, *Schooling as a Ritual Performance* (New York: Routledge and Kegan Paul, 1986).

26. Simon, "Empowerment," p. 372.

27. David Lusted, "Why Pedagogy?" *Screen*, 27:5 (September-October 1986), pp. 4-5.

28. For an important analysis of similar issues, see Kathleen Weiler, *Women Teaching for Change* (South Hadley, Mass.: Bergin and Garvey, 1987).

29. For a superb history of curriculum as a field of struggle, see Herbert M. Kliebard, *The Struggle for the American Curriculum, 1893-1958* (New York: Routledge and Kegan Paul, 1986).

30. Henry A. Giroux, "Radical Pedagogy and the Politics of Student Voice," *Interchange*, 17:1 (1986), pp. 48-69.

31. Sharon Welch, *Communities of Resistance and Solidarity* (Maryknoll, N.Y.: Orbis Books, 1985).

32. Simon, "Empowerment," p. 375.

33. For a similar analysis, see David Buckingham, "Against Demystification: A Response to *Teaching the Media*," *Screen*, 27:5 (1986), pp. 80-95; also see Swanson, "Rethinking Representations."

34. Dieter Misgeld, "Education and Cultural Invasion: Critical Social Theory, Education as Instruction and the Pedagogy of the Oppressed," in *Critical Theory and Public Life*, ed. John Forester (Cambridge, Mass.: MIT Press, 1985), pp. 106-07.

35. Michelle Fine, "Silencing in Public Schools," *Language Arts*, 64:2 (1987), pp. 157-74.

36. This issue is well-developed in Michelle Sola and Adrian T. Bennett, "The Struggle for Voice: Narrative, Literacy and Consciousness in an East Harlem School," *Boston University Journal of Education*, 167:1 (1985), pp. 88-110.

37. Paul Willis, *Learning to Labor* (New York: Columbia University Press, 1981); and Samuel Bowles and Herbert Gintis, *Schooling in Capitalist Society* (New York: Basic Books, 1976).

38. Aronowitz and Giroux, *Education under Siege*, especially chapter 2, pp. 23-46.

39. Sara Freedman, Jane Jackson, and Katherine Boles, "The Other End of the Corridor: The Effect of Teaching on Teachers," *Radical Teacher*, 23 (1983), pp. 2-23.

6. TEACHER EDUCATION AND DEMOCRATIC SCHOOLING

1. Arthur G. Powell, "University Schools of Education in the Twentieth Century," *Peabody Journal of Education*, 54 (1976), 4.

2. Ibid., p. 4.

3. George Counts, quoted in Powell, "University Schools," p. 4.

4. As quoted in Lawrence A. Cremin, David A. Shannon, and Mary Evelyn Townsend, *A History of Teachers College, Columbia University* (New York: Columbia University Press, 1954), p. 222.

5. Ibid., p. 222.

6. As quoted by George Counts in Ibid., p. 222.

7. For an interesting discussion of this issue, see Ira Katznelson and Margaret Weir, *Schooling for All: Class, Race, and the Decline of the Democratic Ideal* (New York: Basic Books, 1985).

8. See especially the work of the revisionist historians of the 1960s. Among the representative works are Michael B. Katz, *The Irony of Early School Reform: Educational Innovation in Mid-Nineteenth Century Massachusetts* (Boston: Beacon Press, 1968); Colin Greer, *The Great School Legend* (New York: Basic Books, 1972); and Clarence J. Karier, Paul Violas, and Joel Spring, *Roots of Crisis: American Education in the Twentieth Century* (Chicago: Rand McNally, 1973).

9. See Stanley Aronowitz and Henry A. Giroux, *Education under Siege: The Conservative, Liberal, and Radical Debate over Schooling* (South Hadley, Mass.: Bergin and Garvey, 1985).

10. I am using the term "discourse" to mean "a domain of language use subject to rules of formation and transformation," as quoted in Catherine Belsey, *Critical Practice* (London: Methuen, 1980), p. 160. Discourses may also be described as "the complexes of signs and practices which organize social existence and social reproduction. In their structured, material persistence, discourses are what give differential substance to membership in a social group or class or formation, which mediate an internal sense of belonging, and outward sense of otherness," as quoted in Richard Terdiman, *Discourse-Counter-Discourse* (New York: Cornell University Press, p. 54).

11. Aronowitz and Giroux, *Education under Siege*; and Ann Bastian, Colin Greer, Norm Fruchter, Marilyn Gittel, and Kenneth Haskins, *Choosing Equality: The Case for Democratic Schooling* (New York: New World Foundation, 1985).

12. Zeichner, "Alternative Paradigms of Teacher Education," *Journal of Teacher Education*, 34 (1983), 8.

13. Some of the more representative writing on this issue can be found in Diane Ravitch, *The Troubled Crusade: American Education 1945-1980* (New York: Basic Books, 1983); John H. Bunzel, ed., *Challenge to American Schools: The Case for Standards and Values* (New York: Oxford University Press, 1985); Diane Ravitch, *The Schools We Deserve: Reflections on the Educational Crises of Our Time* (New York: Basic Books, 1985); and Edward Wynne, "The Great Tradition in Education: Transmitting Moral Values," *Educational Leadership*, 43 (1985), 7.

14. Some of the best analyses are Lawrence C. Stedman and Marshall S. Smith, "Recent Reform Proposals for American Education," *Contemporary Education Review*, 53 (1983), 85-104; Walter Feinberg, "Fixing the Schools: The Ideological Turn," Issues in Education, 3 (1985), 113-38; Edward H. Berman, "The Improbability

of Meaningful Educational Reform," Issues in Education, 3 (1985), pp. 99-112; and Aronowitz and Giroux, *Education under Siege*.

15. Barbara Finkelstein, "Education and the Retreat from Democracy in the United States, 1979-1982," *Teachers College Record*, 86 (1984), 280-81.

16. Berman, "Improbability," p. 103.

17. I am using the term "influential" to refer to those reports that have played a major role in shaping educational policy at both the national and local levels. These include The National Commission on Excellence in Education, *A Nation at Risk: The Imperative for Educational Reform* (Washington, D.C.: GPO, 1983); Task Force on Education for Economic Growth, Education Commission of the States, *Action for Excellence: A Comprehensive Plan to Improve Our Nation's Schools* (Denver: Education Commission of the States, 1983); The Twentieth Century Fund Task Force on Federal Elementary and Secondary Education Policy, *Making the Grade* (New York: The Twentieth Century Fund, 1983); Carnegie Corporation, *Education and Economic Progress: Toward a National Education Policy* (New York: Author, 1983); and Carnegie Forum on Education and the Economy, *A Nation Prepared: Teachers for the 21st Century* (Hyattsville, Md.: Author, 1986).

Also considered are other recent reports on teacher education reform: The National Commission for Excellence in Teacher Education, *A Call for Change in Teacher Education* (Washington, D.C.: American Association of Colleges in Teacher Education, 1985); C. Emily Feistritzer, *The Making of a Teacher* (Washington, D.C.: National Center for Education Information, 1984); "Tomorrow's Teachers: A Report of the Holmes Group" (East Lansing, Mich.: Holmes Group, 1986); and Francis A. Maher and Charles H. Rathbone, "Teacher Education and Feminist Theory: Some Implications for Practice," *American Journal of Education*, 101 (1986), pp. 214-35. For an analysis of many of these reports see Catherine Cornbleth, "Ritual and Rationality in Teacher Education Reform," *Educational Researcher*, 15:4 (1986), pp. 5-14. The Holmes Report has been the subject of a number of articles; some of the most insightful are to be found in *Teachers College Record*, 88:3 (Spring 1987).

18. Marilyn Frankenstein and Louis Kampf, "Preface," in Sara Freedman, Jane Jackson, and Katherine Boles, "The Other End of the Corridor: The Effect of Teaching on Teachers," *Radical Teacher*, 23 (1983), pp. 2-23. It is worth noting that the Carnegie Forum's *A Nation Prepared* ends up defeating its strongest suggestions for reform by linking teacher empowerment to quantifying notions of excellence.

19. Stedman and Smith, "Recent Reform Proposals," pp. 85-104.

20. I am not automatically opposed to all forms of curricular software and technologies, such as interactive video disks and computers, as long as teachers become aware of the limited range of applications and contexts in which these technologies may be put to use. Certainly, I agree that some prepackaged curricula are more salient than others as instruments of learning. Too often, however, the use of such curricula ignores the contexts of the immediate classroom situation, the larger social milieu, and the historical juncture of the surrounding community. Furthermore, classroom materials designed to simplify the task of teaching and to make it more cost-efficient often separate planning or conception from execution. Many of the recent examples of predesigned commercial curricula are largely focused on competencies measured by standardized tests, precluding the possibility that teachers and students will be able

to act as critical thinkers. See Michael W. Apple and Kenneth Teitelbaum, "Are Teachers Losing Control of Their Skills and Curriculum?" *Journal of Curriculum Studies*, 18 (1986), 177-84.

21. Linda Darling-Hammond, "Valuing Teachers: The Making of a Profession," *Teachers College Record*, 87 (1985) p. 209.

22. Ibid.

23. For an excellent theoretical analysis of this issue, see Freedman, Jackson, and Boles, "The Other End of the Corridor." For a more traditional statistical treatment, see Darling-Hammond, *Beyond the Commission Reports: The Coming Crisis in Teaching*, R-3177-RC (Santa Monica, Calif.: Rand Corporation, July 1984); National Education Association, *Nationwide Teacher Opinion Poll*, 1983 (Washington, D.C.: Author, 1983); and American Federation of Teachers, *School as a Workplace: The Realities of Stress*, volume 1 (Washington, D.C.: Author, 1983).

24. Dennis J. Schmidt, "Translator's Introduction: In the Spirit of Bloch," in Ernst Bloch, *Natural Law and Human Dignity*, trans. Dennis J. Schmidt (Cambridge, Mass.: MIT Press, 1986), p. xviii.

25. John Goodlad, *A Place Called School: Prospects for the Future* (New York: McGraw-Hill, 1983); Theodore Sizer, *Horace's Compromise: The Dilemma of the American High School* (Boston: Houghton Mifflin, 1984); and Ernest Boyer, *High School: A Report on Secondary Education in America* (New York: Harper and Row, 1983).

26. For an overview and critical analysis of this literature, see Henry A. Giroux, "Theories of Reproduction and Resistance in the New Sociology of Education: A Critical Analysis," *Harvard Educational Review*, 53 (1983), 257-93.

27. Popkewitz and Pitman, "The Idea of Progress and the Legitimation of State Agendas: American Proposals for School Reform," *Curriculum and Teaching*, 1 (1986), p. 21.

28. Ibid., p. 20.

29. Ibid., p. 22.

30. Zeichner, "Alternative Paradigms"; and Jesse Goodman, "Reflections on Teacher Education: A Case Study and Theoretical Analysis," *Interchange*, 15 (1984), pp. 7-26. The fact that many teacher education programs have defined themselves as synonymous with instructional preparation has often given them a debilitating practical slant, leading to a limited conception of teaching as exercises in classroom management and control. Isolated courses on classroom management have had a tragic effect on how teachers are able to critically interrogate the political implications of curricular decision making and policy development. This predicament can be traced to a history of the academic politics that grew out of the separation of colleges of education from the liberal arts tradition and the arts and sciences faculty; see Donald Warren, "Learning from Experience: History and Teacher Education," *Educational Researcher*, 14:10 (1985), pp. 5-12.

31. For an excellent analysis of this issue, see National Coalition of Advocates for Students, *Barriers to Excellence: Our Children at Risk* (Boston: Author, 1985).

32. As quoted in Frank Lentricchia, *Criticism and Social Change* (Chicago: University of Chicago Press, 1985); see also John Dewey, *Democracy and Education* (New York: Free Press, 1916) and *The Public and Its Problems* (New York: Holt, 1927).

33. Dewey, "Creative Democracy—The Task Before Us," in *Classic American Philosophers*, ed. Max Fisch (New York: Appleton-Century-Crofts, 1951), pp. 389-94; and

Richard J. Bernstein, "Dewey and Democracy: The Task Ahead of Us," in *Post-Analytic Philosophy*, ed. John Rajchman and Cornel West (New York: Columbia University Press, 1985) pp. 48-62.

34. Zeichner, "Alternative Paradigms"; Henry A. Giroux, *Ideology, Culture, and the Process of Schooling* (Philadelphia: Temple University Press, 1981); and John Sears, "Rethinking Teacher Education: Dare We Work Toward a New Social Order?" *Journal of Curriculum Theorizing*, 6 (1985), pp. 24-79.

35. Of course, this is not true for all teacher education programs, but it does represent the dominant tradition characterizing them; see Zeichner, "Alternative Paradigms."

36. See John Ellis, "Ideology and Subjectivity," in *Culture, Media, Language*, ed. Stuart Hall, Dorothy Hobson, Andrew Lowe, and Paul Willis (Hawthorne, Australia: Hutchinson, 1980), pp. 186-94; see also Julian Henriques, Wendy Hollway, Cathy Urwin Couze Venn, and Valerie Walkerdine, *Changing the Subject* (New York: Methuen, 1984).

37. Henry A. Giroux and Roger Simon, "Curriculum Study and Cultural Politics," *Journal of Education*, 166 (1984), 226-238.

38. Stanley Aronowitz, "Schooling, Popular Culture, and Post-Industrial Society: Peter McLaren Interviews Aronowitz," *Orbit*, 17 (1986), p. 18.

39. Foucault, "The Subject of Power," in *Beyond Structuralism and Hermeneutics*, ed. Hubert Dreyfus and Paul Rabinow (Chicago: University of Chicago Press, 1982), p. 221.

40. T. J. Jackson Lears, "The Concept of Cultural Hegemony: Problems and Possibilities," *American Historical Review*, 90 (1985), pp. 569-70.

41. Gary Waller, "Writing, Reading, Language, History, Culture: The Structure and Principles of the English Curriculum at Carnegie-Mellon University," unpublished manuscript, Carnegie-Mellon University, 1985, p. 12.

42. I am primarily referring to the French school of discourse theory, as exemplified in the writings of Foucault; see his *The Archaeology of Knowledge*, trans. A. M. Sheridan Smith (London: Tavistock, 1972); see also the following works by Foucault: *Language, Counter-Memory, Practice: Selected Essays and Interviews*, trans. Donald F. Bouchard and Sherry Simon (Ithaca: Cornell University Press, 1979); and "Politics and the Study of Discourse," *Ideology and Consciousness*, 3 (1978), pp. 7-26.

43. For an introduction to such issues, see Umberto Eco, *A Theory of Semiotics* (Bloomington: Indiana University Press, 1976); Roland Barth, *Elements of Semiology*, trans. Annette Lavers and Colin Smith (New York: Hill and Wang, 1964); Roland Barth, *Mythologies* (New York: Hill and Wang, 1957).

44. Waller, "Writing, Reading, Language," p. 12.

45. Ibid., p. 14.

46. Foucault, "Two Lectures," in *Power/Knowledge*, ed. Colin Gordon (New York: Pantheon, 1980), pp. 78-108.

47. Waller, "Writing, Reading, Language," p. 14.

48. Giroux, *Ideology, Culture, and the Process of Schooling*.

49. As quoted in Harold Rosen, "The Importance of Story," *Language Arts*, 63 (1986), p. 234.

50. For a thorough analysis of this, see Arthur Brittan and Mary Maynard, *Sexism, Racism and Oppression* (New York: Blackwell, 1984).

51. Steve Tozer, "Dominant Ideology and the Teacher's Authority," *Contemporary Education*, 56 (1985), pp. 152-53.

52. Arendt, *The Human Condition* (Chicago: University of Chicago Press, 1958).

53. Attempts to link classroom instruction to community contexts are nowhere more important than during teachers' clinical experiences. On these occasions, prospective teachers should be assisted in making connections with progressive community organizations, especially those affiliated with local governmental council meetings, and in interviewing community leaders and workers in various community agencies linked to the school. This enhances the possibility that prospective teachers will make critically reflective links between classroom practices and the ethos and needs of the surrounding social and cultural milieu.

7. CONCLUSION: BEYOND THE POLITICS OF ANTI-UTOPIANISM IN EDUCATION

1. George Lukács, *History and Class Consciousness* (Cambridge, Mass.: MIT Press, 1968).

2. Walter Benjamin, *The Origin of German Tragic Drama* (London: New Left Books, 1977).

3. Ernst Bloch, *The Principle of Hope*, volumes 1-3 (Cambridge, Mass.: MIT Press, 1968).

4. David Gross, "Left Melancholy," *Telos*, 65 (Fall 1985), p. 113.

5. Bloch, *The Principle of Hope*, volume 1, p. 8.

6. Theodor Adorno, *Minima Moralia: Reflections from Damaged Life*, trans. E. F. N. Jephcott (London: New Left Books, 1974), p. 247.

7. See Stanley Aronowitz and Henry A. Giroux, *Education under Siege: The Conservative, Liberal, and Radical Debate over Schooling* (South Hadley, Mass.: Bergin and Garvey, 1985). This issue has been recently taken up by Russell Jacoby, who argues that a whole generation of intellectuals have abandoned their role as public critics for the sectarian discourse and comforts of the university. Russell Jacoby, *The Last Intellectuals: American Culture in the Age of Academe* (New York: Basic Books, 1987).

8. I analyze the work of some of these theorists in more detail in Henry A. Giroux, "Solidarity, Struggle, and the Public Sphere," *The Review of Education*, 12:3 (Summer 1986), pp. 165-72; "Solidarity, Struggle, and the Discourse of Hope," *The Review of Education*, 12:4 (Fall 1986), pp. 247-55.

9. For example, see Dan Liston, "On Facts and Values: An Analysis of Radical Curriculum Studies," *Educational Theory*, 36:2 (1986), pp. 137-52.

10. A typical example includes Nicholas C. Burbules, "Radical Educational Cynicism and Radical Educational Skepticism," *Philosophy of Education, 1985*, ed. David Nyberg (Urbana: Philosophy of Education Society, 1986), pp. 201-05. For a criticism of this position, see Peter McLaren, "Postmodernity and the Death of Politics: A Brazilian Reprieve," *Educational Theory*, 36:4 (1986), pp. 389-401.

11. For example, see Robert R. Bullough, Jr., and Andrew D. Gitlin, "Schooling and Change: A View From the Lower Rung," *Teachers College Record*, 87:2 (1985), pp. 219-37. See also Robert V. Bullough, Jr., Andrew D. Gitlin, and Stanley L. Goldstein, "Ideology, Teacher Role, and Resistance," *Teachers College Record*, 86:2 (1984), pp. 339-58.

12. See, as one instance, Dan Liston, "Marxism and Schooling: A Failed or Limited Tradition?" *Educational Theory*, 35:3 (1985), pp. 307-12. I have argued against this position in Henry A. Giroux, *Theory and Resistance in Education* (South Hadley, Mass.: Bergin and Garvey, 1983) and in Henry A. Giroux, "Toward a Critical Theory of Education: Beyond a Marxism with Guarantees," *Educational Theory*, 35:3 (1985), pp. 313-19.

13. Philip Wexler, "Introducing the Real Sociology of Education," *Contemporary Sociology*, 13:4 (1984), p. 408.

14. Bloch, cited in Anson Rabinach, "Unclaimed Heritage: Ernst Bloch's *Heritage of Our Times* and the Theory of Fascism," *New German Critique*, 11 (Spring 1977), p. 11.

15. Ibid., pp. 74-74.

16. Sharon D. Welch, *Communities of Resistance and Solidarity: A Feminist Theology of Liberation* (Maryknoll, N.Y.: Orbis Books, 1985), pp. 82-83.

17. Michael Lowy, "Interview with Ernst Bloch," *New German Critique*, 9 (Fall, 1976), p. 37.

18. Michel Foucault, *Power/Knowledge: Selected Interviews and Other Writings, 1972-1977* (New York: Pantheon, 1980), p. 132.

19. Ibid.

20. The educational Left is notorious for its reductionist treatment of ideology. For one example, see Michael Dale, "Stalking a Conceptual Chameleon: Ideology in Marxist Studies of Education," *Educational Theory*, 36:3 (Summer 1986), pp. 241-57. For an analysis of this position, see Peter McLaren, "Ideology, Schooling, and the Politics of Marxian Orthodoxy," *Educational Theory*, 37:3 (1987), pp. 301-26.

Index

Index

Index

morality, 6-7; on recovering a radical ethical stance, 39
Bourdieu, Pierre: on cultural hegemony, 87
Boyer, Peter J.: on the new American male, 27
Brameld, Theodore: on democracy and schooling, 8; on educator's role, 10

Capitalism: and public schools, 113, 115
Carnoy, Martin: on democracy and social movements, 110
Child centeredness, 129
Childs, John: on citizenship education, 10-11; on democracy, 82-83; as reconstructionist, 80; on teachers, 86
Chomsky, Noam: on democracy, 69
Chopp, Rebecca: on importance of narrative as a structure of memory, 97-98
Citizenship: and authority, 88; critical theory of, 32-34; defined, 3-4; in film and television, 16, 23-28; as historical process, 7; and literacy, 33-34; in the *1980s*, 15-16; versus patriotism, 17; as political process, 7; and schools, 7-8; theoretical qualifications of, 7
Citizenship education: critical theory of, 28-36; radical model of, 6, 8
Clark, Joe: on conservative educational leadership and discipline, 21-22
Closing of the American Mind, The, 117
Comay, Rebecca; on Rorty, 66
Community: new vision of, 152; and students, 200-201; and teachers, 169-70. *See also* Citizenship; Democracy
Connell, R. W.: on curricula for working-class kids, 103-4
Conservatives: on authority and education, 71, 78; on educational reform, 46; on ethics and schooling, 42-53; on history and equity, 46; versus liberalists, 113-14; new, 176-77, 180, 182; on the *1980s*, 44; on the *1960s*, 45; and pro status quo, 50-51; versus

reconstructionists, 232; on teaching and learning, 232; theory of, 113-14, 123
Corrigan, Philip: on literacy, 158; on social forms, 51-52
Counts, George: on democracy and schooling, 8; on democracy and social welfare, 86; as reconstructionist, 80
Crisis of Democracy, The, 4
Critical Literacy. *See* Literacy
Cultural deprivation: and illiteracy, 149; and liberal theory, 126
Cultural Literacy, 117
Cultural politics, 135-37, 141, 142, 212; and curriculum, 165, 192-93; teacher education as, 176, 189, 202, 207; and working class, 203
Culture: defined, 123, 193; dominant versus subordinate, 130, 142, 143, 150, 168, 170, 187-88, 200; and equality, 124, 193-94; and literacy, 150; and power, 130, 133-34, 193; and students, 127, 143; study of, 194-96
Culture industry: as dangerous force in society, 12. *See also* Media industry
Curricula: conservative, 113-14, 179; and corporate ideology, 137, 149, 178; defined, 165; democracy within, 102-3; hidden, 182; organization of, 9-10; radical, 114; as structured around silences and omissions, 100; and student experience, 197-98; teacher education, 185-86, 188-89; teachers' versus managers', 179-80
Cusick, Philip: on positive knowledge, 121-22

Damico, Alfonso J.: on Rorty, 64-65
Darling-Hammond, Linda: on curricula development, 180
Democracy: and authority, 80; and citizenship, 35, 181; defined, 6, 28-31; and ethics, 80-87; and learning, 22; and new conservativism, 181; and politics, 28-31; and popular culture, 120;

Index

public schools as part of, 72, 114, 136, 146, 172, 185, 208, 213-14; radical, 152; and radical theory of education, 39-40; reconstructionist view of, 80-87; and student voice, 199; and teacher education, 183-202, 207; and teachers' role, 175

Des Pres, Terrence: on ethics and history, 228

Dewey, John, 114, 117, 202; on citizenship, 11, 81; on democracy and community, 86; on democracy and morality, 84; on democracy and schooling, 8, 83, 232; on intelligence, 84; as reconstructionist, 73, 80; on teachers as intellectuals, 85-86

Discourse: defined, 219

Discrimination: against students, 126-28, 129

Donald, James: on circumstances and subjectivities within schools, 101

Dorfman, Ariel: on textual analysis, 140-41

Drop out rates, 130, 131

Economics: and public schools, 113, 178

Education: as cultural politics, 9; radical theory of, 37-40. *See also* Schooling
_____, teaching: as cultural politics, 176, 189, 196, 202; in early twentieth century, 174; and educational reform, 173, 183; and knowledge/power, 190-91; and language/power, 191; relative to public education, 184; purpose of, 174, 184, 186; and social inequality, 186-87; and study of history, 192-93

Educational reform: and liberalism, 182; management orientation of, 179; and new conservatives, 177; political nature of, 178; radical, 205-7; and teacher education, 173, 175

Educators. *See* Teachers

Empowerment: defined, 133, 189; and false consciousness, 206; language of, 166; through literacy, 152, 153, 156, 170; through schools, 214; social, 118-19; and student voice, 164, 175

Enlightenment, the, 209, 211

Ethics: and authority, 79-80; and critical theory of schooling, 39; as defined by Foucault, 224; and democracy, 80-87; and history, 40; and schooling, 37, 41-42, 107; and student empowerment, 166; in the universities, 50

Farber, Jerry: on authority of classroom teachers, 75; on patriarchal nature of authority, 76

Farber, Paul: on authority in education, 72

Farley, Margaret: on politics of caring, 96

Feminist theory, 91-92; and authority, 73, 76, 92; and ethic of risk and resistance, 93, 96, 235; on memory, narrative, solidarity, 91-98; and politics of caring and sensuality, 96-97; sources, 234

Ferguson, Thomas: on democracy, 30

Film and television: celluloid patriotism in, 23-28; citizenship in, 16, 23-28; ideologies and images in, 23-28, 223

Finkelstein, Barbara: on citizenship, 32-33; on educational reform, 176; on the purpose of education, 17

Fletcher, Colin: on democracy and learning, 103

Foucault, Michel, 211-12; definition of ethical, 224; definition of moral, 224; on history and knowledge, 99-100; on knowledge, 103; on power as structure, 101

Freire, Paulo, 117, 132; on conservativism, 120; on language, 133, 154; on literacy, 152-54; on political nature of education and teacher's role within, 69

Friedman, Susan: on authority and feminist teachers, 76

Index

Giarelli, Jim: on analytic tradition and philosophy of eduction, 54
Glazer, Nathan: on curriculum, 125
Goodsell, Willystine: on democracy and schooling, 8
Gorz, Andre: on cultural hegemony, 87
Gouldner, Alvin: on cultural hegemony, 87
Gramsci, Antonio: on history, xii-xiii; on intellectuals, 87; on language/power, 147, 154, 191
Greene, Maxine: on teachers creating public spaces in classrooms, 100-101
Grimshaw, Jean: on public versus private spheres, 94, 95

Habermas, Jürgen: on rights and justice, 57
Hand, W. Brevard: on textbook banning and religion in schools, 225
Hanson, Richard: on democracy and citizenship, 6
Harrison, Beverly: on critique and hope, 96; on moral theology, collective naming, and politics of experience, 93-94
Heller, Agnes: on authority and schooling, 72; on ethics and values, 59-60
Heritage Foundation: and blueprint for conservative government, 4
Hirsch, E. D.: on conservative pedagogy, 117-18
History: and dominant culture, 192; and education, 40; and ethics, 227-28; and memory, 81, 91-98, 99; study of in teacher education, 192-93
Holmes, Henry W.: on teaching profession, 173
Holocaust: as example for teaching ethics, 108
Honig, Bill: on character formation in public school curricula, 43
Horkheimer, Max: on ethics, 12, 57-58, 227
Humiliation: in classroom, 127
Huntington, Samuel: on crisis in American democracy, 4

Ideology: defined, 24, 34
Illiteracy, 155; Aronowitz and, 157; defined, 149; Freire on, 156-57; politics of, 156-57, 158; as promoted by media, 12

Jameson, Fredric: on history, 62; on postmodern philosophy, 61
Johnson, Richard: on textual analysis, 140

Kilpatrick, William H.: on democracy and social welfare, 86
Knowledge: conservative view of, 120-21; and language, 131, 133; positive, 121-22; and power, 102-3, 133, 142-43, 147, 152, 165, 181, 190-91, 211, 213, 220; production of, 159, 162, 163-64
Kohlberg, Lawrence: on moral reasoning, 48, 57; right-wing criticism of, 48-49

Labor: in education, 137-38
Laclau, Ernesto: on democracy, 29
Language: dominant, 158; versus experience, 116, 147; Gramsci on, 147, 191; and knowledge, 131, 133; oppositional, 67-68; political nature of, 131; as power, 116, 133, 135, 147, 154, 157, 166, 172, 191, 209; technology of, 116
Lara, Patricia: as a subversive, 22
Learning: and democracy, 22
Lefort, Claude: on homogeneity of social and public spheres, 85
Left, the. See Liberals
Lerner, Michael: and vision of a moral American community, 59
Liberal arts, 186
Liberals: on authority and education, 77-79; versus conservatives, 113-14; and educational reform, 182; on literacy, 148; and morality, 53-60; on student experience, 128-29; theory of, 114-15, 125-26, 146
Liberation theology: and authority and ethics, 73; and memory, narrative,

254

Index

Index

143, 164; and social structure, 143-44; versus teacher voice, 164, 168-69

Teacher-learners, 167-68

Teacher voice: defined, 144; versus student voice, 164, 168-69; Weiler on, 144-45

Teachers: and authority, 80, 90; deskilling of in *1980*s, 45; difficulties faced by, 102, 170-71, 179, 181; versus federal government, 170; as intellectuals, 72, 73, 83, 87-91, 99-101, 108-11, 172-76 *passim*; and other public spheres, 35, 109, 118; as politicians, 69; powerlessness of, 176; roles for, 33, 35, 68; student, 187, 200; undermining of in *1960*s, 45; and values-clarification, 47; view of, 10, 173, 180; working conditions of, 102. *See also* Education, teacher

Teaching profession: 10, 173; and democracy, 73

Technology: economics of, 113; of power, 116

Television. *See* Film and television

Textual analysis, 138-41

Touraine, Alain: on self-production, 141-42

Tozer, Steve, 200-201

Truth, 211

Veblen, T.: on bureaucratic structures, 13

Violence: against students, 123

Voice. *See* Student voice; Teacher voice

Wagner, Tony: on students' worldviews, 15-16

Weber, Max: on bureaucratic structure, 13

Weiler, Kathleen: on teacher voice, 144-45

Weiss, John: on values-neutrality, 49

Welch, Sharon, 210-11; on feminist ethic of risk and resistance, 93, 235; on solidarity, 98

West, Cornel: on Rorty's neopragmatism, 65-66

White, Doug: on humanization of the social order, 90-91

Willard, Horace: on teaching profession, 173

Williamson, Judith: on importance of student experience, 106

Wolin, Sheldon: on citizen as political being, 88-89

Wood, George: on morality and community, 66-67

Working-class students: instructors' view of, 126-28; and literacy, 150, 151, 157

Worldview: construction of, 167

Wright, Linus: on computerized merit pay for teachers, 232

Wynne, Edward A.: on the *1960*s, 45; on schools as places that transmit values, 42-43; on traditional moral values, 71

Yankelovich, Daniel: on prevailing social philosophy, 20

Zeichner, Kenneth: on teacher education, 176

Henry A. Giroux has taught in the School of Education and Allied Professions at Miami University, Ohio, since 1983; he is professor of education, Renowned Scholar in Residence, and Director of the Center for Education and Cultural Studies. A secondary school teacher from 1969 to 1975, he earned his Doctor of Arts degree in curriculum theory, sociology of education, and history at Carnegie-Mellon University in 1977 and subsequently taught at Boston and Tufts Universities.

Three of Giroux's books, *Ideology, Culture and the Process of Schooling, Theory and Resistance in Education*, and *Education under Siege* (with Stanley Aronowitz), were named by the American Educational Studies Association as one of the most significant books in education for the years 1982, 1984 and 1986. He is also the author of *Teachers as intellectuals* (1988), *Popular Culture and Critical Pedagogy* (co-edited with Roger Simon, 1988), and *Schooling, Politics, and Cultural Struggle* (co-edited with Peter McLaren, forthcoming). He contributes to numerous journals, including *Harvard Educational Review, Social Text, Teachers College Record*, and *Educational Theory*. Giroux is a member of the Consulting Editorial Board of The Boston University *Journal of Education* and is a contributing editor of *Curriculum Inquiry*. He is co-editor with Paulo Freire of the series *Critical Studies in Education*, published by Bergin and Garvey Press, and co-editor with Peter McLaren of *Teacher Empowerment and School Reform*, a series to be published by SUNY Press.